OUR EARTH,

OUR CURE

OUR EARTH

A Handbook of Natural Medicine for Today

OUR
CURE

by Raymond Dextreit
Translated and Edited by Michel Abehsera

Illustrated by Judith Abinun

SWAN HOUSE
in association with
BOLDER BOOKS

Copyright © 1974, 1979 by Swan House Publishing Company. Published by The Swan House Publishing Company, P.O. Box 170, Brooklyn, New York 11223, in coordination with Bolder Books, a division of Hampstead Hall Press Ltd., 10 East 40 Street, New York, N.Y. 10016.

ISBN: 0-918282-08-x   (hard)

ISBN: 0-918282-09-8   (soft)

Library of Congress Card Catalog Number: 74 - 83427

Cover design by Jackie Schuman.

Text design by Heather F. White

Assistant Editors: Alessa Wirchberg, Michael Tilles

Tenth Printing.

Printed in U.S.A.

For a better world.

FOREWARD

This book is compiled from the 43 books written by Raymond Dextreit. Of course, not all have been included in their entirety - that would have resulted in an enormous book, with many repetitions. Instead, they were all examined carefully and from each one the important chapters, paragraphs and sentences were selected. The aim was to present the American public with a book that would be complete yet concise, to remain true to the author's intent and the reader's needs.

Raymond Dextreit does not claim to possess the 'elixir of life'; what he brings, however, is a simple, straightforward medicine which is easy to understand and practice and will help many people. There are now many popular schools of natural medicine in America, all of which are valid to some extent since individuals vary so greatly. However, Mr. Dextreit brings something new to medical practice on this continent, a method sure to grow in importance and popularity, for in addition to his authoritative use of food, herbs, and baths, and his extensive knowledge of the human organism, Mr. Dextreit has mastered the use of *clay* for curative purposes.

In addition to the cures obtained through food, herbs and other means, the reader will greatly appreciate the vast medical knowledge of the author. Mr. Dextreit displays such an understanding of the causes of the diseases and of the body functions - whether it is the digestive system, the blood circulation, the liver functions, etc. - that doctors of all schools will certainly acknowledge and learn from his skill.

Some people may not agree with Mr. Dextreit's completely vegetarian way of life, but they will find that nevertheless, there is a great deal to be learned from his deep understanding of the human body. Those who prefer naturopathy know well that accurate diagnoses and clear pathological and physiological understanding of a disease are the necessary first steps towards its cure. We think that everyone - the practicing naturopath and even the M.D. - should refer himself to Mr. Dextreit's view of diseases and their cure, regardless of whether he is a fruit, vegetable, or grain eater. Most people seem to know what they are doing with regard to their respective ways of eating; they lack, however, one important factor: a clear view of how disease takes place in the organism. We chose to publish this book for that reason alone. Mr. Dextreit's 32 years of practice have helped him acquire an excellent reputation in his country where he seems to be 'the doctor of the people' for his medicine is inexpensive and easy for everyone to apply.

A basic principle in Mr. Dextreit's medicine is that when undertaking to heal ourselves, treating the general condition is more primary than relieving a specific manifestation, for 'a local disease is usually the consequence of a general disorder'. In fact, the particular manifested trouble can even be seen as a 'beneficial crisis, leading to diagnosis and treatment of a latent abnormality (of the organism as a whole).'

This is not difficult to understand. Getting rid of eczema, for example, involves more than merely applying a cream to make it disappear from sight; for then it is quite likely to burst out again -- unless suppressed unnaturally by even stronger means.

Here we have the old debate between the naturalists and the modernists: the naturalist searches for his cure in nature, believing that a genuine, enduring cure is possible only through an accord between man and nature, at least during the healing period. The modernist sees things differently. He focuses on repairing the damages, not on their cause. He does not ask nature's advice. Perhaps he thinks nature is too low to teach him anything civilized and scientifically verifiable.

The radical naturalists believe that *all* the answers are to be found in nature, while the extreme modernist believes that everything lies in his analytical understanding of things. It is best not to take either of these positions exclusively, for both must be included. When we put ourselves in trouble by violating spiritual and physiological orders, we instinctively look to correct our errors. This involves first searching for the cause of our mistakes in the place of our downfall: the earth with its hosts. In other words, we humble ourselves by seeking advice from nature our servant, performing in that gesture a normal act of gratitude to this world and its Owner.

CONTENTS

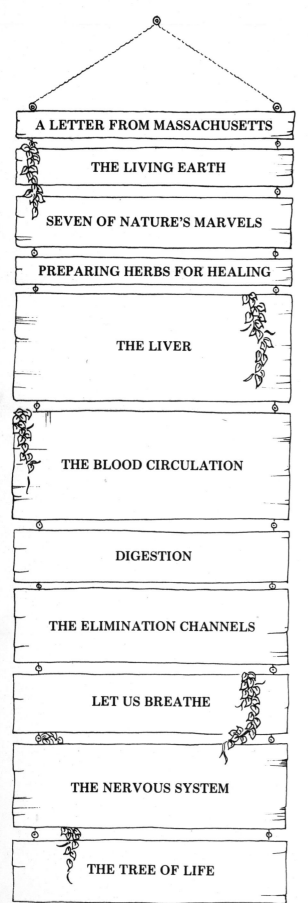

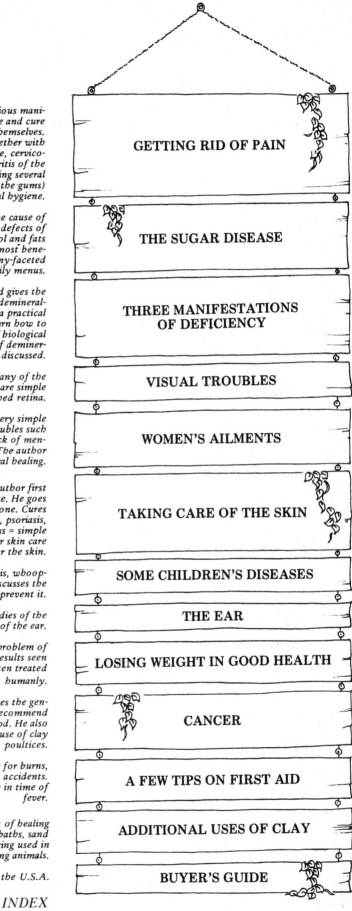

A LETTER FROM MASSACHUSETTS

Jan., 1974

Dear Sirs,

I would be very glad to write down my experiences with Mr. Raymond Dextreit's Harmonist Method. I would have done it earlier but my brother's family was visiting from France, and also, I am expecting a baby in a few months and it seems I am not as efficient as usual. Anyway, I shall be pleased to tell our story, although I am afraid it will not be very dramatic as we are a healthy family and so there aren't any spectacular incidents to recall.

I became a harmonist ten years ago - my mother had been one for many years already, so I was already somewhat familiar with it. What really convinced me was once when I had a rather severe nervous breakdown and had to go home to Paris and my mother -- my husband, being a medical student could not afford to support an unworking wife! I put myself entirely in my mother's hands. I had no choice; otherwise it would have been hospitalization. She treated me with the Dextreit method: herbs, clay, strict vegetarian diet. The result was fantastic. I was pregnant then with a disastrous cell count. At the end of my pregnancy my blood test was excellent and I gave birth(natural childbirth) to a healthy boy. Unfortunately, under the absurd advice of a pediatrician I gave up breast-feeding. My son was fed with bottles of carrot juice, fruit juices, and home-made vegetable broth, until he was big enough for solid food. He then ate all kinds of vegetables, fruits, eggs, cheese, and whole grain cereals.

I wanted so much to have my second child at home, which I did with the help of a midwife who knew and agreed with Dextreit's method(I was still living in Paris). Everything went beautifully and I breast-fed that second child for seven months.

My children have never had any antibiotics or any medicine at all, except for their vaccination(they are 8, 7, and 5 years old - the third was born in the U.S. - 1968). I do not agree with vaccination at all, but they had to go to school. After each vaccination I would put a thin clay poultice on the spot and make them drink a lot of lemon juice and they never had any bad reactions.

I put cabbage leaves on their liver for intestinal disorder to help with eliminations. It is an excellent 'tranquilizer'! They actually ask for it if they have a headache or some discomfort - as they ask for clay to put on their scratches, burns or bumps! I use it of course mainly in case of fever or any infections.

My confidence in clay is such that when I had a miscarriage last February, I just put clay poultices on my abdomen day and night. One week later there was no more bleeding and everything was back in order. With clay I never fear infection, or complications.

Once, my oldest boy scratched his cornea with a stick while playing. He was in great pain - I just put clay on his eyes. It calmed the pain immediately and 48 hours later the cornea was clear and healed. I also have used it to treat some of my children for ear infections successfully. The first time the infection cleared up in 24 hours; it still amazes my husband who is quite a traditional physician and an eye-ear-nose-throat specialist. He checked their ears and can see the result after a few clay poultices - cleared of all infection. I could go on and on. . . .I don't think I have to go into details about the way I treat colds, flu and other virus infections, for I just do what Mr. Dextreit suggests in his books.

My first years in the U.S. were difficult. I did not find such a large variety of fresh fruits and vegetables as in France, health food stores were scarce(we were living in Connecticut) and I had to have many things sent from France(I still get many of the herbs I need for the decoctions from

France - that's the only thing), and of course I was passing for some kind of a nut! But I could see the result in our health and I was not going to give that up for any plight to conformism - I never have.

At the time my third son was born(1968) my husband, for whom I still cooked meat, declared that he felt better with our diet and stopped eating meat. He also stopped smoking. I have never seen him sick more than twenty-four hours. Usually an attack of flu or colds that he - the doctor - asks me to 'treat', which I do by making him drink cup after cup of various herbal teas and decoctions. He is an excellent patient! Although being a physician and an American, he does not fully agree, or understand the harmonist method, he has always left me free to do whatever I wanted for the children's health -- the results speak for themselves. Our children are rarely sick or even tired. At 4, the younger one could take a walk with his father for three hours in winter and come home to get on his tricycle for another couple of hours.

My children have had cold baths since birth. They do not have heat in their room at night(even before the energy shortage!)and they sleep with their windows open and are never cold -- and you know how the winters are here in New England. They have never seen a doctor since they finished their immunization shots. When they have a cold or are coughing, they are accustomed since they were babies to take a spoonful of pure lemon juice, alternated with a few spoonfuls of honey. I also use camphor oil liniment on their chest. For more severe coughing, I mash some garlic cloves in it and give them a good rubbing with this mixture; they sleep through the night.

As for diet, which is the base for all good health, we are strictly vegetarian, eating according to Mr. Dextreit's teachings. I have had to make a few adjustments to this country; for instance, I make sandwiches for lunch(I bake my own wheat bread). We always start meals with some fresh fruit and then salad(raw cabbage, carrots, tomatoes, lettuce, etc.)before the main vegetable or spaghetti or rice or other kind of cereal dish. Then a home-made dessert. I use soya oil for cooking and salads, sea salt, lots of honey, spices(no pepper). We also eat some eggs and cheese, yoghurt, peanut butter, nuts and dried fruits. I buy most of my groceries in health-food stores. I use frozen vegetables but never any canned products.

For snacks, my children have apples or raw carrots which they share with their dogs -- the two older are known to refuse candies and lollipops and not being used to them, they don't even like them. I try to teach them to have respect for each person's way of living; they don't seem to have any problems up to now for being brought up differently than their schoolmates.

As the years go by, I am more and more confident in this way of living and more and more sure of myself. Of course, it would be easier and less tiring to swallow some pills than to prepare decoctions and poultices. . . . .in addition to all the time I spend peeling vegetables and baking my own bread. I simply could not do differently now. For me it is the way life is meant to be, with nature giving us all we need to take care of ourselves. For that reason, I consider Mr. Dextreit a benefactor to humanity and I consider myself very lucky to have been introduced to his methods.

I have also a personal gratitude toward him and his wife, for whenever I needed their advice, it never failed to be right and always it was given so clamly and reassuringly! A few times since I have been in the U.S., I was uncertain of what to do and I never hesitated to call them. And when my youngest boy, then 3, had a fever of 105° for 6 days, and did not seem to respond to the usual treatments(he also had bronchitis), I kept a humidifier in his room and day and night did all I knew and could think of. Finally I called Mrs. Dextreit and asked her advice.

Following her instructions, I dampened some bath towels in cold water and wrapped the child in it, with plastic and a blanket around him. He gave one scream and. . . .fell asleep - peacefully and immediately. That night the temperature was normal and it stayed that way - the child recovered quickly.

I am happy to have been of some help. All of this is so familiar to me, I may have missed some points. I shall always be glad to give you any information you might want about my personal and constant experimentation with clay and the rest of Mr. Dextreit's methods.

Sincerely yours,

M.G.

P.S.   When I arrived in this country six years ago, I tried to get clay in ceramic studios and suppliers - they usually sell it in small packages with labels that gave me doubts about the purity of the clay. I wrote to a friend who lived near Boston and she shipped me a 50-lb. bag of Jordan dry clay. I found that clay very good and have been using it very successfully since. It is a brownish kind of clay - I always purchase it in 50-lb. bags at about $5.00 a bag in wholesale ceramic supplies stores(in the yellow pages). I find that the green 'French' clay mixes more easily with water and may be less sticky than the Jordan dry, but the result is the same. Also in France, you can find some clay that comes in very fine powder, drinkable once diluted with water - I have never tried to drink the Jordan dry clay.

I always have some clay ready for use - that is, mixed with water. I use an earthenware bowl. Plastic and metal should not come in contact with clay - enamel is alright. I add enough water so it reaches the consistency of some kind of wet, soft putty. You can check the consistency with a wooden spoon or spatula. The clay should not be mixed. Just pour the water on it and let it be absorbed.

To prepare the poultices, I spread the clay in a thick layer on a paper towel. I always attach the poultice for two hours minimum with elastic bandages of various sizes.

I do not think it matters where you keep the clay that already has been prepared as long as you keep it moist by adding water when necessary. Room temperature is all right. It will dry up more in winter with the heat in the house - I keep mine under my kitchen sink - the bowl covered with a plate. I leave my big supply of dry clay in a dry place.

M.G.

THE LIVING EARTH

The Miracle of Clay

The earth is the source of infinite means for restoring and maintaining good health; its fruits, vegetables and grains renew one's flesh and blood; its aromatic plants provide vital elements which stimulate the organic functions; its herbs can help restore subtle balance in times of illness; its rivers and streams supply life-sustaining pure water for drinking, cooking and healing baths.

The study of nature is infinitely marvelous and rewarding. Unfortunately, however, the most precious and simple natural remedies are generally neglected by people who go searching for complicated expensive ones.

These days, more and more people in rapidly growing numbers are aware of the healing properties in food, herb, and water, but as yet, very few know that *the earth itself, receiving its vital energies from sun, air, and waters, is a most*

powerful healing agent of physical regeneration. Clays, muds, sands - these different forms of earth all participate in life-giving, health-restoring processes.

Clay treatment alone is, of course, not enough; it is far more important to establish correct eating habits. However, since the miracle of clay is a healing phenomenon so relatively unknown, it seems necessary to begin this book with a few words on the properties of clay and its uses. May the reader soon come to understand how our earth is our cure.

PROPERTIES OF CLAY

What is meant here by 'clay' is a greasy sort of earth, retaining that quality even when wet and impermeable. It is the same clay used by sculp-

tors and potters. There are many varieties of different colors, each with its own properties. It is sometimes found in garden subsoils, about one yard deep, but generally it is dug out from quarries and sent to the different industries which utilize it, such as tile and brick factories, and pottery and ceramic plants.

For healing and therapeutical purposes, clay may be used externally and orally. As will be shown, eating clay (dissolved in water) can be a wonder-working cure! Applied in poultices and compresses, clay provides numerous benefits. It can heal sores and ulcers and aid in the rebuilding of healthy tissues and cells, and even of fractured bones and vertebrae.

Clay (together with lemon, which will be discussed later) acts on capillaries, liberating them, dissolving crystals and 'flakes'. Its natural tendency is to absorb toxins. For example, it is useful in neutralizing intoxications caused by poisonous mushrooms and chemical acids.

In the presence of clay, microbian flora disappear; in a clayish medium, pathogenic germs, that is to say parasitic organisms, cannot proliferate. The presence of worms in excrements has sometimes been observed after drinking clay. These worms have not, of course been produced by the clay; rather, the treatment has drawn them out from the bowels and other organs where they were lodged.

Taken orally, clay initiates a many-pronged effect. In cases of organic disorders its intense activity eliminates and destroys unhealthy cells and activates the ·rebuilding of healthy ones. Besides the colloidal properties of clay, it acts as a cleansing agent eliminating all noxious substances. The same sedating, relaxing, absorbing and healing action is seen in treatment of the inflammation of the intestines as well as amoebic and other types of dysentery.

All this is the 'direct' action, the immediate action on the digestive channel. But clay activity, goes much further: clay not only cures minor problems, such as diarrhea and constipation through local application; it acts on all the organs - on the whole organism. Everything unhealthy and emitting negative radiations is irresistibly attracted to clay (a brilliant positive pole) and becomes subject to immediate elimination.

It continues its purification of the blood, which it cleanses and enriches. The same teaspoon of clay can cure an obstinate carbuncle and a tenacious anemia equally well. Curing the carbuncle is explained by clay's absorbent power...but anemia! Does clay contain a profusion of mineral bodies, in particular iron? No. According to the analysis made in the National Center of Scientific Research (in France), clay contains the following oxides and chemical elements in compound: Silica(31.14-41.38), Titanium(0.47-1.89), Aluminum(40.27-48.13), Iron(0.11-0.78), Calcium(0.05-0.13), Magnesium(traces to 0.05), Sodium and Potassium (0.25-0.85).

The analysis of its composition is not sufficient to explain its rebuilding action of red blood cells, but that it produces results is easily confirmed by a red cell recount. In a month, you can expect an impressive increase in red blood cells.

Wherever there is a deficiency, clay seems to supply the needed substance regardless of whether or not the clay itself is rich in that substance. In the analysis of wheat consumption, the mineral bodies identified in the wheat are found in identical proportion in the organism. This is not so with clay. It is because clay does more than restore a particular substance lacking in the body. It is possible that synthetic replacements may act this way, but clay does more than merely remedy a deficiency.

If an organ does not function well or the function is carried out only partially, it is not sufficient to supply a remedy that introduces into the organism the lacking substance; it is necessary to go further, as clay does. It stimulates the deficient organ and helps the restoration of the failing function. How it does this will be discussed later.

One of clay's peculiarities is based on its physical-chemical domination. From a thermodynamic point of view, we must admit that clay cannot be the sole source of energy of the phenomena it produces. Clay is effective through a dynamic presence far more significant than a mere consideration of the substances it contains. It is a catalyst rather than an agent in itself. This is possible because clay is alive -- 'living earth'.

It would be presumptuous to attempt a precise and concrete explanation of the basic action of clay. Among the properties to which we can attribute its effect is radioactivity. Clay is radioactive to a degree (as is everything), but this radioactivity is generally imperceptible to the testing apparatus at present used in laboratories. Some muds are an exception.

Radioesthetically, the matter has been extensively discussed. Scientists differ widely as to the significance of this radioactivity in clay. The problem is further complicated by the differences between one clay and another.

This complexity is not limited to clay; it has not been easy to find a consistent scientific explanation of the effects of such radioactivity. Some scientists would have the gas, *Radon* as responsible, for the noxious radiations of the so-called 'cancer'. For others the same *Radon* is the origin of benefactory vapors. According to this view, Capri Island and many mineral waters would owe its therapeutic properties to it.

It seems that clay has, among other properties, that of either stimulating a deficiency or absorbing an excess in the radioactivity of the body on which it is applied. On an organism which has suffered and still retains the radiations of radium or any other intensive radioactive source, the radioactivity is first enhanced and then absorbed. A clay could, in this way, ensure the protection of organisms over-exposed to atomic radiations. This radioactive effect has been researched: today, when everyone is forcibly submitted to many artificially provoked radioactive aggressions, such as dust in the atmosphere from bomb testing, everything increasing this danger should be avoided. Experiments made with the Geiger counter have demonstrated that dry clay absorbs a very important part of this surrounding radioactivity.

The absorbent power of clay is extraordinary. Raw eggs covered with clay lose three times more weight than if they remained in the open air, without causing any damage to the egg-shell.

It can be confirmed by employing its deodorant action on a part of the body, or by mixing foul-smelling substances with clay; the odor disappears, absorbed by the clay. When in the home of an invalid in bed, it is sufficient to place clay in the bottom of the bed-pan and the evacuations will be quite deodorized.

Clay has the power to attract and either absorb or stimulate the evacuation of toxic and non-useful elements. In general, clay has remarkable resistance to chemical agents and only the most energetic ones can attack it. As a bacteria-destroying agent, it can render contaminated water innocuous. Its absorbent power has contributed to the elimination of the chemical taste of chloride in Paris

water! This action is not limited to deodorization but it persists along the digestive path and uproots many unwelcome intrusive bodies, including gas.

These absorbent properties, certainly due to micro-molecular structure of clay, explain its action - but only partially. We cannot always penetrate Nature's secrets, we must merely acknowledge and use them.

There are substances which do not destroy themselves in action; they are the diastases and enzymes; clay is particularly rich in these. Some of these diastases, the 'oxidase', have the power of fixing free oxygen, which explains the purifying and enriching action of clay in the blood.

The knowledge of these properties would be insufficient to explain clay's active power if we did not know that clay is a powerful agent of stimulation, transformation and transmission of energy. As every filing which comes from a magnet keeps its properties, every piece of clay retains a considerable amount of energy from that large and powerful magnetic entity which is our planet earth. This radioactive action transmits to the organism an extraordinary strength and helps to rebuild vital potential through the liberation of latent energy. We have extraordinary energy resources which normally remain dormant--- clay awakens them.

We must not confuse this action with the stimulating effect of drink and food which do not act on the energy potential but simply on the foreseen energy of coming days, driving us to mortgage that near future.

Clay acts symbiotically in the body; since it is impossible to see and control what happens with living organisms, we are limited to hypotheses. Nevertheless, clay's action and the results obtained permit a rather precise idea of its properties. In this way, it is remarkable for its organo-therapeutic value.

How has this healing power of clay been ignored for so long? Or has it been? When we look back in time we discover that clay has been used for thousands of years by many people who put all their confidence in its results.

The Egyptians used it for the mummification of their dead because they knew of its purifying powers. It is therefore, nearly certain its use was not only reserved for the dead.

The doctors of antiquity did not hesitate to make use of it and many of them, such as the Greek Dioscorides, attributed an 'extraordinary strength' to the vital properties of clay. Long before this, the 'Prince of the Doctors', the Arab Avicena, and the Greek anatomist, Galen, used it widely, mentioning it in terms of praise. The Roman naturalist, Pliny the Elder devoted a whole chapter of his 'Natural History' to it.

The tendency of many is to assume that these ancient peoples used clay only because they lacked the other and more active medications available to us today. However, the reputation of clay has been restored, while at the same time deficiencies in the treatment of ill people by use of drugs and chemicals has been revealed. The great German naturopaths Kneipp, Kuhn, Just, Felke and others of the last century have contributed to this revival of the use of clay in the framework of natural treatments.

The priest Kneipp strongly advised a mixture of clay and natural vinegar for packs and poultices. In some western countries this method had survived but was applied mainly to animals - when one was seriously ill, it would be daubed with a paste made of clay and vinegar.

At the end of his life, Kneipp transmitted valuable observations on clay to Adolph Just, another naturopath; under his direction, the clay treatment was widely extended and the Earth of Just, called 'Luvos', was soon known and appreciated. In the early part of this century, a Berlin doctor, Professor Julius Stumpf, used it successfully in the treatment of Asiatic cholera.

During the First World War, the Russian soldiers received 200 grams of it along with their rations and it was added to mustard in several French regiments, who remained free of the dysentery which ravaged nearby regiments.

In villages which we call 'primitive' because they still live in close contact with nature, the use of clay is common. All around the world can be found people and even whole tribes who eat earth. . .in Mexico, in India (Mahatma Gandhi advised the use of clay), in Anglo-Egyptian Sudan, in South America, or among the High Orinoco villages of the Cassiquare, of the Meta and Rio Negro; they knead the earth in balls or lumps and then dry and bake them when they wish to eat them.

In Switzerland and Germany, doctors made use of it and in Davos, an important center for the treatment of tuberculosis, patients were usually treated with clay; the whole thorax was daubed with a paste of very hot clay and this pack was kept on all night. This treatment frequently was credited with miraculous healings.

Under the name of 'Cutler's earth', clay was used in some districts of France - and perhaps it is still used - as a resolutive and against burns from first to third degree. It is also known under the names of Luvos, aluminum silicate, colloidal white clay, balus, and others.

More recently, its use for therapeutic purposes has been extended in France in such a way that it is impossible to argue about its properties. Recent experiments have treated sores and ulcers with aluminum; not only is clay in a great part formed by Aluminum silicate - its healing action is increased due to the fact that its components are in a state of natural dosage.

Scientific experience has now also embraced the use of previously disdained substances such as marshy mud. Those 'biogenic stimulants' applied on the skin or even to the cornea of the eye - are sometimes products taken from marshy mud. These muds contain highly active ingredients, able to induce cellular rebuilding and to hasten all organic processes. This problem of rejuvenation is only solved with the help of life's resources - Nature and her elements - rather than with synthetic products.

Any similarity between clay and chemical medicine is only apparent. There is a basic difference between clay and chemical antiseptic actions. Any chemical product is a dead substance which acts blindly and destroys all bacteria indiscriminately: the good and the bad, the healthy and the ill, the useful and the harmful. It is possible that the dangerous germs get extinguished, but the reconstructive elements are not respected and the treated tissues of sores and ulcers are reproduced in a much slower time than those not treated.

Scientists are trying to find out what is responsible for the healing value in mineral waters. They have tried to rebuild a synthetic water, using the chemical composition of the mineral waters. An amount of water has been reactivated, drawn out after a certain period of time sufficient to make it lose its radioactivity. All these experiments have failed.

Observation of nature convinces one that duplicating its properties, through chemical or physical means is impossible. Chemistry and physics cannot rebuild life. This is a fact which many methods of modern science ignores. We must humbly recognize the existence of many untranslatable problems for mere man. We must observe, verify, take note and admit. We must accept the facts even if we do not understand their origin. And clay does act with wisdom - it goes to the unhealthy spot. Used internally, whether absorbed orally, anally or vaginally, clay goes to the place where harm is, there it lodges, perhaps for several days, until finally it draws out the pus, black blood, etc. with its evacuation.

From helping to prevent the proliferation of pathogenic germs and parasites to aiding with rebuilding of healthy tissues and cells, clay is a 'living' cure.

PRELIMINARIES TO CLAY TREATMENT

Choosing Clay

Clay may be obtained from herbalists and other merchants, as well as from the quarries and the industries which use it in large quantities. In fact, it is good to always have some ready-made clay on hand, convenient for camping, car, etc. It is sold ready-made commercially (in health-food and herbalist shops) in tubes (see 'Buyer's Guide). If clay is obtained from a ceramics supply outlet make sure that it is 'virgin' clay; that is, that it was extracted from the quarry without having undergone any treatment. Never use prepared clay baked or mixed with medicinal substances or any other additives.

There are many varieties of clay, and many different colors (green, red, yellow, grey, white, etc.). It is important to find the one most suited to the ailment or to the temperament of the patient. When we use nature's products we are not running to an inert substance, but to life. We must look until we find 'sympathy'.

Clay is alive. There are kindred links between clay and living beings, whether plant, animal or man. The same clay can produce a marvelous result in one person and seem 'inoperative' in another. Actually, it is always active, but only to a degree that is a function of the relationship between the person and the particular clay. When it seems inoperative, it is important to realize that it is that one particular clay which is not being very active, but not 'clay' in general. It would undoubtedly be possible to overcome this 'intolerance' by gradual habituation, but it is probably advisable to switch to a different clay. It may be necessary to get it from other districts or try many kinds in order to find the origin or color which is favorable. As a rule, clays obtained from the district you live in, act more in 'sympathy' than those from a far quarter, although there are exceptions. It would be best to try a few different kinds before determining which is the one for your specific needs.*

Assuming that nothing in clay's composition explains its action on the organism, it will be necessary to refer to empirical evidence and opinions based on experience for guidance in selecting the most efficient variety of clay. In general, it seems that greenish clay is the most active. However, it is also the least tolerated in cases of hypersensitivity. Certainly it can be used initially, reserving the possibility of changing to another in the case of any disagreeable manifestations such as nervousness, cooling, etc.

Before Using

The more clay is exposed to sun, air and rainwater, the more active it will become. It allows clay to exercise its property of absorbing and storing a remarkable part of the energy of other elements, above all, the sun. It is possible that its particles, infinitesimally small, constitute as many condensors capable of freeing witheld energy at the appeal of an opposite pole. Assuming the revitalizing action of clay, it may be possible to say it has the property of attracting the sun's magnetism upon initial exposition to light. It is this energy which it reconstitutes and gives out upon use. Perhaps it is this revitalizing action which accounts for its ability to fix the oxygen in water added to it.

*For information on obtaining clay in America, see 'Buyer's Guide' and 'Letter from Mass'.

The time for exposing clay to sunrays is just prior to an immediate need. For storing clay in its initial condition darkness is better; it can be kept indefinitely. It will grow no older in a dark container than it would have in the quarry from where it was taken out.

At this point, it is necessary to add that even taken out and applied without an intermediary and long exposition to light, clay already possesses most of its wonderful properties. A graphic proof is that clay is quite irreplaceable for sustaining life in cavernous species that dwell in pitch-dark. These cave-dwellers, especially certain shrimps (Niphargus), can only reproduce and develop themselves in clay. These animals would disappear and die if they were deprived of clay, although they are able to stand a lack of food for a long time.

Two Precautions

Clay does not adapt itself to the presence of other pharmaceutical medicines (even homeopathological ones); therefore, it is not advisable to combine its use with medical treatment. Sometimes patients under medical treatment are eager to know whether they can begin to use clay before finishing their treatment. It is not recommended, especially if used internally, as clay generally is inhibited by medicines. It is better for them to wait until ready to definitely and exclusively use the natural method of drinking clay. However, it is sometimes possible to combine external clay applications with medical treatment, especially for those people who still doubt clay's effectiveness.

As clay is so powerful, it is advisable to precede clay treatment with at least ten days of purifying teas (many kinds will be described in the course of the text) and food (mostly raw fruit and vegetables; no meat, sugar, alcohol, or chemicals) in order to reduce the amount of harmful toxins in the body. In all cases, clay treatment should be accompanied by sensible and healthy eating habits.

Internal Use of Clay

The idea of clay taken orally is now accepted and does not produce unjustified feelings of repulsion as it did when it was unknown. This is due, in part, to the fact that its benefits are becoming better known also because it turns out to be not at all disagreeable to take. The visible evidence of the effectiveness of clay applied externally also inspires confidence in its internal use.

It is interesting to note that when mixed with water, clay does not granulate unless there is the unfortunate presence of sand. So, for drinking purposes, it is best to choose a fine greasy clay which does not crack in the teeth: that is to say, without sand.

The clay should be prepared, if possible, several hours or even a night in advance. Put a teaspoon of clay into half a glass of unboiled water. *Do not leave a metallic teaspoon in contact with clay.* It is best to drink clay in the morning after waking or at night on going to bed; however, even 15-20 minutes before eating is possible, although at least an hour would be better.

Clay modifies itself -- its action changes according to the method of preparation (clay poured into water or vice versa, water onto dry clay, etc') and according to the manner of drinking it or application. So it is possible to observe a tendency to 'obstruct' the bowels if drunk before breakfast, while quite a different effect may be manifested if it is taken in the evening. This action on the bowels is the normal and quick 'direct' effect but, if we are looking for a sedation of stomach pains after eating, then we have to take clay immediately before eating.

The first treatment of clay last three weeks, then after a rest of a week, treatment is renewed continuing during the following months at the rate of a week of treatment alternating with a week of rest.

Clay does remarkable work in restoring deficient organs and organic functions. It does not accomplish this by supplying the missing elements, but by aiding the organism to be able to fix and assimilate those elements where previously it was failing. These catalytic substances need only be present in infinitesimal doses. Therefore, it is unnecessary to absorb large quantities of clay; a teaspoon daily is a sufficient average.

We know that certain substances such as lycopodium, inoffensive and inoperative in large doses, becomes one of the most active medicines when taken in infinitesimal doses. Similarly, clay should be used in relatively small doses. *It is useless to take large doses because its action, as already said, is due to its radiations and not to quantities of particular elements.* It is not merely a pain-reliever; it must be used prudently especially in internal use.

As has already been said, the average dose is a teaspoon for adults and half for children under 10 years. Although, in some bowel infections (tuberculosis, dysentery, etc.), the dose may be increased to two or three teaspoons a day.

When ingestion of clay is poorly tolerated, it is necessary to avoid injury by accustoming the organism to it slowly. Begin by drinking only the clayish water; introduce clay gradually until the daily dose of a teaspoon - the average per adult - is acceptable. Anyway, the absorbed quantity is only relatively important; there are people who, being unable to swallow clay and water, prefer to drink only the water after most of the clay has settled at the bottom of the glass, and they get satisfactory results.

If clay absorption produces nausea, mix it with a little water in order to form a kind of paste, make small balls like peas and let them dry. Swallow these instead of clay powder. For children, prepare this paste with some aromatic infusion (mint, eucalyptus, etc.) instead of water; and give the balls to suck as if they were caramels. People inclined to constipation can prepare the balls with a concoction of senna or rhubarb.

Babies will take a teaspoon of clayish water before three feedings every day.

In the case of rheumatism or sore-throat, suck clay in pieces or balls or simply take a teaspoon of powdered clay.

Sometimes clay sends forth a taste of petroleum, which does not alter its properties; quite the contrary, naphtha is a powerful antiseptic and clay is sometimes in contact with it in the ground.

As clay enriches the blood, it is advisable not to take too much when blood pressure is rather high - take only one or two small doses a day with water

If clay causes constipation, dissolve in in a little more water and take it several times during the day, between meals. Or else, if the constipation persists, replace clay with a laxative tea. This trouble can be eliminated by drinking a lot between meals so that the volume of liquid is sufficient to dilute three solid residues and evacuate them. In order to avoid this inconveniency - which is not all that common - in the beginning drink only the clayish water, leaving the sediment in the bottom of the glass.

Clay bricks are hardened and impermeabilized with an emulsion of a petroleum derivative. Thus, during clay treatment it may be prudent to restrain the use of domestic oils, whether or not this is really necessary.

In fact, this is a precautionary measure, because no incident has ever been reported involving the use of clay and the consumption of vegetable oil. In terms of experience, only the consumption of mineral oil is to be mistrusted. On the other hand, it is advisable to drink a lot between meals (lemonade, teas, etc.).

All these precautions apply especially concerning afflictions in which clay is in direct contact through the digestive channel (stomach or duodenal ulcer, enteritis, etc.).

Clay for External Use

Clay should not be prepared in a small bowl but in a deep bowl, wash-basin or a deep mixing bowl or even in a large wooden trough, as with clay it is best to have a large amount. Use a container made of enamel, earthenware, porcelain, wood, or glass, but never of metal (aluminum, copper, iron) or plastic materials. For storing dry clay, plastic may not be unsuitable, especially considering that nowadays plastics are manufactured for every kind of food product and considered perfectly stable. However, for the mixture of clay and water, it is advisable to use only those materials of recognized traditional stability.

Place clay inside, matching the surface distribution as much as possible. Keep a little dry clay nearby in case the mixture is too clear and has to be thickened; it is preferable for the mixture to be rather clear, as it is easier to thicken it by adding clay than to thin it by adding water. It is logical to prepare clay for several days use. For storing, just pour on a little water every day without touching the clay. If clay for poultices begins to harden before use, let it harden and when clay is quite dry, grind it prior to a new preparation. So do not be afraid to prepare too much at one time. Prepared in advance, clay lays out for better homogeneity. You will observe that when well-prepared and regularly soaked in water, it is easier to use.

Add unboiled water to the clay in the container until it reaches a half inch or so over the clay - initially, it may take a few trials because all clays do not absorb the same percentage of water. Let clay rest for some hours *without touching it.* When it is stirred up, it becomes sticky and difficult to handle. It loses its porosity becoming smooth and, in consequence, impermeable. Its possibilities of absorption are then very much reduced. It is not necessary to touch it before use; it dilutes itself alone quite well. Handle it as little as possible when placing it on the supporting cloth. Do not smooth its surface it will settle naturally when put into place.

The prepared clay has to be a smooth, very homogenous paste and not very concentrated - just enough to avoid falling apart. When possible, place the container in the sunshine, covering it with a gauze in order to avoid impurities.

Clay Temperature

Clay may be used cold, tepid or hot, depending on the specific problem. Each time it is used on a feverish or over-active or naturally-warmed organ (e.g. lower-abdomen). it must be cold. A few minutes after applying the poultice, it should feel tepid. If the cold sensation persists, it is not advisable to continue the cold poultice. On the other hand, if the poultice starts to feel very hot, it is necessary to change it after 5 or 10 minutes of application. When clay is used for revitalization purposes, for osseous rebuilding, for kidneys, for gall bladder, liver, etc., it must be warm or, at least, tepid.

The guiding principle is that 'every action is immediately followed by a reaction'. Thus, if we use the poultice on a feverish, angry or congested part, we have to refreshen it; but, if used with the goal of strengthening or revitalizing, we have to warm it. Applied on a weak or feeble organism or organ, it is possible to make cold applications of cold water, air, or mud, but the overheating, which is the goal of this application, must follow rapidly.

For fever or congestion, where the cold treatment may be compared with the system of water circulation for cooling car engines, overheating is dangerous and must be avoided. In other cases,

however, this cold treatment must bring about an overheating of the body due to the stimulation of organic functions such as oxidation and circulation. This means the body's temperature must rise slowly; *only when it produces this effect is the cold treatment beneficial.*

As with every rule, there are exceptions and there are weak or feeble people who will maintain poultices longer than necessary or remove them before the clay has had time to dry. In such cases as when clay produces a disagreeable feeling of cooling or even when it does not warm on contact with flesh, it is advisable to place a bag of boiling water near the poultice or beside the patient's bed. There cannot be a good defense without heat.

In some cases clay may at first weaken the patient. This obstacle is not insurmountable and after a long or short period of adaptation, clay becomes more bearable. In fact, it is a phenomenon of revitalization that energy so developed produces an immediate, but temporary reaction, reflecting latent reserves. Do not force things; apply small poultices in several places until a favorable position is found where clay can be easily supported. Put regular poultices around these areas, gradually increasing the size and duration of their application, eventually reaching the desired zone of treatment.

It is interesting that a clay poultice can be active on a point far from the application site. It is not necessary for clay poultices to be in direct contact with the affected part, for clay acts on the whole body. In a dental crisis (an abscess or such), clay may be put in direct contact with the gum - but it has actually been proven more efficient to apply a large poultice on the cheek.

How to Heat Clay

It is necessary to avoid placing clay in direct contact with a powerful source of warmth. A double-boiler is the most convenient way that will still preserve all of the clay properies.

Place the container with clay paste within another larger container filled with water to at least half the height of the clay container. Place everything on a fire and leave it there until the desired temperature is reached.

By placing it in the sunshine or by another source of mild warmth, such as a radiator or a warm stove-top, it is possible in certain cases to sufficiently heat the clay.

If you have prepared enough clay in advance for several poultices, do not heat the entire quantity - only warm what is necessary for one poultice because clay cannot be warmed twice. In this case, place the poultice fully prepared on the covered lid of a pan with hot water.

A good method to induce natural heating of the poultice is to apply very hot wet compresses on the area of application in advance or simply use a bag of boiling water. The slight problem with heating the poultice initially is that this sometimes does not avoid cooling, but only prevents the patient from feeling the disagreeable sensation of cold clay in contact with skin.

Preparing the Compress

Sometimes the use of a weaker clay compress is preferable to that of a poultice. To prepare it, it is necessary to make a clearer paste by combining less clay and more water than for a poultice. Just before using, stir it up in order to get a good mixture. It should adhere to a piece of cloth upon contact. Dip the piece of cloth into the clay, wring it out a little and place it on the part to be treated, using an intermediate cloth if necessary.

How to Prepare a Poultice

Place a piece of cloth folded in two or four parts on a table, bearing in mind that it has to be rather larger than the part to be treated.

With a palette-knife or a wooden spoon (neither metal or plastic material) spread an even layer of clay onto the prepared cloth. The thickness can vary from 1/4" to 1", according to need. Applying it as if it were an ointment will not get good results. Except when it is for a boil or similar treatment, clay can easily cover a surface of 4" x 8" with a thickness of 1" and often covers a surface of 8" x 12".

There are people who, for better handling of clay, prepare the poultices by mixing clay with wheat bran or flaxen flour in gauze. This is not correct, not only for reasons of comfort(as very dense clay is easy to handle) but also because the clay loses at least partially, its beneficial properties. Besides, the traces which clay leaves are easily removed; even on an ulcer or open sore where clay must be placed directly onto flesh, if traces remain on removal of the first poultice, they are absorbed by the next one. When a gauze or cloth is placed between clay and skin, the poultice sometimes sticks less, allowing some air to come through, provoking the cooling of the poultice or produces a disagreeable feeling of diminishing the beneficial effects of the clay. For efficient action, it is necessary to place it directly onto the body. We can also help to obtain better contact by pressing on the poultice, causing it to stick everywhere.

This method has another important facet - that of helping to determine the duration of the application. Clay applied in direct contact can do this because, after producing its effects, it falls off as does ripe fruit off the tree. On an abscess, boil, anthrax, etc., it takes about 20-30 minutes before the clay detaches itself, even when the poultice has been prepared with clay which is not so dense. When you notice that the clay has detached itself, it is because its action has finished. It is not important to remove it immediately (especially if it is at night, it is not necessary to awaken to control the phenomenon of spontaneous detachment) but it is very important to bear in mind the minimum time of application.

Assuming normal activity, clay should be nearly dry on removal. In this case the poultice is easily withdrawn, leaving a minimum of clay stuck to the skin. If it does not detach easily, pour a little water between clay and skin. Rasp the remaining particles of clay on the skin and wash it with cold or tepid water without soap. Never use alcohol or cologne water. Nevertheless, if clay has to be applied to a hairy or difficultly attainable part or if it has to be applied by a person who is treating himself alone, a piece of muslin, gauze or any other light cloth can be placed between the clay and the skin.

Once the poultice or compress is placed, cover it with a dry cloth then fix it with:
- a bandage of light cloth, such as an 'ace' bandage.
- a small band of flannel or another warm fabric if the application is on kidneys, liver, abdomen or lungs.
- a sticky bandage if the area is not accessible for a simple bandage, or if it is very small.
- a 'T' bandage if the application is perineal or rectal.

If the application is at the nape of the neck, bandage it to the forehead, not to the neck.

With regard to clay for external use, it is advisable to use a cabbage-leaf instead of a cloth for covering clay placed on an inflamed organ, an abscess or another purulent sore. In these cases, clay dries very quickly; the cabbage-leaf slows this drying, as cabbage keeps fresh longer. This may also be put into practice for a large poultice to be kept overnight - otherwise, it would dry very rapidly (particularly with varicose ulcers).

Rhythms of Application

The duration and sequence of application depends on the case to be treated, the extent of the ailment, the temperament of the patient, his reactions to clay, the surface to be treated and all other variables.

The application can last from one hour to all night, according to the case. Thus, when treating a deep organ (liver, kidneys, stomach, etc.) we can leave the poultice for two hours as a minimum, sometimes three or four hours. They should be spaced well before and after meals. It must be remembered that these larger applications determine very important reactions and that the organism cannot withstand them for a very long time without the risk of weakness if they are renewed frequently, especially if the patient is continuing his normal pace of activity. One poultice a day is usually proper. Two poultices a day may be applied to a patient who is in bed or inactive, if he can withstand them without fatigue or excessive reactions.

If the application has the goal of revitalizing an organ, or rebuilding an osseous decalcified tissue (vertebrae, etc.) it may be left overnight, but it should be removed during the same night if it disturbs or if it becomes cold.

On the other hand, if treating an abscess or purulent ulcer, for example it is necessary to change the poultices every hour whenever possible, night and day, until the end of the period of suppuration. Then leave the poultices for an hour and a half. At night, apply compresses of clayish water, renewing them once or twice. Finally, when tissues begin to be rebuilt, apply poultices every two hours with dry dressings during the night.

Clay is not a standard remedy to be applied indiscriminately disregarding specific considerations of the patient, his condition and the location and method of application. For a good result, it is necessary to individualize the methods of application and to make some trials prior to the

application of a determined treatment.

The season, as well as the climate, can be of great importance in determining the temperature of the poultice; for instance, a cold poultice, well supported in summer or in a warm region, can become unbearable upon change of season or climate. A congested liver can present a good reaction to cold clay while a blocked-up gall bladder will generally need a hot application.

On the lower abdomen, where fermentation of improperly digested food occurs, leading to rises in temperature, cold poultices about 1" thick should be applied (place clay in direct contact with the skin, or with a gauze in between on hairy areas. Poultices should be large). On the other hand, in certain afflictions, especially those of the bladder or ovaries, cold clay on the lower abdomen may be poorly tolerated, causing colic or other troubles. In such cases, tepid or even heated poultices must be applied.

With clay applications on the lower abdomen, as with the liver and especially with the stomach, it is necessary to apply them long after eating - essentially, completely out of the digestive period. Wait at least two hours after eating before applying a cold poultice; a hot one can be applied after one hour. Both must be removed at least one hour before eating in order to prevent clay reactions at the moment of beginning the first digestive phenomena. In general, the lower abdomen is where clay treatment must begin before any other application. However, do not put clay on the abdomen if menstruating except if there is an increase of temperature (fever).

Clay succeeds by performing a powerful drainage action and attracts all the substances of negative radiation. It is perfectly understandable then that all the toxins of the body will direct themselves towards the treated part when clay is applied. Therefore, it is possible and even probable that, on beginning the treatment a flaring up of the ailment will be produced; this is only an apparent and not a real worsening; it is due to the cleansing of the ulcer or treated part.

Can clay provoke reactions?

With every natural remedy helping either to directly rebuild the organism, or to liberate and eliminate those substances which harm it, it is always possible that there will be disagreeable reactions. For example, a varicose ulcer will at first enlarge itself, the dead flesh of the periphery will fall off, the surface inflate and pus or blood can appear. Pain may even increase for some time but it will decrease later and finally disappear with a definite closing of the ulcer and rebuilding of healthy tissues.

This is why it is advised before beginning a natural treatment to be sufficiently informed of its possibilities and its development. When a reaction is foreseen, it is more easily controlled. We must not be afraid of these reactions on the contrary, they are desirable, for they are a sign that the organism is responding to this intervention.

Of course, violent reactions are never desired; do not hesitate to temper brutal reactions. Eventually, replace the clay poultice for another of wheat bran and ivy leaves if pain is very violent. Remove the clay poultice if it is the origin of disagreeable manifestations – (nervousness, itching, burning sensations, cooling, etc). When the disturbance is gone, recommence to whatever extent can be tolerated. More frequently clay will

amount of toxins in the organism. It is only after ten days of this preparation that clay treatment can begin.

Once begun, do not interrupt a clay treatment, not even provisionally (presuming there are no adverse reactions). Clay is a very active agent; its application produces phenomena which start a chain reaction in the whole organism; to disturb the reactions once it has been started is hazardous. Just as it is useless to start a train, and then suddenly stop it - it must reach its destination. Here, the terminal is good health.

Since the clay has a very powerful action (in the reactions it produces and the energy it frees) it is impossible to apply it on two different places at the same time. If, for example, a poultice is applied on the lower abdomen, it is advisable to wait one hour or more after it is removed before applying another on any different organ. This waiting period may be reduced to 30 minutes or less in certain cases.

act quite the contrary-by calming intense pains.

Because the first action of clay is to drain abnormal particles towards the treated part and to cleanse ulcers, sometimes its immediate effect is to extend the ulcer, as mentioned above. In case of internal ulcers, as in any deep cancer (stomach, uterus, etc.) it is necessary to avoid such extension that could touch essential neighboring organs or drive the vital reserves of the patient to exhaustion.. Therefore, it might be best to begin with a mild action, applying a very small, thin poultice (less than 1/2"). After a few days, increase the size of poultices, and after that the thickness may be increased. Arrive gradually at a poultice measuring about 8-12" long, 6-8" wide and 3/4-1" thick. Don't increase both size and thickness simultaneously, but in accordance with the tolerance of previous applications that were without trouble, disorders or adverse reactions.

It is also advisable to precede the treatment with laxative teas, a fruit or lemon treatment, vegetarian nourishment and the absorption of clay by oral route, in order to greatly reduce the

In principle a clay application must not produce trouble or a sensation of pain. If, for example, a poultice placed on an abscess or boil dries it in half an hour, take it off without waiting the hour. If on the spinal column the poultice produces a cool feeling, even when applied hot, then take it off immediately and do not leave it overnight. When the application is made on a feverish or overheated part, it is necessary to take it out before the clay becomes warm; while if the goal is revitalization, that is to say, overheating, it is necessary to take it off before the clay cools.

Sometimes an obstacle arises in clay treatment which can hinder its continuation: the appearance of red patches or eruptions accompanied by unbearable itching. The explanation is that perhaps acid substances flowing from internal regions pass through the tissues attracted by clay. The fact that this itching stops after clay applications would confirm this hypothesis.

There may be other phenomena but they have no importance if the treatment can continue. Try to diminish these eruptions and appease the itching by applying a soupspoon of tepid water stirred progressively into clay to pomade density, and applied after the poultice. Protect clothes and bed sheets with a cloth. If the poultice has been applied in the evening and left all night, this ointment should be applied in the morning.

The following evening try to apply the poultice again; in the case of disagreeable phenomena, several continued evenings. Recommence the clay application when everything is normal. In additions, drink an herbal tea. Even at the end of treatment, do not suddenly stop clay applications but space them progressively (every day, then twice a week, etc.). It is necessary to continue the applications more or less intensively to the last disappearance of the problem, until even the smallest piece of new skin over scars has properly grown in. Do not stop until the process is completely finished.

MISCELLANEOUS USES OF CLAY

Pregnancy

Clay, in combination with a natural diet, is highly beneficial for the formation of the foetus and in the preparation for childbirth.

Take a regular daily teaspoon of clay for one or two weeks.

If the child is badly situated, do not hesitate to apply clay poultices on the belly. For the sake of prudence, it is preferable to apply it systematically during the last month of pregnancy. Also place tepid clay poultices on the lumbar region if pains appear.

Cold poultices applied on the stomach just after the childbirth will prevent all subsequent troubles (principally, the risk of infection) and is the best remedy for the imperfect elimination of the afterbirth.

Clay drinking favors nursing.

Headaches

With all head troubles, whether sinusitis, migraines, ear inflammations, persistent headaches, etc., regardless of specific location, the treatment consists of applications of clay on the nape of the neck alternating with local poultices.

In case of migraine headaches, use poultices

alternately on the nape of the neck and forehead. On the forehead, apply light poultices of cold clay to be left for one hour. The surface of the clay in contact with skin can be sprayed with lemon juice. On the nape, apply thick tepid or cold clay poultices to be left for two hours maximum.

Keep alternating these until the total disappearance of the trouble. Complement the treatment with hot foot-baths, except in the case of varicose veins, where hot hand-baths are used instead.

Clay on the nape is also beneficial for, pineal and hypophiseal glands, as well as for thyroid problems.

In the event of sensations of giddiness or similar disturbances, interrupt the applications on the nape and do not renew them until having applied poultices on the lower abdomen for several days. Once wastes are eliminated and general toxicity is reduced, local treatment can be resumed.

Post-operative Complications

Clay applications give the best results for the reabsorption of adhesions, healing and other post-operative complications. It is not necessary to act immediately after the operation, but one or two months later.

Begin with very thin poultices (1/2-1 cm.) leaving them on for at least two hours. Then gradually increase to 2 cm. thick poultices.

If poultices are well-tolerated and if they do not fall apart, dry quickly or cool, they can be left in place overnight. At first, try cold clay, but warm it in a double boiler if heating does not occur rapidly after application.

After Use

Throw clay away after use, because it will be devitalized and impregnated with the toxins it absorbs. Whether it has been used on an ulcer or not, it is not able to be used again and is best thrown into a place where it cannot be touched. Wash the cloths which can be used again when dry.

It is possible to speculate that, exposed again to the elements and to its natural 'nourishment', clay will recover from its overcharges and regain the greatest part of its potentialities. This has yet to be tested and proven. Anyway, it is certain the clay would need a long rest period. Nor is buying price all that high as to inhibit the replacement of used clay.

When clay is needed for lengthy and difficult treatment look for a source of cheap clay such as in quarry, brick factory, or a ceramic plant. Of course, handling this clay, generally in big damp blocks, is not very convenient.

IN CONCLUSION

We have limited this chapter to a simple exposition of facts and practical instructions, abstaining from the enthusiastic praises clay inspires in us. Expression of enthusiasm, admiration or thankfulness must not be shown by dithyrambic phrases, but by results achieved.

It is not possible to foresee exactly what will happen with clay applications, especially at first, but in every case, there is a remarkable improvement, if not complete healing. As there are no dangers to fear, there is no reason to oppose giving it a try, even for an extended period of time.

Let us repeat: apparent inconveniences at the beginning do not represent any danger; on the contrary, it is a sign of the efficient and beneficial action of clay.

You must remember to precede the treatment with laxative teas, a fruit or lemon treatment, vegetarian nourishment, and the absorption of clay by oral route, in order to greatly reduce the amount of toxins in the organism. It is only after ten days of this preparation that clay treatment can begin.

For those who are not acquainted with clay, these affirmations may seem rather bold. How can a natural remedy as simple and cheap as clay perform such complex actions as: to void an abscess, to heal a sore, rebuild a vertebral column, reabsorb a cyst (even internal), relocate a badly placed foetus, help to rebuild destroyed tissues? How? No one knows. Those who would pinpoint it are bold indeed. Besides, the answer to this question is of but relative importance in the light of clay's effectiveness. We should be satisfied testing these powers. And so it is; more and more people are trying it every day. Is this not the essence?

Why not begin by experimenting with slight ailments, extending its use only in accordance with the extent of confidence in its effectiveness?

Perhaps one day scientific researches will be motivated towards the study of clays -- hopefully in applications which are not a violation of nature and her laws.

Since 1957, the date of issuing the first edition of this work, tens of thousands of clay users have appreciated its amazing properties. We were so astounded with each new result, and results were so often beyond expectation, that we realized clay has many more healing possibilities which are as yet unexplored. This is why there will always be a need for more research and more writing about clay.

SEVEN OF NATURE'S MARVELS

Lemon, Garlic, Olive Oil, Sea Salt, Carrots, Cabbage, Thyme

Nature provides many simple powerful remedies which are as valuable as they are inexpensive. Where nature sends a disease, nature must also provide a cure!

Here are seven of the most valuable, six from the earth and one from the sea.

LEMON

While many fruits are beneficial to good health, it remains indisputable that first place be conceded to the lemon. It is true that, medically, opinions on lemon have covered the spectrum from enthusiastic endorsement to tenacious general condemnation, including such statements as "Lemon decalcifies, lemon makes you tuberculous, lemon spoils the stomach"; nevertheless, experience and personal experiments have shown its true worth.

Lemon is one of the best aids to digestion because of the biliary reaction it stimulates. It also favors the fixation of calcium and is highly recom-mended for losing weight without incurring deficiency.

Lemon stimulates, decongests, and cleanses the liver. Also, the potassic salts and glucose of lemon tonify the heart. It is excellent for fluidifying the blood, and yet it does not act to prevent coagulation at all.

Very high blood pressure, very dense badly-circulating blood, hardened arteries, distended veins, fragile blood vessels.....all these troubles are healed with a good lemon cure. In fact, there are many people who cannot tolerate herbal remedies and yet feel at ease with a lemon cure. In addition, it is one of the most effective and quickest of blood purifiers. The organisms of parasites, dysentery, typhus, cholera and similar bacterial diseases do not stand up to lemon action. And if toxins, crystallized, are lodged in the joints or surrounding areas, as in cases of arthritis and rheumatism or even in the kidneys and bladder, it is only necessary to use lemon for dissolving and eliminating them.

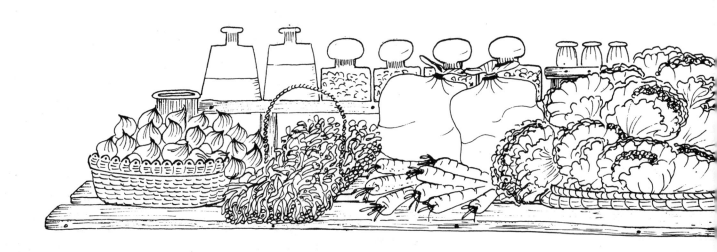

Of course, it is not advisable to go overboard and recommend immediately drinking 6,8, or 10 lemons or more without considering the condition and temperament of the individual. A lemon cure should be carried out without useless haste, increasing or decreasing quantity slowly. It must begin with 1 or even ½ a lemon every day until the body is acclimated, and then increase by 1 or ½ a lemon every two or three days.

The average daily quantity varies according to the case, the temperament, the climate and the distance from where the lemons were grown. For treating rheumatism or arthritis, it is possible to arrive at 8 or 10 lemons a day. In localities where lemons are grown, a daily absorption of 20 or 30 lemons is less dangerous than 6 or 7 which were picked before ripening and ripened in the course of transport, as happens in most regions.

After arriving at the limit permitted by the organism, it is necessary to taper off at the same rhythm, until maintaining a consumption of 2-4 lemons daily.

Lemon has many external uses as well. For example, a few lemon drops into the nose relieves migraine; use the inside part of a lemon peel to massage and strengthen the gums; pass a lemon cut into two sections over the pricks of gnats, fleas, lice, and other small insects; use the inside part of lemon rind for curing hand or facial skin problems. Lemon juice is a preventive for chilblains and it can strengthen the sensitive skin of feet; it also has enormous antiseptic power - rub sores with lemon juice -- it stings a little but how beneficial it is!

The best way to take lemons is with water (½ a lemon in 4-8 oz. of water)for drinking during the day between meals or with a little hot water, before, during**, or after** meals. Honey may be added, but never sugar. In fact, lemon and honey is a very nutritious mixture, capable of treating aphtas and oral irritations.

For strengthening the liver, it is useful to add a little grated lemon rind to raw salads. It is equally efficient for the stomach's tone. Lemon juice should replace vinegar in all the seasonings. Eating lemon seeds quickly eliminates oxyrus. He who eats lemon with rind, pulp and seeds has made good work for his organism.

Many people who were decalcified, tuberculous, obese, anemic, dyspeptic, acidic, arthritic, rheumatic, or troubled by parasites or ulcers owe their return to health to lemon, combined with the practice of natural medicine and sensible eating habits. An absolute intolerance to lemon is very rare; it is usually due to fear, prejudice or reminiscence and most likely is only temporary. Acting with prudence and moderation, there is no reason to refuse the precious and varied properties of lemon. Lemon is truly one of nature's marvels.

GARLIC

Garlic is a powerful remedy and an efficient preventive. It is also very inexpensive and easy to

---

**One exception: cereals and lemon juice are not a favorable combination.

procure.

Containing, among other elements 'allyl'(volatile sulphurous essence), sulphur iodine, and silica, garlic is a natural antiseptic and a wonderful disinfectant, especially for the lungs. Its elements enter the blood stream very rapidly. Natural association with these substances forms a protection of the whole organism against illness, glandular imbalance and many other troubles.

Garlic can help dissolve the parasitory calcifications such as uric acid crystals found in arteriosclerosis. It is also a powerful germicide and it is sufficient to wear a garlic necklace or to put it into a small bag around a child's neck to make body parasites disappear. Internally, it fights worms and prevents putrefactions, as well as purifying the blood. In the south of France, children are strengthened by using garlic as suppositories.

Garlic is also useful for rheumatism and arthritis - rub the painful parts with a mixture of camphor oil and chopped garlic(2:1).

Garlic increases gastric secretions and the mobility of the stomach walls, and thus stimulates appetite and digestion. For internal use, garlic may be put in all dishes. It is necessary to take it raw, as cooking destroys most of its active forces. If garlic is not well-accepted by the stomach, it is because the mucous membranes of the digestive apparatus are very inflamed or ulcerated. In the first case, it is necessary to be careful to chew thoroughly, or else, for a safer and more efficient action, to do the following:

Chip 2 - 4 cloves of garlic(begin with one) and put them in a glass with hot water; leave to steep and dissolve overnight. In the morning, filter it, discard the garlic and drink the water.

In his book, *Healing Vegetables and Fruits*, Leonce Carlier gives this interesting recipe: 'crush one or two cloves of garlic with parsley in the evening, adding olive oil. In the morning, spread the paste on bread as if it were butter for breakfast.' We add this precaution: crush the garlic well into the oil with a fork in order to avoid the evaporation of sulphurous essences of garlic which are very volatile. Another agreeable way of taking it is to spread a mixture of butter and chopped garlic on a slice of bread.

It would be a pity to be deprived of garlic as it is certainly one of the most important and powerful of all of nature's remedies.

OLIVE OIL

Olive oil is one of the best and sweetest of curatives. It should always be cold-pressed, using no heat or chemical solvents. Cold-pressed olive oil retains all its natural ferments and is very digestible.

Olive oil is the source of the most healthy type of fat for the human organism. In addition, its cholesterol is a protective and constitutive substance for the cells and is completely different from the dangerous cholesterol obtained by eating the flesh of animals.

It is an excellent natural laxative and of great benefit to the intestines, for it lubricates the mucous membrane of the intestines and yet does not seal it off and prevent nutritive elements from being absorbed.

Olive oil also stimulates the secretion of hepatic and pancreatic juices. It is very helpful to the liver in particular, especially in cases of gallstones and liver congestion. There are even instances known of doctors who have been successful in

eliminating gallstones by administering to their patients a single massive dose of olive oil - quantities of up to half a quart or even more! Nevertheless, it is far preferable to proceed slowly but safely; this is nature's way.

Olive oil is most effectively beneficial when taken in the morning on an empty stomach. Up to three teaspoons may be taken, depending on age and tolerance. It is usually advisable to mix it with an equal quantity of lemon juice, which serves to emulsify it.

SEA SALT

The constitution and osmotic pressure of sea water is similar to human blood ('Quinton's plasma', an artificial blood serum is a mixture of sea and fresh water). This similarity and also its mineral richness, is reproduced to a certain degree in sea salt.

Sea salt also contains clayish particles; it is an intermediary between earth and sea. It associates very well with clay, reinforcing its action, for it also has the property of attracting and absorbing unhealthy substances.

It is not possible to give a general rule on the use of salt in feeding because it is quite a strictly individual question to be solved in accordance with various abundances or deficiencies (sodium, magnesium, iodine, etc.). Sometimes it is necessary to give a deficient baby a teaspoon of sea or salt water before meals.

The sodium chloride of sea salt balances with the addition of potash to fields and its magnesium lessens the toxicity of chemical fertilizers. For avoiding 'cancer' the live magnesium of sea salt is a thousand times more precious than all commercial inorganic salts. Iodine, equally alive in sea salt, acts favorably on the thyroid and is without the dangers of iodine obtained by chemical methods. At the same time, its bromide soothes the nerves without weakening the nervous system. In addition to these useful substances sea salt still has traces of many other catalyzing elements(gold, copper, nickel, cobalt, etc.).

Unrefined sea salt can be of precious assistance as an auxiliary for a humoral glandular or nervous disorder caused by deficiency.

It is possible to remedy glandular disorders with complete baths of heated salt water and 'sea-weed broth' (pre-soaked seaweed). Thin poultices may be prepared with seaweed and salt.

The tonic action of a salt water bath is already known; only remember that for children up to ten years old, about 2 pounds of sea salt is sufficient for a warm bath of 15-20 minutes duration. One bath a week is enough. Increase or reduce the dose according to age and height.

Hot foot-baths with two or three handfuls of sea salt produce a tonic action which reverberates throughout the organism. (In the case of varicose veins, replace the foot-bath with a hand-bath).

Ablutions over the whole body with very salted fresh water produce a light and beneficial excitation.

Its healing and antiseptic properties make unrefined sea salt excellent for gargling in all instances of mouth or throat trouble. Put 1 tablespoon in a large glass of unboiled water. Do this three times a day.

Always use mineral-rich sea salt for cooking and eating purposes rather than common table salt.

CARROTS

Carrots are one of nature's most useful aids to good health, for in its juice form it is well-tolerated and appreciated even by those who are not accustomed to eating vegetables raw. Carrot soup is suitable even for babies with fragile intestines.

Carrots can be an effective cure for diarrhea, as they are very beneficial for the intestines. Even cases of diarrhea with blood in the stools have been known to quickly disappear when carrot juice was taken to the extent of one pint a day. As a matter of fact carrot juice can operate as an excellent remedy for constipation as well, particularly in those cases of constipation caused by liver insufficiency, since carrots help to fluidify the bile. Thus, the importance of carrots as a source of vitamin K is increased, since this vitamin becomes active only in the presence of bile in the digestive tube. In addition, its carotene helps the liver to isolate vitamin A.

Carrots should be used raw as often as possible in vegetable dishes, grated and seasoned with lemon and olive oil. Preferably, it should not be peeled as the peel is rich in important ingredients. Use organically grown carrots, or scrub the carrots very well with a stiff brush; do not soak, for many of its vitamins are water soluble.

Carrot juice is a powerful remedy and tonic, as has already been mentioned. Up to two glasses a day may be taken, either before or after meals, but always on an empty stomach. Some water should be added before giving it to infants.

The various uses of carrots and carrot juice are numerous and effective, they are to be found throughout the entire book.

CABBAGE

Cabbage is one of the most valuable of nature's plants. Simply used as a food, it already has certain special qualities: it is rich in sulphur and contains arsenic, calcium and iodine; it serves as an aperitive, remineralizer and reconstituent. For those who worry about nitrogen deficiency due to an absence of meat in their diet, cabbage supplies this element in generous quantities. In addition it is rich in vitamins, it is antiscorbutic and revitalizing; it beautifies the skin. The chlorophyl in cabbage favors the production of hemoglobin, and is an aid in the treatment of anemia.

Cabbage is also effective in cases of nephritis and when troublesome threadworms and intestinal worms are present in the bowels. Its germicidal power is particularly located in the raw juice(extract it with a fruit-press and drink about 1 oz. a day).

Contrary to appearance and prejudices, cabbage is a specific for the bowels, where its mucilage, sulphur and potassium salts do marvels, on the condition that they are not spoiled or misused in cooking. Boiling cabbage deprives it of most of its richness. On the contrary, steamed or raw, cut in thin slices with olive oil, a little salt and lemon, its nutritive elements are untouched, inoffensive and beneficial.

It is interesting to realize that ancient peoples recognized the value of cabbage and held it in great esteem. Their authors mentioned many picturesque recipes, for example, "the water in which cabbages are boiled helps wonderfully our nerves and joints. If we wish to cure old or new sores, or

cancers not healed by any other medicament, treat them first with hot water, then apply well-crushed cabbage. Cabbage heals colic - boil twice, the second time adding oil, salt, cumin-seed and boiled barley flour. If we eat it so seasoned without bread it will be very useful."

Hippocrates advised those affected with heart disease, dysentery, tenesmus(constant and nearly useless desires to evacuate), to eat cabbages boiled twice with a little salt. Caton the Ancient, of Rome, advised the application of cabbage poultices in all cases of diseases with fever and for eruptions, wounds, ulcers and arthritis.

The Celtic and Germanic tribes also greatly appreciated cabbage for its nutritive value as well as its curative properties.

In general, raw cabbage can be used for numerous afflictions by placing the leaves directly onto the skin, as well as being both nutritive and delicious when eaten raw in salads.

THYME

Thyme is an excellent natural health-aid, although it is not at present very well known. Its antiseptic power reaches pharmacies mainly in the form of extracts of "essences" which are more or less devitalized. It is much better to use the whole plant in its natural state in decoctions and infusions.

Thyme used as a spice aids digestion as well as adding an agreeable taste to the food it is cooked with. Its pleasant flavor is an additional bonus to its numerous virtues.

The benefits of thyme tea in decoctions and thyme inhalations, thyme powder and thyme compresses are scattered throughout the book: from thyme tea as an agent against colds and hay fever, to thyme baths for arthritic conditions and even thyme powder as a dentifrice to strengthen the gums. Thyme is tonic, resolvent and anti-spasmodic as well as antiseptic; it is truly one of nature's marvels.

PREPARING HERBS FOR HEALING

Many recipes for the preparation of herbal teas and decoctions are given throughout the book. Plants vary greatly, the method indicated for each particular plant is the one best suited for extracting and protecting its active healing properties.

A decoction is prepared by putting the ingredients in the pot with cold water and then bringing it to a boil. If no time is specified, remove from the fire as soon as the boiling point is reached and let infuse for recommended time.

In an infusion the water is brought to a boil first, and the plants are added immediately upon removing the pot from the fire.

The general principle is that roots are boiled briefly, the whole plant and seeds are brought to a boiling point, and leaves and flowers are infused.

It is best to use a heavy enamel or glass (pyrex) teapot. Stainless steel is also acceptable, but never aluminum, teflon, or anything chemically treated.

If an indicated plant is not available consult a good herbal reference and substitute a different one with similar medicinal properties.

Use spring water whenever possible.

Avoid sweetening the teas when prepared for medicinal purposes. At most, a little bit of honey may be added.

In general, the dose remains the same whether the plant is fresh or dried. Fresh plants are more voluminous than the dried and therefore there will be less of them per measure (teaspoon, handful, etc.), but, on the other hand, the vital properties of the fresh plant are much more active than those of their dried counterpart.

The doses indicated in the recipes are for adults. For children it is necessary to dilute the prepared infusion by adding water.

For a child of less than 1 year use 1 part tea to 4 parts water.

Between 1 and 3, 2 parts tea to 3 parts water.

Between 3 and 5, 3 parts tea to 2 parts water.

Between 5 and 10, 4 parts tea to 1 part water.

For older children it is not necessary to dilute the preparation, but only a small cup should be given.

For some adults it may be necessary to reduce the dosage as well, depending on the sensitivity. The basic method is to begin with a half-dose and gradually increase it in accordance with individual tolerance.

Smaller amounts than specified in the recipes may be prepared, but in reducing the amounts of plants and water, take care that the proportions remain the same.

* *

pinch	= 2 or 3 grams	
Teaspoon	= 5 grams	
Tablespoon	= 10 grams	
Full tablespoon	= 15 grams	= ½ oz.
Handful	= 30-40 grams	= 1 - 1½ oz.
	25-30 grams	= 1 oz.

THE LIVER

The Unknown Organ

Many readers will be surprised at what we have to say about the liver. They are to realize that what is written here is not just something whimsical or original - what follows has been learnt from years of experience and observation.

The reader will have to become familiar with certain important facts that will prepare him for a better understanding of this natural medicine. He must learn not to attribute his disease to any mysterious bacterial agents, however microscopic, but to himself, his style of life and his way of eating. He will also learn that taking care of the liver is the best way to assure good health, for the heart and other major organs depend on the liver to produce the good quality blood they need for nourishment and invigoration. To accomplish this, he will acquire several natural healing methods in addition to the use of clay. After reading these next few chapters, he will fully realize that good health is at hand.

A malfunctioning liver plays a large contributing part in nearly every disease of the organism. Many of those diseases will be listed here to show that connection, even though they will all be discussed at greater length later on in their respective chapters.

The reader must realize that there is no cure of any disease, no true health, without a healthy well-functioning liver.

The importance of the liver and its significant part in the origin of all disease remains largely unknown because it almost never feels painful - except during cases of inflammation of the gall bladder - and so nobody pays any attention to it. Yet, a person with a healthy, well-functioning liver is a rare exception; the modern liver is a victim of bad food and chemicals, sometimes it is even already overworked at birth.

The liver is approximately as heavy as the brain. Its weight varies from 3-4 pounds, depending on the amount of blood that it contains. It is the largest gland and is involved in several functions.

The liver is an organ of digestion along with the stomach, the small intestines, the salivary and gastric glands, the pancreas and the duodenum. Some of its secretions enter the digestive tubes, others enter the blood directly.

The liver is not simply a filter situated between the intestines and the heart, but is a biliary organ and an endocrine gland; it plays a role of great importance in that it maintains or re-establishes the general equilibrium. The primary liver function is blood formation; other functions are the transformation of protein and fats, the fixation of materials for maintenance and building, the neutralization of certain poisons, the production of several enzymes and the fulfillment of the functions of regulation.

The liver does not merely distribute material; it also has the important role of biologically transforming these materials, 'humanizing' them before their utilization. Without this process, the best food can become poison for the organism.

The liver also produces particular substances needed to establish and maintain basic body defenses against infection. The absence or insufficiency of these substances promotes the appearance or the perseverence of the infection.

VARIOUS FUNCTIONS OF THE LIVER

Digestion

Every two hours the liver secretes from 500-1000cc. of bile, used primarily for the digestion and assimilation of fats. Biliary salts emulsify the fats, helping the action of the enzymes and of the pancreatic lipase.

Nutritive substances are definitely 'humanized' and metabolized only after they have been acted upon by liver secretions. Without this transformation, almost all foods would be toxic. The toxicity of a chemical remedy can be attenuated if the remedy is taken through the mouth or even through the rectum, rather than by an injection into the blood. Notwithstanding, it will still inevitably lead to the tiring of the liver and even to the destruction of its cells. In addition, it is the liver which must take care of transforming, fixing or eliminating poisons such as the ptomaines of animal tissues, nicotine and caffein, as well as all the waste products and toxins carried by the blood.

Bile completes the process of digestion and assimilation of fats. Fats can be used only after having been emulsified by the bile. It is also through the liver that albumin, sugars, vitamins, etc., are filtered and transformed before use or storage. Carbohydrates that are not immediately used are transformed into fat and stored. Poisons coming from inside or outside are neutralized, cholesterol is transformed, iron is fixed and sulphur oxidized.

It is also due to the liver and its secretions that uric acid can be discharged into the urine after its transformation into urea. It is the same with the ammoniacal salts and the surplus amino acids which are also discharged, for otherwise they would be harmful to the organism, as they would make it too sensitive to any mechanism.

Deficiencies in any of these functions of the liver lead to a state of toxicity and hypersensitivity generally expressed by an attack of rheumatism, asthma, or hives. As soon as a toxic substance is absorbed, the liver intercepts, neutralizes and rejects it with the help of the bile. Even a minimal amount tires the liver and can even cause its failure. A deficient or encumbered liver cannot effectively perform its function of defense. When this is the case, a part of the ingested toxic substances goes directly to the blood, degenerating organs and nervous centers.

Formation of the Blood

If the liver does not actually make blood globules, it still plays a primary role in maintaining blood balance, thanks to its anti-anemic function. Regularizing the amount of iron in the blood cells and the coagulation index of the blood, the liver prevents both hemophilia and excessive coagulation.

When the body's defenses must be mobilized, the liver provides the proteins necessary for the fabrication of white blood cells. The liver synthesizes certain proteins including fibrin and prothrombin which are indispensable for the coagulation of the blood.

The biliary salts also play a great part by preventing the blood from becoming too fluid. They contribute to absorbing the lipo-soluble vitamins such as vitamin K, which is also a blood thickener. In case of deficiency in biliary salts, the fats and the lipo-soluble vitamins are not absorbed. When neither synthesis of prothrombin nor the ingestion of vitamin K takes place, there follows a tendency to hemophilia.

After absorption of a substance made of the combination of two factors: an external one provided by food, and an internal one constituted from gastric secretions, the blood carries this substance to the liver where it is stored. After transformation, this substance becomes a hepatic factor, which, once freed by the liver, goes to the bone marrow where the red blood cells are made. In a liver that is already congested it may become impossible to store these substances, while an insufficient liver is incapable of transforming them. Cirrhosis, for example, does not allow these essential functions. Anemia results from these failures and abnormalities.

The rationale of treating anemia by eating animal livers (or extracts of them) is to provide a hepatic hormone that the liver is sometimes unable to produce. However, to obtain a minute quantity of this hormone, it is necessary to ingest (or inject!) an enormous quantity of toxic bodies which were inevitably trapped in the liver at the moment the animal was killed; what is more, this toxic supplement is even less justified since the deficiency is alleviated only temporarily, without bringing any remedy to an abnormality which will be corrected only with the re-establishment of normal functioning.

The same remarks also apply to blood transfusion. At the time the blood is removed from the donor, red globules are stopped by certain liver cells which transfer their iron pigment to other liver cells; these latter cells are responsible for the transformation of hemoglobin into biliary pigments. A large part of the red globules are used for the fabrications of the hormone that was previously mentioned. Pigments and hormones combined give a substance that is sent toward the bone marrow, where it will stimulate the production of red blood cells.

It is only through this process that the introduction of foreign blood can contribute to the making of new blood, for transfused blood is immediately attacked by antibodies, which are in the plasma. The consequence of that is a fever, followed by diverse manifestations, hives, asthma, etc. The seriousness of these manifestations arises from the fact that, at the moment of the destruction of the foreign red blood cells, the substances which result from their transformation sometimes agglomerate in the small tube of the kidneys and obstruct them. This is the *hepatic crisis of transfusion* which can be deadly. If the transfusion brings about an excess formation of biliary pigments, jaundice is the result.

Along with its function - of securing the coagulation of the blood - the liver seemingly exercises the opposite function of fluidifying the blood. This also contributes to organic equilibrium. In fact, without the intervention of a hepatic secretion(heparin), the blood would coagulate in the vessels (this happens in the case of phlebitis). It is the liver which maintains fluidity in the thinnest vessels.

Hormones

Besides the production of its own hormones, the role of which is not yet clear, the liver effects the transformation of the steroid hormones(mostly sexual) and regulates the folliculin production. This folliculin, if present in excess, lowers the calcium content of the blood, creating anguish and hypersensitivity. Its insufficiency can also be a factor in these troubles.

In case of excess folliculin, other problems also arise which have their origin in an insufficiency or a disturbance in the liver functions. There may be constipation, dark and insufficient urine and hemorrhoids.

Thus it is important that the liver be in the best

possible condition for the accomplishment of all its functions, as its impairment can have grave consequences.

Regulation

The liver contributes to the metabolism of the lipids, to the regulation of carbohydrates and to the synthesis of proteins. It regulates the iron level in the blood stream and helps maintain a constant temperature within the body. Whenever some parts in the organism manifest a tendency to congestion, the liver acts to help by regulating the circulation.

These regulatory functions of the liver play an important part in the processes of transformation and synthesis. They help in the elimination of excess substances. Thus, in the case of cholesterol, which is indispensable to the normal functioning of the organism but is quite dangerous in accumulation, the liver portions out the cholesterol according to need and neutralizes its excess.

The liver is also responsible for the homeothermic balance. Its deficiency leads to the abnormal lowering of temperature. Also, its overactivity or its congestion can be responsible for a constant fever. A person with an overactive liver suffers from heat in the summer, whereas one with an insufficient liver barely tolerates the cold and is not comfortable in winter. When the composition or the density of the blood changes because of a liver disorder, small, bright red specks the size of a pinhead sometimes appear and reappear at different places on the body.

EFFECTS OF A MALFUNCTIONING LIVER

General Liver Troubles

There are many possible troubles and lesions of the liver, each with numerous ill consequences.

Jaundice

The yellow coloration of the skin and the mucous membranes indicate an impregnation of the tissues by excess biliary pigments in the blood. The jaundice can be of an acute form or may be chronic.

There are many types of jaundice, each with their own symptoms of disorder and complications.

Hemolytic jaundice indicates that the excessive destruction of the red blood cells is accompanied by anemia and by an increase in the size of the spleen.

Obstructive jaundice may arise when the bile does not flow normally into the intestines due to the obstruction of the biliary channels.

Jaundice from hepato-nephritis is linked to liver and kidney troubles. This type of jaundice is distinguished by a dark coloration of the feces, whereby a great abundance of pigments thicken the bile and hamper its flow.

Finally there is the *classical jaundice* which is more widely known. The passage of bile in the blood causes the dislocation of the skin and mucous membranes. The urine is also darkened due to the discharge of biliary pigments.

Gastric intolerance is very marked, nausea and vomiting occur quite often and there is complete loss of appetite - which in a way is good, for food would do more harm than good at this point. The patient shivers despite temperatures which may be as high as 95° or 100°. The urine might be dark, but the feces lose their normal brown color, becoming light. In this case the pigments which are eliminated in mass by urinary channels, are missing in the intestines. These symptoms may be accompanied by headaches, pains in the joints, or hives.

Cirrhosis

Cirrhosis is generally characterized by a proliferation of cells, causing an expansion of the liver. Only the principal forms are listed here.

Hepatitis generally occurs from contamination after a vaccination, a blood transfusion or any other injection in the blood. The cure for hepatitis is the same as for jaundice.

In the case of *atrophic cirrhosis,* the decrease in the size of the liver accompanies the hardening and premature aging of the tissues; it is generally the terminal phase of all types of cirrhosis.

One of the most common forms of cirrhosis is the famous *alcoholic cirrhosis,* distinguished by liquid in the abdomen. The abdomen is very voluminous although the body becomes thinner. The legs are swollen; if pressed with the finger, the hollow that has been caused by the pressure remains. The tissue is soft and insensitive. This is a typical case of edema which often accompanies cirrhosis. These signs accompany a dry mouth and a bright red coloration of the tongue. The skin is dry and

scaly. Urine often becomes more and more rare; hemorrhage is likely to occur.

Another type is where *fat* accumulates in the liver tissues instead of liquid.

Biliary cirrhosis is when the liver sometimes increases or decreases in size. In this particular case, a tuberculous manifestation could very well affect the envelope of the heart, the liver and the peritoneum. Here the liver is big and there is edema and dropsy.

Abscesses

The liver is sometimes the seat of slow-developing abscesses; the temperature rises and pain is felt.

Stones

A 'mud' can accumulate in the gall bladder and create 'stones', solidified masses of normal elements in the bile, such as pigments and cholesterol which were badly utilized or not eliminated. The presence of these stones in the biliary ducts is called *biliary lithiasis.* It is when the elimination of these stones begin(occurring often in women) that *hepatic colitis* appears. At the place of the gall bladder, under the right costal edge, great pain is sensed most acutely at the level of the right breast, with irradiations toward the shoulder and the point of the right shoulder blade. This pain is most acute around 3 A.M. Complete inhalation is sometimes impossible. Nausea and vomiting may occur. The mouth is sticky and there is a bitter taste. The second day of the attack, the temperature can reach 105° - this indicates the extent of the defense effort of the organism, it goes down in a few hours. In all, the crisis lasts approximately three days.

A constant temperature indicates the persistency of the abnormal state. In this case a prolonged cure will be required.

Finally the *liver insufficiency* can be due to the partial obstruction of the biliary channels by mud or gall stones. It can also be caused by a failure of the normal function of the liver. A degenerated organ does not always present apparent lesions or abnormalities, yet still is incapable of accomplishing its normal functions.

Overeating causes a slowing down of the liver functions due to congestion of the ducts. The result is the famous 'liver attack' which manifests itself in nausea, vomiting, constipation - or diarrhea, headaches, dizziness, shivering, and an unhealthy complexion. This attack is sometimes preceded by differing symptoms, for example, dislike of food, shivering, feeling of having splinters under the nails and the eye unable to take bright light.

SYMPTOMS OF A MALFUNCTIONING LIVER

Yellow complexion - the skin is yellow, the white of the eye is also yellow.

Spots - Sometimes coloration is not uniform and occurs in the form of dark spots on the face and on the back of the hands. The presence of excess cholesterol is usually exhibited by small protuberances in the eyelids. These little 'bulbs' do not have the same coloration as the neighboring tissue. Other spots appear in the forehead, around the nose. The skin often seems to be dirty.

Red nose - the disadvantageous influence of a deficiency in the biliary functions during digestion often results in a red nose.

The mouth - the mouth is often 'sticky', especially when waking up. There is also a feeling of bitter taste. The breath sometimes smells so bad that it is loathsome. The tongue is thick, with a whitish, yellowish or even greenish coat. The exaggerated insalivation may be caused by an inflammation of the gall bladder.

Nausea - Most of the time a liver disorder is at the origin of nausea and the rising of the bile. Sometimes vomiting may follow. The subject has no appetite, even for food he usually appreciates. He may complain of heart trouble.

Gas - the presence of gas in the intestines is normal, providing the phenomenon is not too frequent and they evacuate through normal channels and do not have an odor. On their way out these gases exercise a useful massaging effect on the intestines, aiding the peristaltic movement. Too often, however, it is not always that ideal; putrid gases form and accumulate, causing painful swelling of the abdomen. These gases can expand in the organism and settle into pockets between organs, or create artificial pockets. This state is due to an insufficient secretion of the bile. Upon reaching the duodenum, food, deprived of bile, spoils; the result of this is a release of putrid gases, which, before passing into the intestines, causes a swelling.

Painful points - it has been said that hepatic colitis is generally the consequence of the onset of an evacuation of gall stones, or of mud that has accumulated in the gall bladder. These stones, or mud, can cause a permanent inflammation, or even an infection of the gall bladder and its ducts. When this happens there is a feeling of acute pain below the ribs on the right side. Sometimes this sharp pain is felt only after pressing there with the fingers. The inflammation of the gall bladder and ducts, and also the congestion of the liver, often causes a feeling of pain around the area of the right shoulder blade and shoulder.

Sometimes the biliary deficiency will manifest itself in the left side, just opposite the gall bladder. This is the result of a gas formation. The presence of gas at this spot occurs frequently, causing sharp pains and palpitations and other uncomfortable troubles.

Headaches - liver troubles which cause constipation are almost always the root of headaches. There is a feeling of heaviness in the whole head; the pain forms a 'circle' around the upper part of the head. There is also a feeling of pressing at the level of the temples. Liver disorder can also cause dizziness and blind spells, and even mental fatigue and nervous depression.

Sleep - Sleeping is often difficult because of a congested liver, especially around one or two o'clock in the morning. The subject sometimes can not fall asleep until the morning. During the hours of insomnia the subject finds relaxation impossible due to annoyance from digestive troubles and negative thoughts which are its natural results. However, a desire to sleep (somnolence, torpor) will occur during the day, generally after meals.

Urine - people with hepatic troubles urinate more during the night than in the daytime. They do not urinate much in general, for the kidney does not receive the necessary stimulants.

The urine is not clear, but rather cloudy. However, if it is too clear, it indicates that the biliary pigments are missing and that the functions taking care of natural elimination are perturbed.

THE DIRECT CONSEQUENCES OF A MALFUNCTIONING LIVER

Bad Digestion

After food has stayed briefly in the stomach for 3 hours, it then goes to the duodenum where it remains 6-7 hours; afterwards it travels to the large intestines where it remains between 10-20 hours. Food, then, is under the influence of the bile for all but three of the 19-30 hours of digestion. A lack of bile makes these phases of digestion impossible.

Bad Evacuation

Poor flow of bile, its lack of necessary elements, or its imperfect composition all have an ill-effect on the process of evacuation. The quart of bile that is secreted each 24 hours, due to its viscosity, assures the lubrication of the intestines. An imbalance in the biliary functions will cause constipation due to a lack in the biliary salts which normally stimulate the peristalsis of the intestines.

Constipation alternating with diarrhea is one symptom of the condition. The feces (and also the urine) may either lose color or be heavily colored. Sometimes they are not so well-formed, or not formed at all, or they may be thin, or have a hard or putty-like consistency.

Intestinal Spasms

The lack of biliary salts in the intestines or a fault in the composition of the bile could be at the origin of an overheating of the intestinal walls. This irritation has a repercussion on the nerve ends of these walls, which sometimes causes spasmodic contractions of the viscera. It has often been verified that the return to normal of the liver preludes the suspension of the intestinal spasms, which might have been a manifestation of the defense effort of an ulcered colon.

Collibacillosis

The abnormal proliferations of intestinal bacilli lead to serious intestinal or urinary troubles, depending on the amount in the intestines or in the urinary channel.

A rich and varied flora flourishes in the intestines and exercises a beneficial activity during the terminal process of digestion if the proper balance is maintained between them. They are: colon bacilli, streptococcus, staphylococcus, bacilli of Aertryck, bacilli of Gartner, aerobics, anaerobics, etc. Any one of these may become dangerous when the balance is upset. It is the bile which regularizes this medium, conditioning the state of equilibrium. If something is missing in the bile, it creates a disorder in the intestinal flora. Species in the flora may disappear, others may proliferate to an alarming number. It goes without saying that the best way to bring the condition to normal is not to destroy the unwanted species, but rather to re-establish a normal medium.

Worms

What ought to be done here is not to destroy the worms in panic, but to encourage a medium that would not allow them to survive. When there is a sufficient amount of bile in the intestines, and the bile contains all its normal and required elements, the worms cannot continue to prosper, or even to live. If larvae are ever introduced with food, they will be quickly channelled toward the intestines where a sufficient presence of bile is an obstacle to their survival. When everything functions normally, worms and larvae are neutralized and evacuated rapidly. People often find it necessary to envisage direct measures against worms and body parasites, but such measures can only be secondary. As has been stated, the primary measure consists of returning the liver and other connected organs to normal functioning.

Inflammation, Infection, Fermentations

Certain elements in food, when transformed imperfectly during the digestive process, can cause irritations of the mucous membranes of the intestines, thus creating an inflammation that may degenerate into an infection. Inflammation and infection happen when the imperfectly transformed elements insufficiently impregnated with biliary salts start fermenting dangerously. It is both the elements themselves and the products of their putrid fermentation which favor a dangerous state of irritation, well-known by people suffering from colitis.

Anal Itching

During fermentation, waste products create a sensation of heat when going through the rectum and anus. On the other hand, food that has not been well-digested liberates toxins in the intestines. These toxins enter the blood, causing a dangerous toxic condition. The organism rids itself of these toxins through eruptions in the skin, some of which appear around the anus, causing unpleasant itching. When the toxic condition affects this area, it is an indication that it has reached an advanced stage and that it will take a lot of time and effort to cure it for first the liver must be restored to normal. Worms may be the cause of the itching; in this case, too, the liver must be restored to normal.

Chills

People who suffer from chills will notice that the most unpleasant moments are usually after the meals, that is, during the first hours of digestion. This is a clue to its cause. The great effort that an overworked liver has to make to produce bile often prevents it from fulfilling other important functions. Blood circulation may slow down and oxidation, dissolution, coagulation, reduction and hydration can all be impaired, since the liver plays a role in every one of these functions. Because of this slowing down, a chilly feeling sometimes results: a sensation of cold inside the body. These unpleasant moments are reduced and eventually disappear when the liver functions are reestablished.

Pyrosis (Heart-burn)

A burning sensation starts from the stomach and comes up to the throat. Belching worsens the discomfort as it brings up an acid liquid which burns the throat. These phenomena are often the prelude to a stomach ulcer, but could also very well be interpreted as a sign of hypoglycemia. When sugar metabolism is defective, the blood composition suffers imbalance and accidents may occur. That is why a stomach ulcer is always preceded by a liver disorder. Heartburn and also the upward motion of the acid liquid may often indicate congestion in the digestive duct, having as its origin an insufficient secretion of the bile. Thus, whatever problem pyrosis indicates, the remedy lies in relieving the load on the liver by eliminating wrong foods and by stimulating the liver through natural means.

Demineralization

Insufficient secretion of certain substances (biliary salts, enzymes, etc.) by the liver impairs the transformation of various elements in food. These elements are neither properly used nor eliminated. The outcome of this is a condition of malnutrition to be expressed later as deficiencies and abnormalities in the body constitution and inadequacy in the accomplishment of normal body functions.

A popular reaction in such cases is to worry about a lack of vital minerals: calcium, potassium, magnesium, phosphorus, iodine, iron, etc., and to imagine that the proper remedy is simply to take supplements. However, in reality, it is not enough to introduce food supplements, the organism must be brought to a condition where it can extract what it needs from food in its natural form. Once more, it is a matter of bringing the liver back to

good working order. When food is natural and the liver is accomplishing its normal work, deficiencies are taken care of without any intervention. *A diet reinforced with food supplements will only aggravate the situation by making the liver overactive.*

Anemia

It has already been mentioned how one of the liver's functions is to destroy old red blood cells and also to secrete a substance which helps make new ones. A deficiency in this function, along with the inability of the liver to fix protein when it imperfectly transforms food containing iron and does not secure the storage of this mineral may result in anemia. A malfunction of the liver may lead to the destruction of red cells, old and new. Thus, before even thinking of introducing food which favors the reconstitution of the blood, it is important to treat the liver in order to re-establish its normal functions.

Diabetes

The liver produces glycogen. This glycogen is subjected to the action of pancreatic juices, then transformed into glucose(sugar) due to another function of the liver, whose cells secrete a diastase (enzyme) especially reserved for this purpose. This sugar is passed to the blood if needed or else stored in the liver.

If it should happen that the liver produces too much sugar or that it cannot adequately handle the sugar coming from the intestines, the blood absorbs some of the excess which is then filtered out at the kidneys to be discharged later in the urine. Thus, there is excess sugar in the blood and the urine simultaneously.

Obese people and Underweight people

The liver produces, retains or destroys fats according to the body's needs. A disorder in this function has as a consequence, either retention of too much fat due to being incapable of destroying the excess, or not being able to produce the fats which the body needs.

Also the neutralization and elimination of excess food may not be satisfactory; residues may

accumulate in the organs or in their tissues. This overloading may accentuate the imbalance of the metabolic function (assimilation, and disassimilation); either obesity or a loss of weight could be a result.

Insufficient production of protective substances is the prelude to an invasion of the organism by toxins. Insufficient secretion of elements such as enzymes that help transform food is another cause of malnutrition; this also can lead to loss of weight or obesity, the former because of deficiency and the latter because of the accumulation of food residues that were not metabolized. The same cause may produce effects which are opposite in appearance, it all depends on the individual condition.

Appendicitis

Many so-called cases of appendicitis are merely instances of a congested liver. Even in the case of genuine appendicitis, the role of the liver is not negligible, considering the antiseptic properties of the bile. It is only when the bile is not regularly produced or is insufficient in quantity that the area of the appendix can become inflamed and later infected.

THE INDIRECT CONSEQUENCES OF A MALFUNCTIONING LIVER

Vision Trouble

The liver provides different organs and tissues with pigments. In order to properly absorb the luminous rays that have impressed the retina, the choroid (vascular envelope of the eye) should be rich in pigments. Thus a lack of these pigments harms the eyesight. Also, if, due to a deficiency of biliary salts, nutritive elements in excess are not neutralized, toxic bodies are formed which the blood carries away and leaves in weaker organs. Deposits of toxins may occur in the ocular region; the result is a loss of elasticity of the crystalline lens, followed by all sorts of inconveniences; the person can become far-sighted.

Malnutrition, caused by a liver failure may evidently have repercussions on the ocular function. Poorly nourished, the eye cells become atrophied and the whole of the organ suffers the consequence. This lack leads to other abnormalities such as: myopia, hypermetropia, astigmatism and even diplopia(double vision).

Many cases have been recorded where vision troubles have lessened or even disappeared as a result of successful liver treatment. The chances of cure vary depending on how old the abnormality is. A cataract, which is caused by the opacity of the crystalline lens under the influence of a toxic condition, may be cured completely or in part by cleaning out the liver. It goes without saying that the older the opacity, the harder it is to cure; however, the process of elimination of the substances which cause the opacity and the revitalization of the tissues always remains possible.

Ear Trouble

The ear, too, can be adversely affected by a liver disability. It may become the victim of a deposit of toxic substances, the cells of its mechanism may be poorly nourished, or there may be a disorder of the nervous centers on which the ear depends, all possible consequences of a liver failure.

A liver congestion signals a tendency to a general congestion of the body; blood can accumulate near some organs and disturb their functions. Buzzings and whistlings in the ear may originate as much from circulatory troubles as from a bone disease which resulted from a toxic condition. It is vain to hope for the return to normal by treating only the ear; a direct action should be exercised on the liver.

Swollen Legs

Heart trouble may seem to be the origin of swollen ankles(edema), but often the reason the heart is overworked is because the liver and kidneys are failing to do their work properly. In addition, the liver can be the direct cause, as it contributes in large part to the use and elimination of liquids if only by stimulating the kidneys with biliary salts. A reduction of the swelling often takes place upon treatment of the liver.

Skin Diseases

Many afflictions of the skin which resisted direct treatment for several years have been cured with only a few weeks of natural treatment of the liver; many people with sties, Quincke edema, and hives have been relieved of their misery by improving their liver. Many cases of eczema that had resisted classical medical treatment for years disappeared with a good cleansing of the liver and switching to natural food.

How does this happen? Toxic substances which have not been neutralized by the liver enter the blood stream, often through the capillaries of the skin. Blocked in these capillaries, these toxins provoke the irritation of the cutaneous tissue and the irritation of the nervous ends; this is what produces the itching. Carbuncles and abscesses are always the outcome of toxins trying to get out in any way possible. If they were neutralized in the liver, these toxins would not have to be discharged through the skin as they could leave by normal channels of evacuation.

Rheumatism

This disease cannot be dealt with properly without treating the liver. To do otherwise is not only useless but dangerous since some classical remedies for rheumatism act adversely on the liver, which can become exhausted trying to get rid of them.

Many observations confirm the close link between the cure of rheumatism and the return to normal of the liver. The origin of sciatic attacks is probably a liver disorder. Either its expansion, or because of a deficiency of a substance secreted by the liver which normally ensures the nutrition of the nerves.

Glandular Imbalance

The liver secretes some hormones and neutralizes some others such as oestrogen. During cirrhosis this function is slowed down, and the oestrogen accumulates to such a degree that it produces feminizing effects on male subjects, such as the increase in the size of the breast and other phenomena. A liver disorder may also be the cause of the destruction of folliculin in women, thus creating masculine effects. At menopause, the malfunction of the liver greatly accentuates troubles and contributes to the slowing down of the circulation.

Discomfort During Menstrual Period

Being an endocrine organ, the liver has a stabilizing influence on the other endocrine glands. Knowing the liver's influence on genital glands it is clear that its disorder leads to malfunctioning in the ovaries. In addition, there may be phenomena of reversibility at the time of ovulation during the menses, including nausea, migraine, and dizziness. The return to normal of the menses, in terms of frequency, length of time and intensity can take place only after the liver has returned to normal.

Neurasthenia

Specialists have observed many cases of liver deficiency in people suffering from neurasthenia, instability and neurosis. By its repercussion on the sympathetic system and endocrine glands the liver disorder can be the origin of problems such as nervousness, anxiety and migraine. If the liver does not transform albumin perfectly, it can provoke the formation of poisons, which, when poured into the blood, will cause humoral troubles and sometimes even lesions. Professor Mouriquand, quoted by A. Colin, M.D., wrote the following: "in im-balanced children, before everything else, it is the liver system which is the base of nervous system disorders. It is illusory to hope for a return to a normal nervous system as long as the liver remains troubled".

Flat Feet

Attempting to remedy this abnormality with orthopedic methods may be an error with dangerous consequences. The feet should be taken care of with local clay poultices and by bringing the liver functions back to order. The arch of the foot collapses when the muscles and tendons are weakened, this being caused by poor nutrition of the tissues.

Adenoids and Tonsils

When the liver is no longer able to achieve the neutralization of the toxins carried in the blood, other organs try to make up for this deficiency. That is how tonsils sometimes have to contribute to this purification process. When they become overloaded and then intoxified, to surgically remove them is but a temporary and inadequate cure.

It has been remarked that a jaundice may appear after removal of the tonsils. This indicates the new location of the abnormality. In this case the tonsils were trying to assist the failing liver; the interruption of that assistance provokes the return of the toxins to the liver which, because of too much work, cannot prevent jaundice or other abnormal manifestations from taking place.

An imbalance in one place can lead to an imbalance in another. The excitement of the salivary functions, as in cirrhosis caused by alcohol, can lead to a hypertrophy of the parotid glands, for the latter indicates the glandular tissue's effort to adapt to the worsening condition.

Sinus Trouble and Head Colds

It is a waste of time to treat these locally without treating the liver at the same time. The harmonist experience has widely demonstrated the relationship between the various troubles in the upper respiratory channels. Head colds always follow a period of excessive indulgence, such as at

Thanksgiving and other holidays. The cold weather is usually incriminated as the cause of 'catching cold' because people don't consider the factor of overeating. Why are head colds more prevalent at certain particular times during the cold season? Because the liver is so overworked that it does not filter toxins properly, thus forcing the organism to attempt to rid them through other means. When there is also organic weakness which helps the toxins obstruct various channels, inflammation and infection is a common result.

A normally functioning liver pours protective substances into the blood which neutralize dangerous residues. If the liver does not drain the organism successfully, substitute discharges take place, in the nose and back of the throat, for instance.

It is not enough to clean out the nasal tract with salted or clayish water or put drops of lemon in the nose in order to get rid of sinusitis or head colds: the liver must be treated as well.

Chronic Bronchitis

Congestion of the liver always has repercussions on the bronchial tract. It is the cause of the inflamed condition of the mucous membranes in the lungs. A deficiency of various protective substances supplied by a normal liver creates an excess secretion of mucous in the bronchia. The need to expel this mucous provokes coughing, a necessary phenomenon at this point.

Treating the bronchitis directly may bring apparent relief, but far from being ideal, this merely serves to displace the disease to somewhere else in the organism, for its cause is still active. The new location may be far from the original one, but nevertheless, it is not the symptoms that are significant, but the cause. It suffices to take care of the liver to experience an improvement in the bronchia. Specific remedies developed to work directly on the bronchia have only a secondary effect,i.e. on the symptoms.

Those suffering from chronic bronchitis should feel assured by the experience of others that this disease can be truly cured by pursuing a proper treatment of the liver.

Paralysis from Sclerosis

Sclerosis is characterized by the hardening and

premature aging of the tissues. As its source is the liver, it is clear that it could spread to such an extent that it could damage vessels, other organs, bone marrow, etc. Liver sclerosis is manifested by a swelling of the organism, a phenomenon created by the retention of gas, which is provoked by the sclerosis of the liver that hardens and compresses the vessels. Afterwards, there is a retention of liquid(ascite), the veins are swollen and hemorrhoids appear.

Tendency to Hemorrhage: Hemophilia

Vitamin K, which is anti-hemorrhagic, is active only in the presence of bile. An insufficient secretion of bile predisposes to hemorrhaging. It has already been mentioned that the liver produces a substance called fibrinogen, an aid to blood coagulation. This fibrinogen is then converted into fibrin with the aid of the enzyme thrombin. A lack of it may lead to hemophilia.

Proneness to Insect Bites

It has been observed that some plants in the vegetable kingdom resist parasites better than others. The same goes for some human beings who seem to be equipped with better defenses.

Proneness to insect bites indicates a deficiency of protective elements in the body. It has been observed that the overactivity of the hepatic and thus the thyroid gland is at the origin of proneness to mosquito bites, while its underactivity corresponding to hypothyroidism - leads to a proneness to being attacked by fleas.

Observation confirms that those usually prone to insect bites become less receptive as the liver returns to normal.

Tuberculosis

No one with tuberculosis has a good liver; yet despite this obvious connection, it has been demonstrated that standard modern medical treatment of tuberculosis usually increases the liver disorder. It is impossible to speak of a complete cure by the chemical industry. The tuberculous person that is called cured is only 'stabilized'; he is given the advice to behave and take care of himself all his life as a tuberculous person, that he should refrain from exposing himself to the sun, water and cold air, not to tire himself in work and other similar restrictions.

Tuberculosis is the climax of an accumulation of degenerative processes. It can occur only if there exists a hereditary predisposition and if nutrition has been shattered by diet which is imbalanced or composed of too many toxic elements. But it is only after organs such as the liver are degenerated that the abnormality reaches the lungs. A deficient liver is incapable of secreting a sufficient amount of protective substances to prevent the pulmonary system from contracting disease.

In order for a tuberculous person to be cured and then to be able to live a normal life, he needs above all to take care of his digestive system, starting with the liver and its related organs. Then the patient can rebuild the network of his natural defenses, together with the injured tissues. Vital elements for his cells will be obtained, while at the same time food wastes and other toxic substances will be destroyed.

Cancer

As with tuberculosis, there is not one person with cancer whose liver properly fulfills the work that is expected of it. Another similarity is that cancer is the sign of a state of degeneracy in its last stage. In fact, frequent cases of cancers of the lungs have occurred after tuberculous lesions, which had been considered cured or stabilized by chemical remedies.

Cancer appears when all the functions of defense collapse completely. Blocking or displacing diseases such as cancer with unnatural remedies allows the accumulation of abnormal matter and the collapse of vital reserves. Then follows an impregnation of the control centers and disorder in the transmission process. The final desperate defense reaction results in establishing a new equilibrium that is foreign to the normal biological structure. This false equilibrium may be composed of parasitical formations. These accumulations of pathogenic elements have nothing in common with normal arrangements; they endure until the terminal phase occurs.

The re-establishment of a true equilibrium depends on the restoration of the nutritive functions. In that way the concerned centers may have at their disposal vital elements and be assured of the possibility of the distribution and elimination of waste products and cells deriving from abnormal proliferations. This is how treating particularly the liver and its functions can restore the organism to a pre-cancerous state.

Sterility and Impotence

The interaction of liver and genital secretions is known and it is clear that a disorder of the former leads to a disorder of the latter. It is interesting that vitamin E (called the vitamin of fertility), like vitamin K, needs proper bile in order to exercise its full effect.

FOODS THAT ARE BAD FOR THE LIVER

Alcohol - Scientific observation has proved beyond any possible doubt that alcohol has a dangerous debilitating effect on all the organs in general and on the liver in particular. It weakens the ability of this precious organ to clean the blood and provide the organism with protective substances.

Aside from causing cirrhosis of the liver, alcohol increases the cholesterol rate in the blood and therefore contributes to a general toxic condition. Within the body, alcohol deadens the vitamins in food and so causes vitamin deficiency.

Cod liver oil - With alcohol and fat, cod liver oil possesses the distinction of causing cirrhosis and even necrosis (death) of the liver cells.

Meat and animal fats - It is an error to believe that meat is necessary for supplying indispensable proteins. There are several varieties of food in the vegetable kingdom that are as rich in protein as meat, if not richer.

Not only have meat proteins already been partially used by the organism to which they belonged but also substances mixed in with it as products of disassimilation and waste, present in the flesh of the animal at the moment when it was killed. These wastes are poisons that are harmful to the liver and extremely difficult for it to neutralize.

Medications and chemical foods - Any chemical substance is foreign to the human organism and therefore injurious. Once introduced directly in the blood or through the digestive duct, the chemical product inevitably reaches the liver which must 'humanize' what it can, neutralize what is unacceptable and eliminate the residue of the synthesis. It also must provide for the evacuation of the damaged cells.

Scientists have 'invented' products which they call 'antiseptics', the goal of which is to destroy what they consider harmful for the human body. But these synthetic products are lifeless, that is to say, *without intelligence and without memory, and they destroy inconsiderately both harmful and useful properties.*

On the other hand, the true *natural* 'antiseptics' act in quite a different way. *They do not destroy.* They avoid the birth and proliferation of harmful bodies and at the same time they strengthen the organism.

Chemical substances, which contribute to the corruption of the natural medium are sure causes of general imbalance and disease. These foreign chemicals weaken natural defenses by destroying protective substances or inhibiting the centers which command the mechanism of immunization.

This is why some antiseptics or antibiotics, when absorbed through the mouth, create a large amount of microbes, causing a disturbance in the intestinal flora. Almost all the intestinal microbes are destroyed, except those that are particularly resistant. These survivors, which clearly are very strong, now have no neighboring varieties to limit them and so reproduce themselves prolificly and invade the digestive organs. The organism will try to defend itself with diarrhea, but this cannot help as long as the original varieties and balance is not restored.

The disturbance of the digestive flora resulting from the use of unnatural products can stimulate the proliferation of bacilli and render them virulent. If the production of bile is not sufficient, these bacilli are not neutralized in the intestines - they enter the blood and thus reach either the kidneys or the liver ducts. At this point, the bile is not yet complete. As it yet lacks all the protective elements which it will later carry to the intestines, the bile is too easily susceptible to being corrupted by these undesirable hosts. This leads to an inflammation, which can provoke the formation of gallstones. Bile secretion slackens so the purification of the intestines is further diminished. It is the start of an infernal cycle.

This corruption of bile by food or chemical medications and the degeneration that follows contributes to the putrefaction of the intestines, creating wastes that are extremely toxic. These poisons attack the now-corrupted bile, which in turn soils the intestinal duct and increases putrefaction. So chemical foods and remedies must be excluded in order to allow the reconstitution of a normal medium.

Vaccines - Whenever a foreign substance is introduced directly into the blood, it is channelled towards the liver whose function it is to neutralize invaders. Antibodies and other protective substances are emitted by the liver system, but various disorders still often follow vaccinations. Vaccines have a tremendous power of sclerosis on the tissues, especially those of the liver. All foreign substances are poison to the body, and any poison soils the bile which should remain pure to be capable of responding to digestive requirements.

Margarine and Processed Oils - Most of the margarine on the market is made with fat as a base. In order for these oils to solidify after liquidation at a certain temperature, it is necessary that they fix hydrogen. So they are treated with a catalyzer, most of the time nickel, of which some traces may remain in the finished product. This catalytic hydrogenation also has the goal of deodorizing the animal fats in order not to displease the consumer. The traces of the hydrogen-fixing catalyzer has a bad effect on the liver which must expend so much effort to neutralize them. In addition, this hydrogenation process of the fatty oils is made at the cost of destruction of some acids which are indispensable to the formation of tissues. The subsequent condition of the liver and its related organs attests that these products do not replace those substances necessary to the reconstitution of the used cells.

Even when the base of the margarine is of vegetal origin there is no escaping the process of catalytic hydrogenation. The main problem is that the processes of extraction use chemical solvents and temperatures high enough to destroy most of the living elements. Also, the oleaginous substance being used in production has almost certainly had its husks removed in order to reduce the costs of transportation by reducing volume. They become more acid and therefore contribute to make the oil which is extracted of them even more acidifying.

Since the liver is partly responsible for the preservation of the acido-basic balance, it is sure to be disturbed by a preponderance of acidifying elements. What is more, as the margarine and oils industrially produced are difficult to digest, the liver will be even further overtaxed.

Coffee and milk - Even alone, coffee and milk are troublesome for the liver. In combination they are twice as destructive. Coffee and milk enter into the intestines undigested and start serious putrefactions that the bile cannot always neutralize. This corruption of the intestines reaches the liver; the bile has been so adversely affected that it is helpless against the putrid fermentation which reaches the neighboring organs.

Industrial sugar - Sugar extracted from beets, like most artificially isolated elements, is an imbalanced product, incapable of sustaining life. Sugar contains neither protective elements nor any ferments necessary to the organism, so the liver is forced to compensate for the deficiency by providing the lacking substances.

Oxalic acid is produced as a result of acidifications in the intestines demanded by the presence of sugar. Oxidated in the muscles, oxalic acid must be neutralized by the liver, which is thus pressured to do even more extra work. Whatever escapes the liver enters the circulation, invades the tissues and is then discharged by the kidneys. However, they are often the cause of pain in the kidneys and blood in the urine. It should also be mentioned that crystals of oxalic acid are present, as is uric acid, in rheumatism, migraines, nervous troubles and fatigue.

White bread - As it is composed mostly of starch and saturated with chemical yeast, white bread is completely devitalized and has no nutritive value whatsoever; it contributes mainly to the formation of gases.

By eliminating the bran, one throws away 80% of the phosphorus and calcium, together with many ferments needed for the digestion of the nutritive elements in the wheat. Moreover, the bran itself is the most vitalized part of the wheat kernel, as it is the most exposed to solar radiation. But what has even more unfortunate consequences on health is the extraction of the germ, in which is contained all the B vitamins.

These deficiencies in ferments and vitamins force the liver to make a huge effort in order to produce these essential phenomena. The task is so great that eventually internal injuries and cuts may occur and even more serious accidents may happen.

Tobacco - The terrible effects of tobacco on the blood vessels include hardening, loss of flexibility, excessive fragility, and decrease of the interior diameter of the vessel. This means the liver must produce elements of defense, but since the organ itself and the blood vessels are injured by the toxic effects of tobacco, its defense ability decreases until total suspension of reaction occurs. The number of amputations due to tobacco poisoning are too numerous to count.

BAD HABITS WHICH AFFECT THE LIVER

Excess fatigue - Whether it be of a physical or intellectual nature, overwork leads up to the production of toxins which are very dangerous for the organism. The liver makes a huge effort trying to neutralize these toxins. If it is just a temporary situation the troubles will not be very pronounced, but if activity is brought beyond the possibilities of the organism, the consequences could be very serious. The toxins in the muscles or nerves will impregnate the tissues if they are not rapidly neutralized and eliminated. Their accumulation may lead to an unfortunate disease such as paralysis from sclerosis of the nervous tissues or hardening of the bone marrow. This is to be feared when the overactive liver is taxed beyond endurance.

Overcooking - Fermentation is necessary to ensure the transformation of food. Some of these fermenting elements are contained in the food itself. However, cooking can destroy a large amount of ferments and enzymes. With a diet composed mostly of cooked meals, the liver has to greatly extend its efforts to produce the missing ferments and maintain this effort to neutralize substances which, due to lack of fermentation, are not being digested.

One should stay away from cooking which involves too much pressure. Cooking with a pressure-cooker, for example, means using high temperatures; this nullifies the value of some amino acids, some of which are indispensable to the liver functions.

Overeating - Too much food strains the liver because of the constant effort demanded to get rid of the excess. In order to neutralize the nitrogenized excesses, the liver transforms them into acid; these acids in excess can disrupt the acido-basic balance if the kidneys do not eliminate them rapidly. The liver will have to intervene again and make an extra effort in order to re-establish the endangered equilibrium. The liver becomes tired; some manifestations are drowsiness(even in children), or a state of nervousness which could lead to a crisis.

Sedentarism - The lack of exercise is detrimental to the organism and endangers its balance. The liver is one of the organs which suffers most from this lack. First, the lungs are not stimulated to eliminate properly, then, whatever is not eliminated in the lungs is channelled to the liver which is forced to compensate for this unforeseen problem.

Lack of exercise is especially detrimental to people who are easily constipated, and that again means more work for the liver, to which the waste products which have not been evacuated are recycled. Regular exercise facilitates and accelerates elimination by reducing the mass of residue to be neutralized.

TREATMENT OF THE LIVER BY HARMONIST NATURAL METHODS

Curing a bad liver can take weeks, months, or even years of constant care. There are quite a few things to be done, the first and most important being to lead a healthy life. Especially great care must be taken with eating habits. Later it will be seen how important and helpful exercises and sunshine can be.

FOOD TREATMENT

Changing Eating Habits

Change of food should be gradual; it is not always ideal to throw away bad habits too suddenly. However, this excludes the destructive elements such as alcohol, meat, animal fat and canned food which must be eliminated as soon as possible.

The notion of 'regimen' and 'diet' is detrimental to the restoration of a depressed state of mind. *He who follows a diet remains a sick person, physically and mentally.* There are not multiple ways of feeding ourselves; there are only two, the good way and the bad way, this being valid for everyone, the sick as well as for the healthy.

It seems to have become a habit among people to index foods, with some being prescribed and others definitely taboo. How many elements of primordial importance are thus neglected! Food can not be evaluated by its name alone; factors such as freshness, quality, source, season and chemical content must be taken into consideration. Also, in order to be utilized, food must be properly assimilated, and to assure proper stimulation of the digestive process, food must first act on the senses, either before having reached the mouth, or at its first contact with the gustative papillae. Sensitive

food preparation and presentation is extremely important. The demands of the environment and the physical condition of the person eating, plus his emotional and spiritual needs must all be involved.

Many marvelous *'food remedies'* are offered by the vegetable kingdom. Food should be eaten raw as often as possible. If raw vegetables are not well-tolerated, begin with a small amount and later increase their intake gradually. Irritated intestines have trouble with raw food; however, this condition will be ameliorated with natural treatment. In the meantime, the curing process can be accelerated with juices and vegetables. Carrot juice benefits liver secretions by fluidifying the bile. Drink one glassful on an empty stomach, in the morning and/or before meals. In season, strawberry, currant, gooseberry, grapes or half a glass of cabbage-juice may be substituted if preferred. Cooked vegetables and cereals, whole-grain bread, and small amounts of dairy products may be eaten, but care must be taken to prepare them properly, and also not to combine them improperly with other foods. See menu, p.111.

GOOD FOODS FOR THE LIVER

Natural Foods

Certain foods are beneficial to the liver in particular and to health in general. However, they sometimes provoke reactions at first.

Apparent troubles after eating spinach, green peas, string beans, onions, artichokes and other vegetables do not indicate that these vegetables are hostile to the liver; rather they indicate that the liver is not in a condition to receive some of their constitutive elements.

It is possible to gradually become used to vegetables that could not be tolerated before. For example, if olive oil provokes nausea, do not force its use. Instead introduce it in small amounts in the seasoning, mixed with a preferred oil. Little by little, increase the quantity of the olive oil until the point is reached where it can be used by itself.

Someone who does not appreciate black olives can take them in small quantities with some natural fresh butter, or incorporate them in cooked dishes.

Spinach which is not tolerated by certain people, as well as walnuts, onions, and other vegetables, can also be introduced slowly with meals. A good method is to serve spinach raw in salads; this will provoke less of a reaction, due to the fact that a smaller quantity is used when served raw, even though previously it had seemed indigestible cooked.

Fresh fruit and vegetable juices are an excellent preliminary to the introduction of raw vegetables. However, when the attempt to introduce a natural food is unsuccessful, it is better to wait and see that the treatment using that food has given some results before trying them again. However, certain foods can never be tolerated by some people; if, for example, a spoon of honey or a mouthful of cheese causes nausea, it would be inadvisable to insist on its use.

Olive Oil

Without a doubt, the oil that benefits the liver most is olive oil; however, it should be obtained cold-pressed, using no heat or chemical solvents.

Most oils available to the consumer without "guaranteed cold-pressed" on their label are obtained with heat and chemical solvents. These oils are then refined, which makes them even less nutritious since the refining process causes the loss of the vitamins A and E and of substances (anti-oxygen bodies) which prevent them from turning rancid. True natural oil will not turn rancid since the anti-oxygen bodies are well-preserved.

Cold-pressed olive oil retains all its available natural ferments and is very digestible and is the best source of healthy fats and cholesterols for the human organism. It is a good stimulant and remarkable remedy for the liver, especially in cases of gall stones and all other manifestations of liver congestion. It is also one of the best of natural laxatives. (see p. 90).

Olive oil is most beneficial when mixed with an equal quantity of lemon juice and taken in the morning on an empty stomach. One to three teaspoons of olive oil may be taken, depending on age and tolerance.

There are doctors who have been successful in immediately eliminating gallstones by administering to their patients a single massive dose of olive oil - quantities of up to half a quart and even more! In this case, the presence of a doctor is certainly necessary in case of any severe or unpleasant reactions. It is preferable to do it moderately. It takes longer, but is as efficient - and as it will not cause any alarming manifestations, emergency precautions are unnecessary. The leading principle of the natural method is non-violence, a return to Hippocrates' precept: "above all, do not damage." It is always preferable to stay away from a spectacular but ephemeral result and proceed slowly on solid ground.

In certain cases it is possible to gradually increase the intake of the oil-lemon mixture, being sure to keep the volume within the limits of tolerance. After three weeks, cease the treatment for a week. Resume on alternate weeks, for a period of three months.

Whole Wheat Bread

The term 'whole' is not precise enough - people often use it without knowing what it involves. Real whole wheat bread must be made with a complete flour, which means a flour that has not gone through any processing whatsoever, neither adding or subtracting anything. It goes without saying that the wheat from which it is made should be cultivated *biologically* -- or *organically,* as it is presently

expressed. Sometimes a light sifting may be tolerated, at the time one starts eating natural food, but this sifting should not take away more than 10-15% of the bran.

"Whole wheat bread" made from a mixture of white flour, bran, wheat germ and occasional chemical 'enrichments' is valueless; it differs from ordinary white bread only in that it generally costs more.

Even if it were made with good whole wheat flour, bread is still not what it ought to be if it is not baked in an oven equipped with an external heating system. Direct heating systems such as gas can be dangerous for they leave residues in the bread.

Fruits

In general, fruits are favorable to the liver. If some provoke unusual reactions(such as strawberries)it is most likely a curative manifestation, and any disorder is only temporary.

Some fruits are particularly beneficial. Lemon should be given first place for it stimulates, relieves congestion and cleanses the liver. There are people suffering from liver troubles who cannot tolerate herbal remedies and yet feel at ease with lemon cures. It can be taken in many ways. For example, mix the juice of half a lemon in a cup of hot water with or without honey. Lemon is the best aid of digestion because of the biliary reaction it stimulates.

During the day, take lemon juice mixed in fresh water - the quantity that can be used daily depends on tolerance. Lemon should replace vinegar in all seasonings. Even the peel of this wondrous fruit, when grated and added to a raw salad, is a good remedy for liver insufficiency.

Oranges, which have ripened naturally stimulate all the liver functions; the same is true of *grapes* which aid the elimination of gallstones while simultaneously stimulating evacuation.

The beneficial qualities of the *olive* have already been discussed in the section on olive oil. Of all kinds of olives, *black olives* seem best since they can be eaten without preparation. Their conservation in brine does not seem to alter their qualities. However, they should be briefly rinsed in hot water to take away the salt, and then served in a bowl mixed with olive oil.

Fresh *berries* are an excellent food. Currants are worthwhile; gooseberries work even better in helping evacuation. Strawberries are a good cleansing agent and chestnuts are particularly helpful for those suffering from the presence of bile in the blood. Raspberries are recommended in cases of fever caused by bile or gastro-intestinal troubles. Huckleberries have no equal as a disinfectant for the intestinal tract. They are astringent, but they do not cause constipation; on the contrary, they regularize the frequency and consistency of the stools.

Almost all other fruits are excellent, except for artificially ripened bananas (or any bananas which were picked before they were ripe), for they are only slightly related to the naturally ripened fruit.

Even the *tomato* which is half-way between a fruit and a vegetable, helps the liver in its function of neutralization of poisons and proper channeling of the waste products.

Vegetables

Many vegetables are protective agents and sources of energy. Like fruits, vegetables should be used raw as often as possible in order to preserve their living elements.

The *artichoke* is most particularly recommended; it is a tonic for the mucous membrane lining of the liver, and also reinforces the anti-toxic function of the liver.

Asparagus, which contains nitre, aids in reducing inflammation, while thanks to its manganese, it also participates in cleansing the liver.

Beets are a tonic.

Carrots help to build blood and also to fluidify the bile, increasing its secretion. Its carotene helps the liver isolate vitamin A.

Chicory also stimulates the secretion of bile.

Celery is a good cleanser of the liver; its leaves can help remedy jaundice.

Leeks are rich in mineral salts, they help regenerate liver cells. Their antiseptic properties aid the bile in keeping the intestines clean.

Dandelion is excellent for stimulating all liver functions. It increases bile production and also participates in the elimination of cholesterol and of blood impurities. It is also a highly active remedy for gallstones, thanks to its manganese.

As *radishes* are effective in getting rid of toxins present in the liver, they are particularly excellent for curing jaundice.

Onions, like leeks, are very rich in mineral salts and help increase glandular secretion. They also contain several protective elements and can contribute to the healing of diabetes.

Garlic and *cabbage* and onions are rich in sulphur, the mineral needed by the liver in its operation of synthesis.

All other vegetables may be used freely, except if they provoke strong reactions, in which case they may be introduced gradually with meals.

Dairy Foods and Animal Products

Milk, in its natural raw state is not good for the liver, especially an adult's, whose stomach no longer secretes the ferment necessary for a rapid pre-digestion of the milk. To drink raw milk safely, soon after its ingestion take some lemon juice which will activate the process of coagulation. Once coagulated, milk is easily digestible and quite healthy.

Buttermilk is good for constipation. However, if consumed regularly, it is advisable to strain out the acidifying juice and drink only the coagulated part.

Yoghurt is as acceptable as buttermilk, but only if properly made.

Cheeses may be taken in moderate quantity, but only once a day, and if they are naturally fermented. Avoid the industrially-processed cheeses that are widely sold on the market.

Raw butter on a slice of bread may be taken on occasion, but only if it is natural and if it has not remained stored in the merchant's freezer for months. The best is the kind obtained from a farm that does not use antibiotics or pesticides.

Eggs have great nutritional value. Their proteins are the only ones in which are found all the amino acids identified to the present day. However, in order to be acceptable, they should not come from farms whose chickens are subjected to a constant artificial daylight and nourished unnaturally, such as with mash made out of fish, flour and waste, and often mixed with medications such as antibiotics. Eggs should be taken in moderation since they are extremely rich; three or four a week is the maximum - they may be prepared in any manner.

Honey stimulates the liver with good results. It contributes to a real rehabilitation and cure of the liver.

Rosemary honey is preferable to other honeys because it benefits all the liver functions; it is particularly recommended for ascites and a fat liver, cirrhosis, jaundice and congestion.

The Aromatic Plants

An important place should be given to these plants which contribute to the smooth operating of the psycho-sensorial functions, thus actively participating in every stage of nutrition, such as digestion, transformation, synthesis, distribution, fixation, neutralization of waste products and elimination.

These plants help keep the intestines clean and promote a normal digestive flora. They stimulate the endocrine and salivary glands. Some of them are especially recommended as benefitting the liver functions. Rosemary comes first on the list, followed by thyme, chervil, celery, tarragon and onion. Others such as stone leek, chive, fennel, cumin, caper(not in vinegar), nutmeg, clove, horseradish, serpolet(wild thyme), and saffron are also excellent.

CLASSIFICATION OF FOODS

Recommended Foods

All fresh fruits in season: sweet or acid
All dried fruits: sun-dried
All cereals: whole wheat, hulled barley, brown rice, millet, rye, oats, corn, buckwheat, whole wheat bread made with natural leaven (sourdough - not yeast), whole wheat or buckwheat noodles, cereal creams, whole wheat or buckwheat cookies, whole rye breads
All vegetables: raw or cooked, soups, vegetable broths
Aromatic plants

Black Olives
Oils: cold-pressed - preferably olive oil, but any pure vegetable oil is acceptable
Sea salt
Honey: if possible, mountain honey, rosemary honey
Fruit juice: natural, on an empty stomach only; carrot juice; lemon juice mixed with water.
Herbal teas: thyme, rosemary, etc. Decoctions and infusions appropriate to condition. See various recipes throughout book.

Foods to be used in Moderation

Fresh eggs: 2-4 a week, from chickens nourished naturally with grains
Lentils, peas and beans: fresh. If dried, aged no more than one year.
Couscous or *semolina* or *bulghur*

Homemade pastry: naturally sweetened
Dairy: buttermilk, cheese, fresh butter (very little - on a slice of bread or a dish of vegetables)
Coffee substitute: cereal or fruit coffee
Jam: not made with sugar

What is Harmful

All kinds of meat
All types of animal fats or industrially made fats
Cooked butter, pasteurized butter and *oils* made in an unnatural way (not cold-pressed)
Meat broth
Fish
Canned food and *food cooked in a pressure-cooker*

White bread and all products made with white flour
White rice and other denatured cereals
Industrial sugars, sweets
Refined salt, pepper
Milk
Dehydrated vegetables and all fruits artificially dried
All alcoholic drinks, chemical products, tobacco

MENU FOR A DAY

Breakfast

One of the following:[1]
—fresh or dried fruits
—whole wheat bread and honey (or butter)[2]
—vegetable soup
with thyme or rosemary tea
or simply one of the following:
a decoction, a glass of water,
(perhaps mixed with clay), or
a tablespoon of olive oil mixed
with some lemon juice

Lunch

—fruit in season
—raw salad (see below)
followed by cereal or cooked
vegetables[3] and some raw lettuce with any one of the
following: cheese, buttermilk,[4]
dried fruits, honey or some
homemade pastry.

Dinner

—fruit in season
—vegetable soup (optional)
—raw vegetables, shredded
—cooked vegetables (optional)
—cereal[3]
—buttermilk[4] or honey

[1]Any of these constitutes an ideal meal. There are many here only to give the ailing, convalescent, or healthy person a selection.

[2]Use complete flour. In case of liver or digestive troubles, the bran may be sifted to 85-90% or else make rye bread. In any case, use natural leaven (sour dough).

[3]see recipe below

[4]Take cheese or buttermilk only at one of the daily meals.

SOME BASIC RECIPES

WHEAT CREAM

Use wheat which has not been too finely ground. Grind it yourself with an electric coffee mill, or a hand mill, or even a blender. If possible, do it just before cooking it, for the fresher it is, the better. Put in a saucepan, add a pinch of salt and water in sufficient quantity (try 1 part wheat to 3 parts water). Place saucepan over a high flame and keep stirring continuously with a wooden spoon in order to prevent burning. It will be cooked as soon as the cream changes color and bubbles appear at the surface. Pour in a bowl and add a teaspoon of honey and crushed almonds. Especially good for constipation.

RAW VEGETABLE DISH - "LA BASCONNAISE"

This dish is usually made from many kinds of raw vegetables, such as grated carrots, turnips, beets, black radish, and salsify, sliced mushrooms, onions, zucchini, tomatoes, and radishes, or slivered (green or red) cabbage, spinach, and swiss chard. Season all the vegetables together or every element separately with oil (preferably olive) sea salt, lemon juice, black olives, crushed garlic, or chopped parsley, chervil, some onion rings, rosemary or tarragon leaves. It is a good idea to put the accent on a different vegetable each time to obtain a variety of dishes.

CEREALS

In an enameled cast iron pot, put some olive oil, some chopped onions, some mushrooms (optional), tomatoes (in season), then the chosen cereal, either brown rice, hulled barley, wheat or buckwheat, millet or couscous. Add water (try 1 part grain to 1½ parts water or slightly more), sea salt, an aromatic plant (thyme, bay leaf, walnuts, nutmeg, etc.). Cook at low flame until done.

COOKED VEGETABLES

Use preferably the vegetables in season. Cook them in a small amount of water, in a cast iron pot (enameled) or in a clay pot, or a steamer, but not a pressure cooker. Put some oil in the bottom of the saucepan or add it before serving. If there are no vegetables available, have whole wheat or buckwheat noodles, potatoes, or some other cereal preparation.

RECOMMENDED PLANTS AND HERBS

Be sure to read p.29 before using any of the following recipes.

Rosemary is one of the most efficient remedies for liver troubles. Its soft action and pleasant taste make it accepted even by children. As it stimulates the liver and fluidifies and increases the bile, rosemary is particularly recommended for liver congestion, bile insufficiency, obstructive jaundice, cirrhosis of Laennec, and common dropsy accompanying an expanded liver.

The whole stem with the flower is used at a dosage of a teaspoon (or one fresh blade) depending on the age and personal taste in a cup of boiling water. Let it steep 10 minutes. Take a cup before or after the meals. Add some rosemary honey if possible. This tea is a pleasant and active aid to digestion. In addition, rosemary is an elegant addition to cooked dishes.

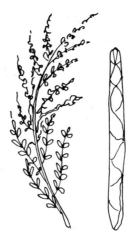

rosemary

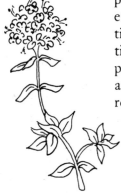

thyme

Thyme also makes a very pleasant drink, as well as benefitting digestion and assimilation by stimulating the secretion of bile and preventing putrid fermentations. Prepare and take the same way as rosemary.

Artichoke leaves stimulate the liver and tonify its cells. It allows the natural cholesterol produced by the body to build up in the blood. It is especially recommended for diseases such as jaundice, dropsy and kidney troubles related to a liver or bile deficiency. Let infuse for 10 minutes in a cup of boiling water (2 fresh leaves) and take before each meal.

Asparagus root can be used successfully in case of jaundice or any other affliction of the liver. Put 2 oz. of the root in a quart of water. Leave on a low flame 10 minutes and drink all the liquid over a period of one or two days.

asparagus root

Marigold flowers are especially recommended for jaundice and liver congestion. They purify the blood and stimulate the liver functions. Put one teaspoon in a cup of boiling water; let infuse 10 minutes. Take a cup before each meal. The fresh flower can be mixed in salad.

Lilac leaves can be used for a congested liver. Put 3-6 leaves in a cup of water. Boil 2 minutes, infuse 5. Take a cup before each meal.

Box-wood tree leaves are highly effective in cases of liver troubles accompanied by intermittent fever. Put 1 teaspoon in a cup of water. Let it boil 2-3 minutes and infuse 10 minutes. Take a cup before each meal, 2-3 times a day.

box-wood

Fumitory The whole plant is used, stem and

flower. It is excellent for jaundice and for cleansing a congested liver. Put 1 teaspoon in a cup of boiling water. Let infuse 10 minutes. Take it before the meal or at night before retiring.

Woodruff stimulates the liver and increases the secretion of urine. It is especially recommended for jaundice and kidney infections that are related to the liver. Put 1 teaspoon in a cup of boiling water; let infuse 10 minutes. Take 3-4 times a day.

woodruff

Pennyroyal (a wild mint) This plant is a good stimulant for the biliary functions. Take 2 or 3 cups a day between, before, or after meals. One teaspoon for a cup of boiling water. Let infuse a few minutes.

Olive tree leaves favor the liver functions and facilitate the discharge of gallstones. Put a handful in a quart of water. Bring to a boil, simmer a few minutes and let infuse 10. Drink anytime.

Shepherd's purse This plant helps to dissolve and eliminate gallstones. It is specifically recommended for hemorrhages of biliary channels. Put a handful in a quart of water. Bring to a boil and remove from flame after a minute or two. Infuse 10 minutes. Take between meals, 3-4 cups a day.

Chamomile flowers are excellent for the obstruction of biliary channels where there is an expanded liver and large spleen. Infuse 3-4 flowers in a cup of boiling water and take it before the meal or a long while after the meal.

chamomile

Goose-grass This plant is excellent for jaundice or when a liver affliction is accompanied by dropsy. Put 1 teaspoon in a cup of boiling water and let infuse 10 minutes.

Dandelion Its taste is bitter, but it is well worth using its root and leaves. Put 1-2 oz. in a quart of water. Bring to a boil and leave on the fire a few minutes. Take 3 times a day before meals. Dandelion is particularly recommended in case of congestion, inflammation of the liver, atonia of biliary channels or liver insufficiency.

Centaury There are two recommended varieties of centaury: the American and the European. Each gives good results for the congestion of the liver. Put a handful of the American centaury's root in a quart of water. Boil 2 minutes; infuse 10 minutes. Take a cup of the decoction in the morning

american centaury

before breakfast and before the two principal meals.

With the European centaury's leaves, put a handful in a quart of boiling water. Let infuse 10-15 minutes. Drink 3 cups a day, before meals.

european centaury

Agrimony It is mostly for chronic afflictions of the liver that one uses this plant. Drink from 3-5 cups of it a day between meals. Put a teaspoon of chopped leaves in a cup of water. Bring to a boil and leave on fire 2 minutes. Remove from fire and let infuse 10 minutes.

Wild soapwort (saponaria) Excellent for obstruction of the liver. Put 1 teaspoon of leaves or roots in a cup of water. Boil for 2 minutes and remove from fire. Pass through a strainer immediately. Take a cup of this drink before each meal (3 times a day).

wild soapwort

Veronica is used when the liver is congested, or the bile passes in the blood or in case of jaundice. Put 1 teaspoon in a cup of boiling water and infuse briefly. Take 3 times a day.

Meadowsweet (steeplebush) is most particularly indicated for liver insufficiency in nervous patients. Boil a cup of water and add a teaspoon of chopped leaves. Let infuse 10 minutes. Take 3-5 times a day.

Chicory is indicated for those having a 'bilious' temperament and also for people suffering from a passing of bile into the blood. Put a tablespoon of either leaves or roots (chopped) in a cup of water. Boil and leave on fire 5 minutes. Take a cup before each meal.

chicory

* * * * * * * * * * * * *

FOR CONSTIPATION LINKED TO LIVER INSUFFICIENCY

Buckthorn - this plant is one of the most simple and active stimulants for the liver and intestines. For preparation, see p.90.

Rhubarb is an excellent laxative, a stimulant for intestines and liver. See p.91.

Barberry The root and bark of this plant are laxative and exercise a stimulating effect on the liver. Put a handful in a quart of water. Bring to a boil and infuse 10 minutes. Use as a drink.

Female Fern Root is the laxative for children and adults who suffer from liver insufficiency. Put a handful in a quart of water. Bring to a boil and simmer 20 minutes. Let infuse 10 minutes. Drink over a period of two days whenever desired.

Dandelion Same preparation as above.

Bindweed is a laxative that is particularly recommended for liver insufficiency, liver congestion and cirrhosis. See p.90.

* * * * * * * * * * * * *

COMBINED HERBAL PREPARATIONS

Sometimes an association of herbs works more efficiently for a liver insufficiency than one plant taken alone. However, one should take great care in mixing them; there are certain rules to be followed, and these are learnt only through experimentation.

In the following mixtures, there are plants which were not mentioned above. These plants are added in order to have complementary effects on the related organs, such as the kidneys, for example. If a particular ingredient is missing, a good herbal reference book should be consulted and a plant with equivalent properties substituted. The best treatments are always those which work on the entire organism. If you wish to try combining herbs on your own, start with only two or three. The number should be increased only after experience. For details on conversion tables and preparation see p.29

Infusion for Stimulation of the Liver

Horsetail	30 gr.	Yellow Bedstraw	
Licorice root	30 gr.	(flowered tops)	30 gr.
Rosemary		Marigold	
(flowered tops)	30 gr.	(flowered tops)	20 gr.
Woodruff		Mint leaves	20 gr.
(flowered tops)	30 gr.		

Put 2 teaspoons or 2 tablespoons (depending on the age) in a cup of boiling water. Infuse 10-20 minutes. Take a cup after each meal. Sweeten if necessary with some honey.

Infusion for Liver and Gall Bladder

Gromwell	20 gr.	Broom	10 gr.
Horsetail	20 gr.	Dandelion	10 gr.
Licorice	20 gr.	Fernroot	10 gr.
Woodruff	20 gr.	Marigold	10 gr.
Asparagus root	10 gr.		

Two tablespoons per boiling cup of water. Let infuse 10 minutes.

Decoction for Obstruction or Congestion of the Liver

Licorice root	30 gr.	Black Currant	
Woodruff		(Gooseberry) leaves	10 gr.
(flowered tops)	30 gr.	Horsetail	10 gr.
Artichoke leaves	20 gr.	Rosemary	
Bearberry leaves	10 gr.	(flowered tops)	10 gr.
Marigold flowers	10 gr.	Small Centaury	10 gr.
Yellow Bedstraw			
(flowered tops)	10 gr.		

A heaping tablespoon of the mixture in a cup of water. Bring to a boil, simmer 2 minutes and infuse 10. Take a cup 15 minutes before each main meal.

----

[1] Diuretic

Decoction for Jaundice and Cholemia

Woodruff		Yellow Bedstraw	
(flowered tops)	30 gr.	(flowered tops)	25 gr.
Artichoke leaves	25 gr.	Dandelion root	25 gr.
Asparagus root	25 gr.	Meadowsweet	15 gr.
Barberry root	25 gr.	Scolopendrium	
Butcher's broom,		officinale[2]	15 gr.
root[1]	25 gr.		

Use one tablespoon of the mixture per cup. Bring to a boil. Simmer 2 minutes and infuse 10.

Infusion for Constipation from Liver Insufficiency

Elderberries	30 gr.	Fern root	15 gr.
Rhubarb root	25 gr.	Flax seeds	15 gr.
Buckthorn	20 gr.	Combretum leaves[3]	10 gr.

One tablespoon of the mixture for a cup of water. Bring to a boil, put the mixture in, turn off the flame, and infuse 10 minutes. Take a cup at night before going to bed or in the morning on an empty stomach.

Infusion for Obstruction of the Biliary Channels

Woodruff		Marigold flowers	20 gr.
(flowered tops)	40 gr.	Rosemary leaves	20 gr.
Boldo	30 gr.	Yellow Bedstraw	
Licorice root	30 gr.	(flowered tops)	20 gr.
Horsetail	25 gr.	Mint	
Asparagus root	20 gr.	(flowered tops)	15 gr.

Put 1 or 2 tablespoons in a cup of boiling water. Infuse 20 minutes. Take a cup after each meal, 2-3 times a day. Add honey if necessary.

----

[2] If unavailable, may be replaced by herb with similar effect such as huckleberry, quince, knotgrass or Wild Alum root

[3] If unavailable may be replaced by boldo or any herb with similar properties

It absorbs impurities, revitalizes the organism, and stimulates the glandular functions. Clay is an excellent healer of the liver and must therefore be included in every natural treatment.

It may be that a deficient liver cannot accept clay at a first attempt. In this case, after mixing the clay with water (1 teaspoon in ½ cup), let the mixture sit for awhile, then strain out the clay and drink only the clayish water.

It is also possible for clay to bring constipation. although in some people it works the opposite way. If constipation occurs, take only clayish water and complete the curing process with a laxative decoction, either every night or from time to time, depending on the condition. Read carefully the chapter on clay.

EXTERNAL TREATMENT

Together with a change in diet and use of plants, it will often be necessary to have recourse to external remedies, adapted to the particular situation.

For almost all 'direct' liver troubles, such as pains where the liver is situated or covering a larger areas (from the right to the left side), hepatic colitis, or swelling of the abdomen, it will be useful to start the treatment with the application of the following preparation:

Bran-cabbage-onion poultice

Make enough of the preparation to cover an area larger than the one covered by the pain. Use between 3-5 handfuls of bran, depending on how much there is to be covered. Chop 2 or 3 cabbage leaves (red or green) and 2 onions. Put everything in a pot, add water until it holds together and place over a high flame. Leave until total evaporation of the water (5-10 minutes). Spread this preparation on a cheese cloth. Ideally this poultice should not exceed ¾" in thickness. Fold the cheese cloth and apply as hot as can be tolerated (but not burning). Leave in place for 2 hours. This poultice can be applied any time in the day and should be used only once. It may be substituted for the wheat bran-ivy poultice when there are no ivy leaves available.

Note: After the period of application of bran-cabbage-onion poultice or cabbage leaves, over a period which may last from 1 to 4 weeks, begin clay applications for a more deep action on the liver. However, it is not recommended to start these clay applications too early, because of the quick action of clay which might contribute in transferring exist-ing gallstones to the hepatic duct. It is better to first take care of the gallstones by drinking decoctions, olive oil mixed with lemon juice, and applying poultices, than to dissolve them with clay. However, it is only clay that will complete the job already begun.

Cabbage Poultice

Sometimes cabbage alone works well, especially for children. Prepare the cabbage in the following manner:

Cut off the big rib from the leaves (red or green) and flatten each leaf with a rolling pin. Apply the leaves (three, one on top of the other) either fresh or heated a few seconds on a radiator. Cover with wool or a towel to retain heat and fasten in place with the help of a bandage at night before going to bed. Leave all night.

Clay Poultice

One of the best methods for stimulating the liver is to apply a clay poultice every night. In the beginning wait an hour and a half to two hours after eating. After the body becomes used to the clay, it may be applied just after the meal, however, then warm up the poultice slightly. While clay is usually applied cold, with the liver it is often preferable to have it warm, especially in the beginning of the treatment. Begin, therefore, with a cold poultice which can be left in place for as long as it does not present signs of cooling. It should not even feel as if it had been applied cold. At the least feeling of cold, of discomfort, increased or new pains, remove the poultice and warm the clay on the radiator or better yet, in a double boiler; apply the poultice tepid. If this tempering proves to be insufficient, do not hesitate to apply a well-heated poultice.

The poultice should be left in place for 2 hours or more. It may even be kept on overnight if it does not dry up or become cold, or cause any reactions such as increased pain, nervousness, internal cold feeling or excessive heat. It is sometimes possible to apply one poultice in the morning and another in the evening, spaced between meals, especially if the clay is cold.

Once the appropriate degree of clay temperature is determined, apply thick poultices (¾"-1"). However, it is sometimes necessary to begin with thin poultices (less than ½") which are left in place only 1½ hours, in order to accustom the organism to the clay.

A series of daily applications may be made for three weeks or a month. In some cases, for gall stones especially, the treatment may last several months. Do not hesitate to interrupt it for awhile when there are signs of fatigue. However, as soon as strength returns resume the treatment. Sometimes exactly the opposite happens - clay gives strength; in such a case proceed with the applications, or even increase them (3 poultices in every 24 hour period).

It is good to follow clay treatment with massages with olive oil.

The Revulsion Method

This method involves reducing the abnormal action of one part of the body by exciting another. One way is to channel the blood towards the feet. This can be done in a sudden fashion, with the help of mustard (1 handful of mustard powder in water; either room temperature or slightly warmed). Another method which is equally as good but takes longer is a very hot foot bath, prepared by boiling 2 or 3 handfuls of red-grape vine leaves for 10-15 minutes, in a gallon or so of water. The bath can last for 15 minutes. If the foot bath is not well-tolerated, try a hand-bath with the same preparation.

Massage and Heat Treatment

Massaging the liver with olive oil accelerates its functions. Proceed clockwise. Applications of cabbage leaves, as indicated above, complete the massage.

Stay away from hot water bottles, hot irons, and the like on the liver during periods of crisis. These practices have no other effect than a temporary easing of the pain, moreover, not only does it keep the congested condition, but it favors an eventual infection. However, the same process may give best results if one or several leaves of cabbage are placed between the body and the hot object. In case of emergency if cabbage is not available, apply very hot wet compresses, called fomentations. Renew these applications (20-30 minutes in length) every two hours.

Hip Bath

Activating all processes, accelerating the blood circulation and precipitating the discharge of waste products, the cold hip bath is equally important for preventive and curative measures. It suffices to take a cold hip bath for a few minutes for the organism to experience a state of alertness, being ready to respond to possible stimulation, such as multiple daily aggressions. It is a natural vaccination, efficient and without dangerous counter-effects. It is taken in a large receptacle of water, so that once in the bath, the water should reach the groin, but no higher. Water may be sprinkled over the lower abdomen and the kidneys. It is quite acceptable to take this bath in a bath-tub, however, *rest the feet on some object, for they should not be in the water,*

Any kind of water will do, from the tap, well, rain, river, as long as it is not boiled.

If the cold is imposing, the part of the body to be immersed can be warmed up beforehand. Even better, rather than starting with a bathful of cold water immediately, it may be preferable to become used to it gradually. Begin with a small amount of lukewarm water (about 2" deep), 77°F., sitting in it for a minute or two at a time and gradually building up until the five minute mark is reached, adding more water as well (each day add a half-inch of water until it reaches the fold of the groin). Once the five-minute mark has been reached, proceed, using cooler water. Diminish the temperature one or two degrees each day until reaching the limit of 64°F.

The ideal rate for gradually reducing the temperature of the water varies among individuals, of course. The basic rule is, if, at any stage, a bad or abnormal reaction occurs, return to the previous stage.

Even more important than the temperature of the bath is the temperature of the room in which the bath is taken. Indeed, a cold bath is better tolerated in a warm room than a lukewarm bath in a cold room. Under no condition should the body be exposed to cold, except the immersed part. Take care to cover all the other parts well if the room is not warm enough.

The colder the temperature, the more energetic reaction it stimulates. In principle the cold bath which does not last long stimulates, while the bath slightly warmed up, lasting longer, calms.

In order to tonify or stimulate, the bath should last 2-3 minutes, even less if the water is very cold. A very short bath one minute or even 30 seconds long has less chance of creating cold in the whole body than a prolonged one.

In case of fever, the bath should last 10 minutes, approximately; 3 or 4 baths a day; one every two hours in case of high temperature.

The normal bath lasts 3-5 minutes.

Vigorous massages should be administered after the bath, once thoroughly dried.

No bath should be taken during the menstrual period or in case of great fatigue, or if the bath creates cardiac troubles (palpitations, etc.) or brings a feeling of cold to the body.

Exercises

Fill up the chest with air, while at the same time pulling in the abdomen. Make an effort to raise the stomach at the same time, trying to shrink it and push it against the spine. Breathe out, emptying the chest as much as possible and relaxing the abdomen. Toward the end of the expiration let the ribs come down and loosen the abdomen.

TREATMENT FOR A DEFICIENT LIVER

When the liver is deficient, the albumin of some foods (especially dairy food) are not correctly transformed, and can become poisons. These unmetabolized substances now circulating in the organism can cause serious nervous troubles, whose symptoms are trembling fingers, periods of apathy or agitation, and mental confusion. In cases where the body temperature rises, it may be that the secretion of some ferments which are indispensable

Breathing exercises should be done slowly with no sudden effort in breathing or expiring. With experience, proceed with a suitable rhythm: for example, count 4 seconds for inhalation and 4 for expiration and increase progressively to 6, 8, 10 or more. Then try to make a two-second stop between inhalation and exhalation, then between exhalation and inhalation.

Breathing

Natural hygiene, which means exposing oneself to natural elements such as sun, air, water and earth, should be supplemented with deep breathing exercises. Good breathing contributes to the alkalinization of the humors and thus to strengthening the body's defense mechanisms. Proper breathing can even function as a massage of the liver complex.

Sun

The rays of the sun transform the sterols of the skin. That is how a great part of the vitamin D which the body needs is manufactured (the rest being supplied by natural oils). This is how most cholesterol is transformed, which saves the liver from having to synthesize it, or to neutralize it if it is in excess.

As with any natural and habitual practice, moderation and gradual progression is a rule that ought to be respected. Exposure to the sun will start with the legs, then the abdomen, the thorax, and at last the whole body. It is preferable to walk, run, play, or do garden work, but if it is necessary to remain immobile, care must be taken to protect the head from the direct rays of the sun.

to digestion have been interrupted. Then there will be putrefactions liberating gases and toxins which aggravate the condition.

In such a case the following is advised: reduce food intake, keep away from milk products, eggs, cereals and all things made with flour such as bread and cookies. *If there is a high fever, refrain from eating anything at all, not even any liquid (such as vegetable broth, milk, pure fruit juice, etc.).*

However, *drink as much as possible of water mixed with lemon juice,* clay powder mixed with water or the appropriate recommended herbal tea. The blood and the liver must be 'cleansed' without bringing in nutritive elements which at this stage might be turned into poison. When eating is resumed after a few days of fasting, it is best to start with fruit juices or carrot juice mixed with water. Afterwards fresh fruits and raw vegetables can be included.

Modern medical theories give too much importance to 'high-protein diets'; they profess that a lack of protein can incapacitate the liver. What of the fact that people who have been vegetarians for awhile have livers which function quite well, causing no disturbances? So the protein-deficiency theory is no answer to the liver trouble; one should look elsewhere for the real cause. However, it would still be advisable to supply the failing functions of synthesis with some proteins rich in amino acids, such as eggs, introduced in moderate quantity. If eggs are not well-tolerated alone, they may be incorporated in cooked dishes. At any rate, do not eat more than two or three eggs a week, and none in periods of crisis.

The Treatment, step-by-step

In the morning, on an empty stomach: 1 teaspoon of clay in half a glass of water, prepared the previous night.

Before eating: a cup of the decoction for obstruction or congestion of the liver (p.55).
After the meal: the juice of half a lemon in a cup of hot water sweetened with honey.
For drinks: lemon-water, decoctions of rosemary, thyme, mint, meadowsweet, chamomile.
Before retiring: a decoction for constipation, if necessary. Those suffering from jaundice should take the decoction for liver obstruction before the meal. If the liver is very fragile, take the decoction for 'liver insufficiency' which produces softer effectiveness. (p.55).

Whenever it is established that suffering is from obstruction of the biliary channels, take the appropriate decoction after eating; also take clay before one of the meals, lemon between meals and, in the morning on an empty stomach, 1 teaspoon of olive oil with the juice of half a lemon.

Every day, apply the bran-cabbage-onion poultice (p.56) from liver to spleen and if there is fever apply 1, 2, or 3 clay poultices on the lower abdomen. Do this every day for as long as the fever is present.

During the period of greatest crisis it is obviously preferable to stay in bed. This rest will liberate vitamins and amino acids as well as accelerating the transformation of proteins into energy, all necessary for building up the body's defenses.

Once the crisis has passed, it is still good to continue with the applications of bran-cabbage-onion every night before retiring for another two or three weeks.

* *

LIVER INSUFFICIENCY IN CHILDREN

Unfortunately this trouble is too common. Without a doubt there should be a change of diet, emphasizing a turn towards what is natural.

Give clay orally - ½ a teaspoon to 1 teaspoon divided in three equal parts and diluted in water for the morning and between meals.

For a drink, lemon-water.

After meals, give an infusion of rosemary or the decoction indicated for liver insufficiency, which is pleasant and well accepted by children.

Every day, give a cold hip bath 2-3 minutes long. Every night cover the abdomen with 2-3 layers of raw cabbage. Bandage and leave all night.

If the child is constipated give wild senna (cassia): one or several young follicles (one follicle for each year of age). Put the follicles in a cup of water and let soften overnight. Strain in the morning, make it luke-warm if necessary, and give to the child to drink.

* *

BLOOD CIRCULATION

Heart, Artery and Vein Diseases

More and more cases of death caused by heart failure accentuate the concern already provoked by the increasing amount of death caused by cancer. The uneasiness is worsening since this latest plague is not connected with age. Through the press, one is often informed of the death of famous people, mostly artists, who did not attain their fiftieth or even their fortieth year. Once past the age of forty, each man wonders if he will last until the next day.

Most people believe heart failure to be caused by overactivity, fatigue and mental strain, combined with the pressure of responsibility: an 'agitated' life. These same people - the majority of them men - with a bad heart are business people who do not even walk a block or two a day! From the bed to the elevator, from elevator to the car, from car to the elevator and from the elevator to the armchair and back again. Their distractions are the theater, nightclubs, banquets, tea and cocktail parties. What an agitating, destructive life it is, even if considering only the alarming cadence at which all sorts of rich foods and liquids are shoveled down. The disease of business managers and executives is caused by wealth spent on the worst kind of food that no heart can withstand.

The heart is known to be a strong organ. Its muscles are extremely powerful and only a series of diverse malfunctions could badly harm it.

The professors Klein and Wahl examined 1187 people with heart problems and made the following discovery: 316(31%) of these people had gastroduodenal trouble, of which 115 (16%) already had a gastric or duodenal ulcer.

People should know that the heart begins to give trouble only when there is partial or total obstruction of one of the vessels around it (coronaries). These vessels are themselves undergoing the repercussions of the fouling of blood channels in the body. Blood deposits waste products in parts of the body where the tissues show little resistance. The artery of a person with arteriosclerosis is devoid of its layer of silica; here is where deposits of cholesterol fat residue will collect.

In the "Journal of the American Medical Association", the doctors Weiss, Sr. and Jr. discuss having found themselves with the responsibility of decid-

ing for 431 men whether or not they should resume work after experiencing a heart failure. Five years later, a third of them had ceased working, either because of forced retirement or death.

How many people died 'in the prime of their life', some not even forty years old. That train conductor who was stricken with an attack while driving and the twelve year old boy with three doctors in his family who died while playing sports at school are just two examples of how medicine as presently practiced possesses insufficient methods for diagnosing and preventing disease.

Cardiac disease originates when there is both excess and deficiency in the blood. The deficiency is often due to an excessive concentration of certain substances which impede the proper use of other vital substances. It is a vicious circle for the deficiencies will often create room for further dangerous concentrations of products in excess, thus leading to further deficiency. What is needed is a method which will restore perfect health *before* a condition of acute disease is developed.

Does this book offer a good solution? Surely,

since those who live according to the harmonist conception of life have proven to be immune to heart failure, even though many of these people are very active, and handling responsibilities and problems that many executives and so-called 'managers' could not cope with.

THE KIDNEYS AND THE HEART

There are different opinions concerning which of these two organs deteriorate first. Some say that the heart is the victim of the failure of the kidney filters, while others say that overburdening and eventual collapse of the kidneys follow after heart trouble. The two camps are both right - and wrong. Right, because it is possible that it is not always the same organ which breaks down first. Wrong because instead of asking which organ precipitated the failure of the other, one should look farther and try to understand why the heart and kidneys of an individual with a normal constitution do not pro-

vide the regular service expected of them. Undoubtedly, it could be found out that many warning signals were either neglected or not well-treated. Then it would be remembered having had, prior to the declared disease, digestive troubles resulting from a disturbance in the liver function.

Probably it was for a long time that the liver had been giving signs of failure and overwork. The gall bladder becomes incapable of producing normal secretions. Imperfect and insufficient bile is manifested in the imperfect neutralization of the excessive waste products coming from food and from the metabolism. These waste products invade the blood, intestines and kidneys. After this follows gastro-duodenal troubles, which are not always noticeable. Another imperfection will manifest itself in the functions of assimilation. Being deficient, the liver will not be able to do its work transforming the food. The unassimilated protein will then create dangerous poisons, so much so that the sick person will find himself in a situation where, even when eating the healthiest kinds of food, he will nevertheless develop a toxic condition - all this because of the disturbance in the process of transformation of protein.

Only naturopathy - a *natural* way of eating - can bring the solution to all these problems which seem insoluble. If a change in the way of eating - meaning coming closer to the vegetarian way of life - is desirable, it will be beneficial only if the liver functions are normalized. And this normalization can be secured only with steady treatment, which includes healing plants, clay and other natural medicine that has been proven effective.

Together, both the liver and the kidney contribute to the keeping up of the acid-base equilibrium of the blood(pH). When the acid level is too high, the kidney eliminates excess through the urine.

It is the kidney which retains the basic substance of the blood and transforms them into ammoniac. The urine is made of excess liquids, more particularly of those coming from the blood plasma. The urine should contain urea, which is an excremential product made from the transformation of nitrogenized matters, uric acid, oxalic, lactic acids, salts, etc. If the liquids are not well-eliminated they stagnate in the tissues and make them swell, resulting in edema, common dropsy, etc. These liquids may also increase the arterial tension.

Nothing would better compensate this defective or tired heart than normal urine emission.

These emissions can be accentuated by placing the wheat bran-ivy poultice (p. 64) on the kidneys. Alternate poultices - one on the heart, one on the kidney. Take lemon-water (half a glass of water with half a lemon, or more) as well as the special tea for kidneys and bladder.

Decoction for Kidneys and Bladder

Bearberry leaves	40 gr.	Horsetail	20 gr.
Ashtree leaves	20 gr.	Mint leaves	20 gr.
Gooseberry		Wall pellitory	20 gr.
(black currant)		Buckthorn	10 gr.
leaves	20 gr.		

Mix everything well. Five tablespoons per quart of water. Boil for several minutes, infuse 10 minutes. Drink during meals or when desired during the day.

Improve the circulation with foot and hand baths with red-grape vine leaves (p. 65). Take this bath once or twice a day lasting for 15-20 minutes each time. The bath can be used a second time after it has been heated.

Outside of an acute crisis when any kind of food would be unwelcome, it would be wise to go on a temporary special cleansing diet consisting mainly of fruits. For example for 3 days take only grapes, or only apples. Afterwards, introduce other food in the form of vegetables, fruits, greens.

In general, finding a sound general treatment is of higher priority than applying localized cures.

The medicine to avoid

Needless to say, the patient should stay away from tranquilizing pills or chemical medicine of any sort which pervert the truth of the situation. The patient thinks himself to be in a better condition than he really is and runs the risk of committing a fatal imprudence. Avoid any intoxifying agents which stimulate for awhile, but afterwards result in a painful and dangerous depression.

All chemical products are deadly for the blood vessels, and contribute to inducing spasms and lesions. What is left to say about these chemical medicines - certain sclerosing agents which are introduced directly into the blood? The liver becomes exhausted from trying to neutralize them, the kidneys from trying to eliminate them, and the heart from experiencing them.

Any foreign substance entering the blood produces an irritation of the vessel wall. This irritation acts on the nervous filaments which are connected to it. Then follows an aggravation of the troubles, often accompanied by coagulation of the blood which obstructs the other vessels. These alterations of the vital functions lead to the degeneration of the tissues and even to necrosis.

The medical prescription most commonly used (antibiotics) seems very dangerous for the simple reason that they destroy the bacterial flora. The disease already shows the clear fact of a troubled organ or area; the medicine will only precipitate the imbalance. Nothing is more disastrous than a disturbance brought to the bacterial flora. It is here that all abnormal manifestations originate.

Mention should also be made of the particular danger in using anti-coagulants. The problem is not solved by forcefully preventing the blood from thickening, but by fluidifying it and bringing it to normal so that it coagulates outside the vessels and not inside. Provoking hemophilia does not constitute a remedy but a regrettable palliative. It is lemon that is best for fluidifying the blood and still promoting production of necessary coagulants in the case of wounds or other types of bleeding. (for other natural fluidifiers, see p.75).

In general do not give salt at all to people suffering from cardio-venal trouble. Except in cases of serious edema or hypertension, we do not see that there is danger in using a little bit of sea salt. However, salt, which contributes to chlorhydric acid production (necessary most of all for digesting meat) is not indispensable to vegetarians and some do well without it. There is thus no absolute rule in this matter, except to keep away from an immoderate intake. It should be added that salt, in slowing the breakdown and transformation of food (which is why it is widely used in the canning industry) slows down the digestive process, enough to cause putrid fermentation. On the other hand, it promotes some kidney functions. At any rate, use only sea salt - unrefined, of course.

The Food

Meat should be avoided, especially for this type of illness. Eliminating it completely from one's diet would speed up the cure. Animal products may be used (mostly dairy) but in very small amounts.

The principal dish of the meal should consist of raw vegetables (lettuce, carrots, cabbage, olives, etc.) which should be taken after some fruits. The dish may be seasoned with olive oil (guaranteed cold-pressed), lemon juice, garlic, parsley and other fragrant herbs.

With the cereals give priority to brown rice, which prevents high tension and buckwheat, which contains a precious substance (rutin) that fortifies the vessels.

Bread made with complete whole wheat flour would be too rich; it is preferable to sift some bran and obtain and 85% complete flour.

Clay Treatment of Kidneys and Bladder

In the case of lumbago, nephritis or other afflictions of the renal region, it is preferable to apply the clay hot or at least tepid.

Prepare large, thick poultices; place clay in direct contact with the skin if possible. One or two poultices every day - leave for 2-4 hours or all night if there are no problems. Complete with light massages with a mixture of equal parts of chipped garlic and clayish water.

Clay poultices can be applied on the lower abdomen, kidney or on both, alternating in cases of cystitis. However, the best way to alleviate this problem is with a bran-cabbage-onion poultice. For directions on how to prepare it, see p. 56. In addition drink clay-water, and decoctions of strawberry root, plantain, bearberry, corn stigmas, (that part of the pistil which receives the pollen), Rest Harrow root, heath, pellitory.

Clay poultices are the indispensable complement to the treatment of renal (kidney) tuberculosis and to the troubles of the suprarenal glands.

Clay Treatment for the Heart

While poultices may be too stimulating, fresh compresses (60°-68°) are generally well-tolerated by the heart. Begin with compresses of fresh clayish water. The first should be left for only half an hour. The next time it may remain for one hour and eventually, two hours. When compresses are well-tolerated after two hours, try to replace them with clay poultices (rather thin,¼") leaving them for the same length of time.

The thickness of the poultices should be gradually increased to 1", always leaving them in place for two hours. If the evening poultice does not cool itself or does not create a cooling sensation, it is possible to leave it overnight. Apply only one poultice every 24 hours, in this case.

In order to increase the efficiency of the poultice, chip a little onion (which is a heart tonic) onto the surface of the poultice before applying. In the event that the clay cools, warm it in advance in a double boiler.

Treating Troubles due to High Blood Pressure with Clay

Apply thick, cold clay poultices on the nape of the neck as soon as possible. Leave in place for one hour to an hour and a half and renew them as many times as possible until a normal state is reached. In conjunction with these applications on the neck, make equally cold and thick applications on the lower abdomen - two poultices a day, kept on for 2 hours.

If possible, take mustard powder foot-baths every day for 10-20 minutes (a handful of mustard powder in a wash basin of tepid water). If the patient cannot be seated for the foot bath, replace it with a mustard plaster on the calves and poultices of raw chipped onions on the sole.

Even after initial relief, continue the poultices (2 on the nape and 1 on the lower abdomen every day) for some days until the problem disappears.

HEART DISEASE

Everyone knows that the weaknesses, lesions, or malfunctions of the heart are indicated by breathlessness, palpitations, pulse irregularities, sometimes pains in the left part of the chest which radiate through the shoulder and left arm. It can also be indicated by the swelling of the legs, generally the ankle, nocturnal perspiration, blue circles around the eyes, purple lips with a blue color around them, or a complexion which is either very pale or very red.

The principal reasons for these manifestations are, along with circulatory trouble, the inflammation of the serous membrane of the cardiac muscle, mitral or aortic insufficiency, not to mention angina of the chest, and arteriosclerosis.

In the case of mitral insufficiency, the valves of the mitral orifice are not able to close completely. The blood can then flow back into the left auricle of the heart, expanding the internal walls and at the same time impeding circulation.

The narrowing of the mitral also leads to dangerous repercussions for the pressure is greater when the orifice is narrowed. The result is breathlessness, difficulty in running, or even walking relatively fast and difficulty in climbing stairs or in any prolonged effort.

In case of aortic insufficiency, the sigmoid valvules fail to completely close the orifice of each ventricular diastole and the blood that passed through to the aorta can flow back to the ventricle. Someone who suffers from this defect has a pale complexion, a bright eye, and a 'jumping' pulse.

The inflammation of the pericardium (water membrane) of the endocardium (the membrane which covers the cavities of the heart) or of the myocardium (the muscle of the heart) has a serious effect on the functioning of this organ. All these troubles can be aggravated by a weakening of the cardiac contractions accompanied by or even caused by an increase in venous pressure and a decrease in arterial pressure. It usually follows a serious slowing down of the blood circulation. Symptoms of these cardiac disorders are: congestive phenomena in the blood, serious troubles in the working of the intestines and bowels, accelerated and irregular pulse, occurrence of edema, touching first the legs, then reaching up to the abdominal wall with a serious overflow in the peritoneum (membrane lining). The liver becomes hypertrophied and the kidneys tire, letting albumin go through. The lungs become congested, causing painful breathing at every moment. The sick person cannot lie down in bed, and must remain seated.

The Cure

The most urgent priority is to help the heart. Prepare the following tea to be taken internally and apply a wheat bran-climbing ivy poultice.

Put 5 handfuls of bran and 2 handfuls of climbing ivy (fresh or dry) chopped, in a pot. Add some water and cook on a high flame, stirring with a wooden spatula for 10-15 minutes until the water is completely evaporated. Spread the mixture on a cheese cloth, fold and apply ¾" thick and as hot as the patient can tolerate. Bandage and keep on one hour and a half to two hours or overnight if it does not cause any disturbance. It may be used only once; discard after using.

Note: If intestines are painful and irritated, add 2 handfuls of althea to this poultice. If climbing ivy is not available the wheat bran-cabbage-onion poultice may be used instead (p. 56).

Decoction for the Heart and Blood Circulation

Red-grape vine leaves	25 gr.	Barberry	15 gr.
		Dandelion	15 gr.
Shepherd's purse	20 gr.	Germander	10 gr.
Mistletoe	20 gr.	Woodruff	5 gr.
Goose-grass	15 gr.	Hawthorn	5 gr.

Boil a quart of water. Add 5-6 tablespoon of the mixture and let boil for 2-3 minutes. Remove from fire and let infuse 15 minutes. It would be even better if it could be left overnight. Take as a drink at meals or during the day.

When violent pain radiates through the arm, the hand and the left small finger, causing a feeling of cramps, accompanied by anguish and sometimes a brief loss of consciousness, it is certain that the problem is angina of the chest.

Angina Pectoris (Angina of the Chest)

The crisis occurs after an effort or a long walk, climbing stairs or a hill, sometimes even without apparent cause. This crisis, which can be of great intensity, is characterized by violent pains that take different forms in the region of the heart; sometimes it is a stabbing pain on the left side of the chest, sometimes felt as a 'bar' across the chest.

Angina pectoris results from an inflammation or even a lesion of the heart, or the aorta or another close organ. Following the intoxification of the organism, the blood becomes impure and thickens; it carries waste products which can be deadly for the vessels and the heart.

The real angina pectoris, which results from a lesion of the heart, the aorta, or any other neigh-

boring organ, is fortunately very rare. The most frequent chest angina results from neurosis which comes from a hyperexcitability of the cardiac nerve. The pain is less violent and anguish is not so acute. However, some vasomotor troubles occur which are recognized by the abrupt coldness of the hands and feet; there may be dizziness, palpitations, frequent urges to urinate and tremors. The sick person will be able to walk whereas in the real angina pectoris he finds it impossible.

To search for the main cause of this illness anywhere but in the digestive system would be a waste of time. How can digestion influence the heart? When, for any reason at all, the normal process of digestion is slowed down, fermentations take place accompanied by gas emanation. The channel for the evacuations of the gases not always being free, it may happen that these gases form a pocket in the upper part of the abdomen. This pocket, dilating according to the volume of the stored gases, will exercise pressure on the plexus and create nervous troubles which will have repercussion on the function of the corresponding endocrine glands. The nervous troubles reverberate onto the cardiac nervous network.

In other cases, the process is different; the accumulated gases succeed in lifting up the diaphragm (the muscle separating the abdomen from the chest) which may come to touch the point of the heart and sometimes even displace it. It is easy to understand how this causes violent pain which can result in a loss of consciousness. This is not really serious, for after losing consciousness, the state of contraction which had resulted from the pressure on the plexus ends. The gases are channelled out and the crisis is terminated.

The Cure

Whether or not the angina is serious it is urgent to proceed with a detoxification of the organism. This is done by taking refreshing nourishment which will help in getting rid of the waste through normal channels and stimulating the liver. (p. 46)

Whatever the origin of the crisis, 'free' the heart by applying a poultice of wheat bran and ivy leaves (p. 56), first on the left part of the chest under the heart, then directly on the chest. Leave each poultice in place for 1 - 1½ hours.

A foot bath can be quite helpful:

Bring 1 gallon of water to a boil, add 2 or 3 handfuls

of red-grape vine leaves and let simmer 15 minutes. If this foot bath is not well-tolerated, it is advisable to try a hand-bath with the same preparation.

In case of minor chest pain, do the following:

Apply cabbage leaves from the liver to the spleen. Flatten the cabbage leaves with a rolling-pin first so that they adhere well to the body. Put on 2-3 layers.

Along with that, drink herbal preparations - both decoctions and infusions - that are good for cleansing the liver - rosemary, thyme, marigold, artichoke, woodruff. Have light meals.

In addition to this, take a cold hip bath every day, lasting from 3-5 minutes. However, contrary to what most people believe, cold hip baths are not always proper for countering heart troubles; they should be taken with great care (see p.57).

While taking the bath, the patient can massage the heart lightly with camphor oil. If the heart is weak, apply a hot compress after the massage to let the oil penetrate.

Eliminate all alcoholic drinks, tobacco, meat, coffee and milk, white bread and sugar and all unnatural (processed) food. The patient should take particular care to have regular bowel movements. A light but firm massage will help get rid of the gases through normal channels. It would be very helpful to take some clay before one meal - 1 teaspoon diluted in half a glass of water - preferably at breakfast, for the stomach should be empty.

In case of any very serious crisis, do not eat anything solid at all. Only liquids such as lemon-water (½ a lemon or more in a glass of water), clay-water, special herbal teas and vegetable broth (made from greens) should be eaten. Have the patient lie in bed; use three pillows to make him comfortable and also place a pillow under each arm to relieve the heart.

Arteriosclerosis

All that modern medicine has ever told people suffering from arteriosclerosis to do is to stop smoking and to eat less fat. This is as far as the public education ever went. Now it is known that diet is the answer. Let us learn about this 'plague' which kills more people, young and old, than any other modern disease.

The walls of vessels are coated with a pulp composed of a mixture of cholesterol, fat and fatty acid. This pulp eventually calcifies, the large vessels such as the aorta, are transformed into rigid and dilated tubes with deformities.

Little by little, the elastic tissue is replaced by a sclerous tissue, which, when pressed lightly with a finger, has no flexibility; a hardness is felt. The lack of flexibility is always accompanied by a decrease in resistance; the small vessels sometimes break (for example, in the case of a brain hemorrhage). Coagulation occurs and that is how arterial thrombosis of the brain, followed by softening, suddenly occurs.

When, after a sclerous thickening of the internal walls of the arteries, lesions develop (most of all in the small visceral arteries) and when the muscular layers are also thickened, arteriosclerosis is taking place. This term, arteriosclerosis, actually designates the progressive hardening of arteries with all the circulatory troubles which follow. A thickening of the inside wall layer occurs, which can lead to obstruction of the arteries. When this obstruction occurs in the hands and legs, there is a feeling of 'dead fingers'; there are cramps along with an intermittent limping. A cramp would make any movement impossible since there is no proper irrigation in the muscles. When the obstruction of the arteries is complete, meaning severe enough to cause necrosis in the tissues, gangrene takes place.

Sclerosis can extend to a few organs (heart, kidneys) which have degenerated because of improper circulation and nutrition. The disease is called dystrophic sclerosis. The inside diameter of the vessel is quite reduced by the sclerosed plexus, the blood circulation is considerably slowed down, the cells of the vessels themselves are not renewed quickly. Sclerosis is deepening to such a degree that arterial tension collapses, followed by the tiring of the heart and the kidneys.

The symptoms of arteriosclerosis are sometimes mistaken for those of other afflictions and it is sometimes difficult to tell the difference. That is how some pains occurring near the joints can make

one think of rheumatism, arthritis, or the like. In case of arterial tension with or without arteriosclerosis, the person has sudden flashes in front of his eyes. There is whistling or buzzing in the ears.

Ulcers sometimes open; nature wants it that way to allow the elimination of the sclerosing pulp. How great a danger is incurred in attempting to close these ulcers by artificial means!

Diagnosis of Arteriosclerosis

In the case of arteriosclerosis, the vessels become clearly visible through the skin. The radial artery (which starts in the thumb and extends to the elbow) is very protuberant; it is winding, rigid and hard; it rolls under the finger and doesn't flatten as easily as a normal artery; it may present other irregularities as well. The humeral artery (which extends from the elbow to the shoulder) presents similar symptoms. The temporal is equally protuberant; its twists are clearly showing; with each contraction of the heart, the arteries elongate and accomplish a sort of creeping movement that is easily noticeable. Sometimes the pulsations of the arteries become easily perceptible to the touch. One can even feel these pulsations on the top of the head.

The Cure

It is a generally known fact that cholesterol is one of the principal factors of arteriosclerosis. Cholesterol has two origins. The first is external; it is introduced in the organism with the animal fats, milk, butter and eggs. The second kind is internal; it is made by the organism itself for its own needs. It must not be forgotten that cholesterol is necessary to the body function as a protection, and can be a source of D vitamins; it is its excess which is dangerous.

Although the overwork of the neurovegetative system had been presented as being the origin of arteriosclerosis, it is now well-known that by reducing the consumption of food rich in cholesterol (animal meat, fat and dairy food), the chances of thickening the vessels with harmful matter are reduced.

Fat of animal origin is unanimously rejected by authorities for consumption, but the opinions diverge concerning the other types of fat. Concerning the margarines now on the market, the ill con-sequences of their manufacture exclude their possible use. Some oils are promoted because of their low cholesterol content such as sunflower oil, corn germ oil. Without denying their efficiency, nothing seems to equal good olive oil, virgin and cold-pressed. The harmonists who are careful in eating properly balanced food make large use of olive oil *and do not experience the physiological miseries of arteriosclerosis.*

Whole wheat bread enriches the blood so enormously that it should not be used continuously. Instead, alternate it with rye bread (real rye bread, not the one commercially sold on the market). It is known to some that in countries where rye is widely used, arteries are flexible and blood is fluid.

Use plenty of fresh fruits and vegetables. Eat them raw, and always at the beginning of the meal. When cooking food, be careful not to overcook, for a strong concentration - from cooking under high pressure - will produce deposits in the arteries.

The most beneficial plants for arteriosclerosis are the Lime-tree, Hawthorn, Fumitory, and Mistletoe. To maintain the flexibility of the arteries, take a decoction of walnut-tree leaves before the meal and another decoction of common meadowsweet after the meal.

One of the best fluidifiers of the blood is lemon. This does not present any of the danger caused by some medication because while it fluidifies, it does not prevent coagulation. It could be taken from 2-6 times a day for a period of several months and sometimes even several years. Mix its juice in some water (1 lemon in a glass of water).

Garlic also contributes to the fluidifying of the blood. It lowers the arterial tension and brings the balance of the blood to normal.

The absorbent action of clay will help. Take it regularly, 1 teaspoon a day (½ an hour or more before meals) except when there is an increase in tension. Like whole wheat bread, clay enriches the blood, so be cautious and take it only once every three days. (Read the section on internal use of clay, p.16).

It is important to keep an eye on the evacuation - not only from the intestines but also from the kidneys since their action can be slowed down by sclerosis.

Obesity increases arteriosclerosis. *Do not eat too much, not even of nutritious food.* A person is much more likely to become ill from eating too much than too little.

During the warm sunny season, remember the sunbath. This gives the opportunity to utilize sterols such as cholesterol for other purposes than the calcification of arteries. Concentrated sun rays transform these sterols into D vitamins.

BLOOD THICKENING

Blood thickening has the same symptoms as arteriosclerosis with the exception that not only is there no hypertension, but on the contrary, a tension lower than normal. Blood analyses often do not reveal in this case, urea, sugar, or excess cholesterol; simply an increase in potassium rate and some 'glucoprotein'.

So many people believe themselves safe because their tension is low. However, the danger of rupture of a duct is greater with a viscous (thick) liquid without exaggerated pressure than with a higher pressure and a thinner fluid. This is why vascular accidents are frequent with people having thick blood, even if they are still young - 35-40 years old. The factor of mortality from 40 on is considerable. A great number of vascular accidents can be imputed to blood thickening such as brain hemorrhage and infection of the myocardium.

Symptoms

The visible symptoms of blood thickening are: somnolence, heavy sleep, digestive troubles, exaggerated chills, especially in the extremities with congestion of the face and skull and also the slowing down of brain functions and sexual drive.

The Cure

The role of food is considerable in curing this abnormal condition, especially the lack of sexual desire. Dr. de Larebeyrette, who made long studies about this affliction, verifies that just not eating white bread for a few weeks effects an improvement.

This demonstrates that there is both intoxification and deficiency, and as the harm from excess is more dangerous than the harm from deficiency, eliminating harmful elements is even more important than restoring the missing ones. *Elimination precedes assimilation:* this is an important basic

principle; accelerating the former process consequently promotes the latter.

As with arteriosclerosis, taking lemons would be helpful.

Garlic, considered by some people as producing hypotension (below normal), is nevertheless recommended. In reality, garlic is a *regulator* of tension; it will never bring blood pressure to lower than a normal rate - rather it normalizes it. The important thing here is its depurative action due to its precious sulphured essences which enter the blood rapidly. For more on garlic, see p. 25. All the aromatic plants, moreover, are especially recommended. When preparing food, do not forget to add plenty of parsley, chervil, tarragon, savory, basil, horseradish, onion, welsh onion, chive, thyme, bay leaves, rosemary, etc.

The food should include revitalizing, refreshing and nutritive elements. This implies mostly raw food (fruits and vegetables) seasoned with cold-pressed, virgin olive oil, lemon juice, sea salt, and aromatics. Some cooked vegetables should also be included.

Cereals and grains are also recommended. Be sure to vary them. Start with wheat and on other days, use brown rice, hulled barley, oat flakes, couscous, millet, buckwheat groats and flour and rye.

Cheese and eggs may be eaten in moderate quantities, but meat must be completely eliminated. Meat brings toxic substances to the intestines, causing spasms of defense. What is more, meat corrupts the body fluids (blood, lymph, bile) and leads to hardening of the blood vessels, whose walls become progressively coated with unwanted waste products. Each mouthful of meat intensifies the danger of the condition; its poisons increase the thickening of the blood considerably.

To avoid the risk of a rupture of a blood vessel it would be wise to accelerate the circulatory course by taking foot baths prepared with red-grape vine leaves (p.65).

It will be helpful to take herbs that are good for unclogging the intestines and bladder as well as cleansing the liver and kidneys (see sections on plant treatment in 'liver' and 'elimination').

Every day, preferably in the morning, a short hip bath should be taken to help accelerate the circulation, thus speeding up elimination.

Sedentary people should train themselves to take long walks and other physical exercise (gymnastics, gardening, swimming, etc.) being careful to stay away from exaggerated overactivity as often happens on vacations.

A person suffering from thickening of the blood cannot get rid of his pains as easily as someone erases a mistake in a notebook. Perseverance is needed, or rather, more exactly, the evolutions of one's conceptions toward a balanced way of life. Many people following the harmonist method have been restored to a normal condition.

Arterial Hypertension

As the mechanism regulating arterial tension is under the influence of the neuro-sympathetic system, its irregularity is a sign of serious disturbances. In an organ functioning normally, this arterial regulation is secured by the balance maintained between the moderating and accelerating elements. If the 'curbing system' should fail in accomplishing its work, the tension increases and the pulse becomes very rapid and irregular.

In order for all the organs to accomplish functions which balance each other mutually, the cells must be nourished properly and the regular evacuation of the metabolism residues be assured. Food thus plays a considerable role. If by changing food, there is still no immediate favorable reaction, it is because the nervous system is deeply affected, and some time will be needed to restore it to normal functioning.

In older people who have hardened arteries, the hypertension is not so alarming since it is simply an effort made by the organism to guarantee its irrigation. Some people affected with hypertension reach an old age. We know of a professor who lived past 90 in spite of a very high tension.

The Symptoms

We do not attach much importance to numbers; instead, we concentrate on the actual troubles. These are of diverse types and are not all experienced at the same time. It could be a headache which comes periodically, dizzy moments, or even loss of balance. Visual troubles could arise, such as luminous rays, sometimes there is temporary interruption of the vision. There may also be palpitations, beating felt in the arteries, unjustified pantings, and a feeling of oppression or sometimes anguish. The following symptoms are sometimes also felt: a compression in the extremities - the phenomenon of 'dead fingers', cramps and frequent urination during the night. For a young person to be afflicted with hypertension could be a consequence of serious kidney lesions. At any rate, in contrast with what happens with older people, its presence always indicates that the defense system is failing. That is why hypertension often occurs when the organism is tired.

The Cure

The treatment of the general condition must include a strict reform of the inaccurate conception of nourishment, without having to adopt or be restricted to the notion of 'regimen', being enslaved to a system that is too hard to keep. Unless the situation is serious, there is no need to completely suppress salt - especially considering the fact that sea salt is more useful than the medicinal salts. It is advisable, however, to reduce its usage and avoid using it in cooking.

The most propitious foods are garlic, lemon, brown rice, parsley, black currants and pears. Season dishes with plenty of garlic and parsley. In the morning, before eating or drinking anything drink the following mixture: 1 cup of water in which 3 or 4 grated garlic cloves had been soaked overnight. Start with half a clove and increase the dosage.

The most beneficial plants are the olive tree, the hawthorn, Black currant, mistletoe and Shepherd's purse. However, for a specific treatment we prefer the one that aims at restoring the disturbed functions. Thus we give preponderance to the teas for the liver, kidneys and intestines. Weak kidneys and obstructed intestines contribute to an abnormal elevation of the tension. The first thing to encourage a cure is to secure the evacuations of these organs.

Because of hypertension, accidents may occur, especially vessel ruptures. If the vessels irrigating the brain or the heart get ruptured, the consequences are serious. It is important, in conjunction with helping to restore the general condition, to introduce measures of prudence which could prevent such accidents. One of the most efficient measures is the foot bath previously mentioned, made with a decoction of red-grape vine leaves (p.65). Take it once or even twice a day, if necessary for 15-20 minutes each. As soon as the condition is better, reduce the frequency of the baths, but keep taking at least two a week.

If the pain is localized in the head, apply clay on the back of the neck while at the same time applying a 'helmet' of cabbage leaves.

> Detach the leaves of a green or red cabbage, cut off the thick spine, lay three layers of leaves one over the other on the head, then bandage it in place. Keep it on overnight.

Arteritis

Pathogenic substances contained in the blood exercise on the inside walls of the vessels an irritation which could later become a lesion. This condition can be aggravated by a deficiency in silica which is found at the base of the protective thin skin; at the level of these lesions, deposits of fat accumulate together with cholesterol and other waste material from the bodily processes. Circulation is hindered, sometimes even interrupted. This complicates the condition, often ending up in the obstruction of the artery or sclerosis.

A detour will be created to attempt to secure circulation but it will not take the inflammation long to spread throughout the area, and circulation will then be completely blocked. The blood which is in the extremities will coagulate and create danger of gangrene.

The beginning of the manifestation of arteritis is indicated by a period of limping, more or less pronounced, and painful cramps in the calf of the leg during walks, forcing one to rest. The cramps are less painful in the period of rest but as soon as effort is resumed, the intensity of the pain returns. This pain is mostly provoked by a spasm suffered by the lesioned artery. The situation worsens when the pains occur even in the period of rest, or when lying down or sleeping.

If hygienic measures are not taken immediately, further complications - which could lead to the amputations of the legs or even death - are to be feared. However, in acting swiftly and in persevering with the treatment, the danger can be decreased and a normal condition restored.

Here, too, alimentary reform will have to be drastic and will involve not only excluding meat, along with fish and alcoholic drinks, but also a reduction in the consumption of all other animal products such as butter, cheese, and eggs.

Take fruits, then fresh vegetables, preferably raw. If a good rye bread is available, this is preferable to whole wheat bread in this particular case, at least during the period of cure.

Smokers must be warned against this affliction, for it is they who form the majority struck by the disease. Nicotine is a terrible sclerosing agent and the first step is to eliminate this menace.

The beneficial qualities of lemon have already been mentioned. They act energetically to fluidify the blood, while at the same time encouraging a return to elasticity of the arteries. For serious cases, do not stop at 2 or 3 lemons a day, but build up to 9, 10, or 12 lemons a day for one or two weeks.

Other plants that help purify the blood are the lime-tree, the hawthorn, common meadowsweet, mistletoe, and fumitory; they also exercise an anti-spasmodic and sedative action on the pain

To the general treatment which includes the practice of cold hip baths (p. 57) add the foot bath with red-grape vine leaves and clay poultices or cabbage-leaf applications on the legs.

Afflicted Legs - Varicose Veins

People experiencing leg troubles are growing in number. How many legs are red, purplish-blue, swollen, crooked, varicosed, benumbed, etc.!

The error is in believing that there is one treatment for varicose veins, another for arteritis, another for ulcers, and so on. That is not so, there are adaptations for particular cases, but the basic in-depth treatment is one, as is the cause.

Why and how do the legs sometimes get in such a condition? Is it being too often in a standing position, or is it fatigue or worries which cause these abnormalities? Perhaps they contribute, but the principal and real cause resides in the violation of the natural rules of life. Too much heavy food - thickening the vessels with deposits, thickening and acidifying the blood, encumbering the channels of evacuation - that is the origin of all these miseries.

A prolonged condition of intoxification may lead to pathological modifications. This is how the veinous walls can be changed for the worse and the valvules become deformed. Under the valvule, the vein dilates, and its walls become distended and later atrophied. The phenomenon starts in the superior region of a vein, then spreads, moving down, the inferior valvule having to support the blood pressure that the superior valvule no longer retains. It continues on in this way, worsening, the weight of the blood column increasing after every failure of a valvule.

The 'sclerosing' treatment consists of injecting an irritating chemical product, which forms a blood clot which is fixed at the punctured place. An inflammation of the vein then follows and then its hardening. Sclerosis is thus the secondary effect of this artificial inflammation. Often an excema bursts out, which is so hard that it sometimes invades the whole leg, including the thigh. A 'cure' now in vogue consists in the simple removal of the vein. After the treatment one rightfully wonders what will happen to the leg, especially to those parts where blood can no longer nourish nor drain.

The healing process for varicose veins is slow; this fact must not be hidden. However, noticeable improvement can be experienced through natural treatment.

Some varicose veins, such as those which sometimes occur during the time of pregnancy, result either from the compression of a large veinous trunk which is caused by the displacement of the foetus, or, more often, from an excess of folliculin. This excess induces the slowing down of the smooth fibers and of the ligaments. The regulation of the oestrogens (folliculin, etc.) is normally achieved by the liver so it is the failing of this organ that is finally at the origin of many varicose veins.

Treatment

The origin of most afflictions of the legs and veins is the slowing down of the circulation. The slowing down of the veinous circulation is injurious to the normal renewal of the blood, which, being full of carbonic acid become darker in color and communicates this purple-blue color to the tissues. The condition then worsens, for the slowing down also impoverishes the blood of hemoglobin; the tissues become white from malnutrition and asphyxia.

Food

Nothing is more favorable to the restoration of a normal circulation than proper vegetarian food. First choice is fruits. Next certain kinds of vegetables such as garlic and onion, which are particularly valuable because of the sulphured essences that they liberate in the digestive canal. Once absorbed in the interior walls with other elements created by the digestive process, these sulphured essences, gas included, are immediately absorbed into the blood which they help cleanse and fluidify. More-over, these essences exercise a cleansing action on the vascular walls, and a disinfecting one in any area that may be injured.

In order to fluidify and purify the blood, cleanse the vessels and normalize their flexibility, no toxic food may be taken, and strong food must be taken with care. In addition to choosing food which is more nutritious, be careful to take what is less harmful to the veins, that is, avoid whatever might be too concentrated. This would deposit a layer of 'dirt' in the inside walls of the veins.

Whole wheat bread should be taken in moderation. Not that it is detrimental, but it enriches the blood to such an extent that it may speed up some abnormal phenomena. Being necessary for general balance, it should not be excluded, but rather alternate it with rye bread - make it like the whole wheat bread with 85-90% sifted flour and a natural starter.

Cheese, dry fruits and most dried vegetables are to be drastically reduced since they are very concentrated. Also, food should not be cooked under too much pressure as it will be too concentrated.

Give preference to different kinds of fresh fruits and raw vegetables. Have fruits in season for breakfast. Also have some at the beginning of each meal and follow with raw vegetables in abundance (cabbage, carrot, turnip, radish, lettuce, spinach, etc.). Flavor it generously with garlic (or onion), parsley or chervil, tarragon, welsh onion or chives, burnet, sage, savory. Add olive oil, sea salt and lemon juice to taste. Some black olives would also be a welcome addition.

If this meal is not filling, the following may be added: cooked vegetables, sour milk, yoghurt, or cottage cheese. Drink, preferably between meals, either lemon-water or herbal decoctions.

Whenever a particular variety of fruit shows up in the market, it would be wise to have that fruit exclusively for the whole day. With time and experience one will be able to go on for several days with such a cure.

Teas and Poultices

Immediately at the beginning of the detoxification, the benefits of the treatment are felt with distinct relief. The effort must be continued in order to bring about a lasting cure, mostly by being careful with food, but also supplementing with herbs, baths and poultices. Decoctions for the liver and circulation may be taken, and also the following plants: plantain, smartweed(persicaria), witch hazel, milfoil(yarrow), cypress(the fruit), black currant (the leaves).

After 3 weeks of detoxification, use a tea which will have a constrictive effect on the dilated veins.

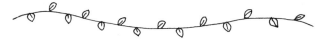

Decoction for Hemorrhoids and Varicose Veins

Hawthorn	20 gr.	Witch hazel	20 gr.
Hyssop	20 gr.	Yarrow	20 gr.
Red-grape		Matricaria	
vine leaves	20 gr.	(wild chamomile)	10 gr.
Shepherd's purse	20 gr.		

Bring a pint of water to a boil and add 4 tablespoons of the plant mixture and steep for 15 minutes. Even better, let it steep overnight. Drink during the day, between meals.

Avoid local applications of clay in the beginning of the treatment. Clay is known to have the property of attracting all the toxins; it would be futile to give this part of the body an additional burden at this time. Premature applications often create a swelling in the treated part. It is preferable to complete the basic treatment with applications of cabbage leaves (raw) and later on, with plantain leaves or Solomon's seal. Use fresh leaves on top of a clay poultice and apply to the skin, the clay being in contact with the affected area. For large varicose veins, anoint with wet compresses dipped in the following solution:

100 gr. of oak bark and 1 quart of water. Bring to a boil and let simmer ½ hour.

As soon as this treatment produces a positive effect, start using the clay alone. Proceed simply with daubs of clay; that is to say, with the hand, take cold clay paste and spread a good and uniform layer over the greater part of the leg.

After 1 or 1½ hours, when the clay is dry, wash the leg and renew the daubs, if circumstances allow. Avoid very hot and thick poultices which could produce considerable drainage of toxic substances over the affected area. Light applications, repeated as frequently as possible, will yield good results with perseverance. At night, use a damp compress with a decoction of plantain or evergreen oak bark (above) or a thin clay poultice, on the surface of which have been placed fresh plantain leaves or Solomon's seal.

Either with varicose veins or for hemorrhoids, clay paste can be prepared with a decoction of plantain, evergreen oak bark or satin leaves instead of water.

From time to time, massage lightly with a mixture of camphor oil and crushed garlic (2:1).

People suffering from varicose veins cannot bear hot foot baths, which often provoke a renewal of the swelling. An exception can be made for the red-grape vine leaf bath which is generally well-tolerated if it is taken moderately warm and only 2-3 times a week. This both activates the circulation (and it does not cause the revulsion which a mustard bath might) and nicely complements the treatment of varicose veins.

Varicose sores and Leg ulcers

Various defense reactions of the body can result in ulcers. There could be a perforation of the vein due to a scab or a varicose issue. Very small ulcers generally correspond to the former case, while other ulcers occupy a very great surface. The degree of pain is not always proportional to the expansion of the ulcer. The very small ulcers (from thrombosis) are generally very painful; they are sometimes harder to cure than ulcers larger than the hand.

No matter what kind of ulcer, there is always a great risk in resorting to immediate local action to heal it. Artificial treatments, especially external ones, are very dangerous. The reason is that the impurities which are eliminated through the ulcer may join the circulatory flow and cause great damage by obstructing a vessel situated close to the heart or the brain.

No natural remedy will permit the obstruction of an exit made necessary by the invasion of the blood by toxic waste products. Only after these dangerous substances are drained towards the natural places of elimination (intestines, kidneys, bladder) can the closing of the ulcer be considered. This explains and justifies the relative slowness of the curing process with natural means. For an ulcer cured with pomades and other medical remedies may open up as easily as it was closed and this closing and opening may continue for years. The natural way may take 'more time' but it is faster in the long run, as it closes the ulcer permanently. Herein lies the superiority of the natural way.

The Cure

The general treatment includes proper food, hip baths, herbal teas for the liver and depuration of the blood, and lemon and clay (taken orally after having been diluted in water).

Then, and only then begin local treatment of the ulcer, either with a clay poultice or cabbage leaves. In the beginning, use both to find out which one works best. If clay is well-tolerated and if its application does not cause later discomfort or pain, use it as often as possible, leaving each poultice on approximately 1½ hours. In the evening, apply cabbage leaves. Sometimes, cabbage leaves are better tolerated if they have been dipped into boiling water before using.

Of course, it is not always that simple, especially with the smaller ulcers, which are painful mostly at night. In such a case, different methods may be tried in order to find the most soothing way. For example, try wet compresses made of an infusion of red-grape vine leaves:

One handful of leaves for one quart of water.
Boil water, add the leaves and simmer 15 minutes.

Lukewarm local baths may also be used, either with a decoction of red-grape vine leaves, or vesiculous varech(a seaweed) or any other kind of seaweed or even a hot saltwater bath (sea salt).

In the beginning, use baths frequently to ensure an enlargement of the ulcer, either in surface or depth. This phenomenon can be explained by the reabsorption of the tissues affected with necrosis, which were likely to be an obstacle to cellular reconstitution. After elimination of the dead or seriously injured cells, the quick regrowth of new tissues can be verified: there are 'buds' inside the ulcer, and they will expand and eventually be able to make up for the hollow created by the ulcer by filling it up.

When the ulcer begins to look better, and the surrounding area seems healthier, it is then necessary to leave it uncovered several hours a day, so that the excitation produced by the external agents stimulates the organism to reconstitute protective means. Use a dry dressing made in the following way:

Lay the very thin skin of onion (found between two layers of onion) over the affected area and cover it with a light material.

After the ulcer has closed, it is advisable to continue the local treatment for awhile to insure the cure. During the day apply a clay poultice for 1½-2 hours. Overnight, put three layers of raw cabbage over the area, previously flattening their spines with a rolling pin.

****

VARICOSE ULCER

One patient, 72 years old, suffered very much from a varicose ulcer on her leg. After many doubts she decided to try applying clay poultices. The ulcer closed completely and the leg recovered its normal appearance - much to the patient's astonishment as she had begun the treatment without any conviction and only because she was suffering so much that clay was a last resort.

****

Hemorrhoids

Hemorrhoids are loosenings of the veins. They are like varicose veins, usually open, placed above or below the anal sphincter, depending on whether they are internally or externally located. People are getting them more frequently now because they are a consequence of blood intoxification and the limp tissues which develop from that intoxification. The blood is so full of non-evacuated waste products that it thickens and is not able to obtain fresh nutrition; the tissues are so undernourished and lacking so much oxygen that they become slack. The veins are in permanent contact with black blood which is thickened and burdened with more toxins than it can carry. The cells of the veins are not renewed as they should be and are kept in a state of oxygen starvation.

The toxins obey the law of gravity. They accumulate in the legs if one is often standing up, or in the anus if one is often seated. However, in all cases *the origin is always the obstruction of the liver filter,* causing more pressure in the portal vein which has the effect of increasing the tension of the veins situated in the lower part of the body and producing a swelling in those located in the arms.

Clearly the first step is to fluidify the blood and thus accelerate its circulation; then find a means of relieving and tonifying the vessels.

Before going further, it is necessary to say a few words on the current medical treatment for hemorrhoids. It is customary, unfortunately, to puncture them. This treatment with needles consists of introducing sclerosing substances which will harden the seat of the hemorrhoids. How can we speak of a cure, since the vessels have been hardened, making them in fact older! It seems logical, if recourse to medication is necessary, that it be with the intention to protect our organs and not make them older prematurely.

If those who have hemorrhoids decide to use unnatural methods, that is their business, only let them be well-instructed in the possible consequences of such treatment. A few years after the puncture, the condition worsens due to the fact that the tissues are irrigated more poorly than before. The used cells are evacuated imperfectly and too slowly. The affected area is thus in an asphyxiated state. It is at this point that surgery must be contemplated with all the risks that it entails. Since hemorrhoids play the role of a security valve, it is always dangerous to treat them with other than a natural treatment. Through this natural method they will be closed and reabsorbed only after a safe elimination of the toxins.

The Cure

Since intoxification is the cause of the hemorrhoid's appearance, the first step is to purify the blood. Take a teaspoon of clay in half a glass of water daily and the juice of 2-6 lemons mixed with water, depending on the tolerance of the individual. A purifying tea may be taken (p. 75) and eventually a laxative one if the stools are insufficient.

Accelerate the blood circulation with cold hip baths lasting 3-4 minutes each (p. 57). Take one or two daily. Eliminate from the food everything that may contribute to a thickening or intoxification of the blood (meat, alcohol, vinegar, margarine, etc.). The meals should consist of fruits, rye bread (homemade) and raw and cooked vegetables.

Some plants are astringent (such as plantain and Solomon's seal) and these may be applied on the hemorrhoids. If they are in season, use them fresh. In the winter, use them as poultices or wet compresses. Apply in the evening and leave overnight.

Clay is also effective for hemorrhoids. Apply small cold clay poultices and keep in place for 1-1½ hours. Less time if hemorrhoids are running. Fix the poultice with a T-shaped bandage. Complete with small hip-baths (or washes) with a decoction of evergreen oak bark (4 oz. of bark per quart of water).

Hemorrhoids sometimes heal rapidly and sometimes not, for their presence is often related to the equilibrium of the glandular system. It is only when the organism recovers its general balance that these painful inconveniences disappear.
Patience is necessary.

Phlebitis

When the organism is defending itself against toxic substances resulting from a defective diet or from an incomplete transformation of some nutritive elements, the lymphatic system can find itself overwhelmed and be overcome by intoxification. Then follows the formation of blood clots in the veins - that is phlebitis.

The tendency is to think that the migration of one of these blood clots is at the origin of embolism. However, it would be more accurate to say that embolism is caused by the formation of another blood clot in a vessel close to the heart. Several modern specialists have mistaken the effect for the cause and incriminated the blood clot instead of the thrombosing substances.

Phlebitis happens most of the time after abdominal surgery (appendicitis, hysterectomy),some times after giving birth, also after a treatment with antibiotics. We are dealing here, in fact, with aftereffects of intoxification by the chemical products used for surgery needs, and by the surgical shock itself.

For the patient in bed, phlebitis usually starts at the place where the vein is compressed by the weight of the leg. The initial symptom is a light acceleration of the pulse and elevation of temperature; the calf of the leg becomes painful.

The Cure

Lemon is an important ingredient in this remedy. At first, take only fruits and as much lemon juice as possible, for the purpose of dissolving the blood clot and avoiding the formation of another.

Accelerate the kidney and intestinal evacuations with the appropriate teas (see section on arteritis). Drink clay - 1 teaspoon diluted in a glass of water, once a day, before eating. Apply clay on the lower abdomen and on the affected areas, alternately. For the night, lay cabbage leaves around the leg. Add comfrey and witch hazel to the teas.

By combining the change of food with hip

baths and the compresses, the problem will be greatly alleviated. For recommended foods and a suggested menu, see p.143.

Do not forget the cold hip baths!

Decoction for Blood Purification

Buckthorn bark	30 gr.	Horsetail	10 gr.
Soapwort	20 gr.	Sarsaparilla	10 gr.
John's wort		Senna follicles	10 gr.
flowers	20 gr.	Wild thyme	
Licorice root	15 gr.	(flowered tops)	10 gr.
Madder root	15 gr.		

Mix everything well. 1 or 2 tablespoons per cup. Boil for 5 minutes and infuse 15 minutes. Drink ¼ cup before the two principal meals.

Decoction for Blood Circulation

Red-grape vine		licorice root	15 gr.
leaves	60 gr.	Horsetail	10 gr.
Buckthorn bark	25 gr.	Hyssop	10 gr.
Couch grass	15 gr.	Walnut-tree	
		leaves	10 gr.

2 or 3 tablespoons of the mixture per quart of water. Boil for some minutes. Drink when desired during the day or with meals.

DIGESTION

Troubles and Cures

It seems as if everyone has stomach problems. These days, digestive troubles are considered unavoidable, but this is simply an error stemming from a poor judgment.

Sometimes stomach disorders occur from social pressure. A single thought can amplify the intensity of the problem, for anything that disturbs the nervous balance, whether directly or indirectly, is obviously detrimental to the normal functioning of the organism. Of course, it may be that the perturbation of the digestive system is caused by functional troubles or by organic lesion. However, not one of these hypotheses is conclusive or even persuasive, surely the principal cause of most digestive troubles is to be found in liver disorders and bad eating habits.

Why should the unexpected hardships of existence cause damage to the nervous system, digestive troubles or any other physiological ailments? It can only happen when degeneration of our organs have ruined our mechanisms of regulation and defense.

When physiological functioning is normal, there is less receptivity to outside solicitations. Thus, the real problem lies in the healing of the organs, starting with the liver and its functions.

When understood, a symptom can be more revealing than a laboratory examination. A sudden pain that erupts and disappears when food is absorbed indicates a strong inflammation of the stomach and excess acidity in the secretions. This also shows a weakening of the mucous membranes, for not enough mucous is being produced to protect the walls with a layer.

If pain occurs just after eating it is no doubt created by an inflammation of the mucous membranes of the stomach, particularly the membrane situated around the pylorus. Not only does there not seems to be any chlorhydric acid, there is not even enough acidity to assure this first phase of digestion.

Such pains are rarely immediate; in many instances, they appear at least two hours after the meal. They are caused by a major irritation of the duodenum, which will ultimately lead to an ulcer.

Being of an acid condition when coming out of the stomach, food goes through a short intestinal zone where the absorption of calcium takes place, then to the small intestines where the second of the principal phases of digestion takes place. At this point it is indispensable that foods be immediately alkalized to prevent any cessation of the transformation process; the phosphorus that food contains must be normally absorbed.

Thus, it is seen that the digestion of various elements in food requires well-determined conditions of the degree of acidity and alkalinity (pH). It is the cooperative influence of the bile and the pancreatic lipase that neutralizes the acidity created by the chyme (end product of gastric digestion) in the stomach, for in order for trypain (coming from the pancreas) to act on the transformation of the proteins, an alkaline medium is necessary.

We have seen that it is in an acid medium that the absorption of calcium is made, while alkalinization is indispensable to the absorption of phosphorus. Without a good functioning liver and gall bladder which assures these necessary secretions these conditions cannot exist; one result is bad digestion.

Under no circumstances should anyone indulge in alcoholized so-called 'aids' to digestion; pills and tonics which, far from helping the digestive process, on the contrary, slow it down by inhibiting the nervous cells. The prescribed varieties are not much better; those alkaline powders, which neutralize the acidity of the gastric secretions also slow down the transformation process. Two in-

conveniences then occur - either food stays in the stomach until renewal of the gastric juice, or food goes on to the small intestines half-digested, potential putrid fermentation - for generating gases and other harmful products.

Although always of the same origin, digestive abnormalities possess different forms and symptoms such as burning sensations, heavy feeling, cramps, spasms, acidity, indigestion, frequent vomiting, lack of appetite or on the contrary over-consumption of food, aerophagia (swallowing of air), swelling of the abdomen, heartburn, etc. Each of these forms may require its own local treatment, while the treatment of the cause inevitably remains the same for all of them.

Food Digestion

The accent should be put on the importance of enzymes, for without these precious auxiliaries, digestion cannot take place. How wonderful to realize that foods of the vegetable kingdom produce from themselves the elements for their *own* digestion! Although some glands do produce a counterpart of these enzymes, a disorder of the digestive function may be followed by a slowing down or a cessation of these glandular secretions.

Ferments are very fragile substances which start weakening when the temperature reaches $94^{\circ}F$. While a meal may include cooked vegetables even though they are greatly lacking in enzymes, this meal must begin with raw vegetables which are rich in enzymes.

When raw vegetables are not well-tolerated, either because the stomach accepts them badly or because a long privation has necessitated a period of re-adaptation, the introduction of fruit juices and fresh vegetable juices will lead to the gradual acceptance of the vegetable in solid form. Start with what is most acceptable, introducing more variety later.

Aromatic plants also stimulate secretions and should not be neglected, for example, add to the vegetables juice celery, tarragon, parsley, or chervil. Do the same with a dish of raw vegetables. When some improvement has been made, introduce some garlic and onion which are among the best stimulants of gastric secretion.

It is always a surprise for a person suffering from gastric troubles to find out that he digests raw cabbage well, seeing as he had been unable to eat it in the past. He perhaps may still experience some difficulties with cooked cabbage, but it is very rare and even exceptional that anyone finds it hard to accept cabbage in a raw form. Even the juice of this vegetable is particularly recommended for intestinal inflammation as well as for ulceration.

Many conceptions have to be studied in a new light. There are theories which oppose the consumption of fruits, calling them 'acid'. Yet often people suffering from an ulcer who eat fruit, far from experiencing an increase of pain, actually see their ulcers attenuated.

The effort should be made to reduce gastric secretions which are too acid rather than to deprive ourselves of precious vegetables and fruits. It is now well-known that animal protein stimulates gastric acidity. This excess acid sometimes succeeds in neutralizing the alkalinity of the saliva, leaving it to the enzymes to take care of the digestion of the starches on their own. In order to limit the putrefactions caused mainly by meat, the stomach gives the meat priority in digestion but neglects the food accompanying it.

The right kind of eating will thus include fruits and raw vegetables, cooked cereal and vegetables, some cheese, eggs, honey and dried fruits. The quantities, of course, are taken in proportion to their toleration. It is dangerous to introduce more than the stomach can take.

SPECIFIC DISORDERS OF THE DIGESTIVE ORGANS

Stomach Acidity

This phenomenon may be objective or subjective. *Objective* stomach acidity is when the acid secretions are overabundant or unbalanced in composition or frequency of production. *Subjective* stomach acidity is when the sensation of acidity in reality is not related to the acid secretion, but is a consequence of some other disorder, such as inflammation of the mucous membrane of the stomach or the small intestines.

Many other factors could be playing a role. For example, the secretions depend in part on the nervous centers which receive the stimuli and pass on the impulse upon which the organic functions depend. However, even if the failure of the nervous system adds to the disorder of the secretions, it remains to be known why the system became troubled in the first place. Almost always it is because toxic substances - generally from food - obstruct and degrade the nervous centers or relays which help in the secretions, preventing them from functioning properly.

Whether the acidity be objective or subjective, it remains a general disorder to which only a treatment aiming at the whole organism can bring true healing to the particular focus of the trouble. Once the treatment in depth is underway, local measures may be administered, remembering that it would be an error to be satisfied with an immediate result obtained by local treatments. Keep track of all reactions in an attempt to discover if the 'acidities' are linked to a particular behavior pattern or perhaps another defective function.

There are some measures which may rapidly bring an end to the pains; this could even happen by simply cutting meat from one's diet. This is easy to understand, since the digestion of meat implies the action of secretions very rich in chlorhydric acid. When no longer receiving the same stimulus, the nervous centers may react by modifying the composition of the gastric juice.

Salt contributes directly to the production of chlorhydric acid, and must be reduced drastically, using just enough for seasoning. It is evident that one should bear in mind the fact that the sense of taste has been temporarily deadened by the heavy use of spices, alcohol and other abnormal elements. A period of re-adaptation must be allowed until more subtle flavorings can be appreciated.

Absorbed orally, clay advantageously replaces the alkaline powders which are normally used to neutralize acidity in the stomach. Clay coats the irritated or injured gastric wall, tonifies it and participates in the regulation of the secretions. If its use causes a slight constipation, correct this by taking 1 or 2 teaspoons of psyllium with some water or broth at the evening meal.

Clay may be taken at any time; it is always good to use it in case of pain. In the regular treatment, take 1 teaspoon in half a glass of water in the morning on an empty stomach, or else before any of the two other meals. During a crisis, clay may be taken up to three times a day.

Experience has shown that bitter herbs give the best results in cases of stomach acidity. Here are some plants which are more specifically recommended: elder bark, elecampane, bitter-orange, gentian, globe-daisy, hop, sweet rush, willow.

Pay strict attention to the order of the meal. Fresh fruits should be taken at the beginning: *nothing is more detrimental than a fresh fruit taken after the meal* - especially if it is a sweet fruit; putrid fermentation is almost a guaranteed result.

In order to aid digestion and, at the same time, stimulate the gastric and biliary secretions, use the following preparation:

Decoction for Obstruction of Biliary Channels

Woodruff	40 gr.	Marigold	20 gr.
Boldo	30 gr.	Rosemary leaves	20 gr.
Licorice root	30 gr.	Yellow Bedstraw	20 gr.
Horsetail	25 gr.	Mint	15 gr.
Asparagus root	20 gr.		

Mix plants well. Put 1 or 2 teaspoons of the mixture in a quart of water. Let simmer 2 minutes. Turn off flame and infuse 5-10 minutes.

Before going to bed, apply a wheat bran-climbing ivy poultice from the liver to the spleen.

Aerophagia

During normal digestion 10-15 quarts of non-putrid gas are released. This gas is normally evacuated by the lungs. However, if too much gas is released, the blood cannot liberate them all through the respiratory ducts. Channelled through the blood vessels, these gases can settle in any part of the body, causing such phenomena as headaches, intercostal pains, oppression. Often lodging under the left costal region, the gas can cause such intense pains there that they are mistaken for angina pectoris; this happens when the gas pocket goes up to the diaphragm in the direction of the heart, compressing and sometimes even slightly displacing it. The simple evacuation of the gas automatically leads to the cessation of the symptoms. It may also happen that the air pocket moves and compresses the solar plexus, which may cause a sensation of anguish or anxiety.

The situation is obviously more serious when the excess gaseous formations are caused by putrefactions (recognized by the particularly nauseous odor of the liberated gases). These putrefactions may be a consequence of either poor digestion or insufficient elimination, such as constipation.

A bile of good quality, when secreted abundantly at the right moment, allows proper digestion without producing any excess gas. It neutralizes potential putrefactions and helps carry waste products toward the channels of evacuation.

Along with the treatment in depth which may include the decoction indicated for stomach acidity, clay taken orally, breathing exercises, hip baths and the elimination of food made with flour, there are emergency measures which can be taken immediately when necessary.

As soon as there is excess gas, accompanied by swelling, spasms or constricted breathing, apply the wheat bran-ivy poultice on the stomach and liver or on the affected area. This poultice may be administered just after the meal; that alone facilitates digestion.

To help get rid of the gases take a cup of the following:

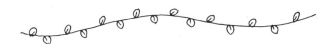

Decoction for Elimination of Gases

Cumin	70 gr.	Fennel	15 gr.
Angelica	15 gr.	Green Anise	15 gr.
Coriander	15 gr.	Caraway	10 gr.

Use 1 teaspoon of the mixture. Bring water to a boil. Add the plant mixture and leave over the fire 2 minutes. Infuse 10 minutes. Also effective against dropsy.

An infusion of thyme is also very useful, especially because of its antispasmodic properties. The infusion of veronica, wild marjoram and angelica also give good results. A decoction of chamomile with some lemon rind would work well, too.

On exceptional occasions, when the pain becomes unbearable it may be necessary to give an enema with a quart of luke-warm water and a tablespoon of sea salt or 2 tablespoons of clay powder; this will provoke the evacuation of the gases.

Gastric Trouble

Gastric trouble is nothing less than an extension of constipation. 'Constipation' does not necessarily denote a lack of fecal elimination (see 'masked' constipation, p. 86) for the liberation of the intestines can very well be imperfect even if one has a regular evacuation. People are surprised to find out - after taking a decoction or having some fresh fruits - that despite their regular bowel movements, their colons were storing quite a bit of waste products. These waste products are the cause of putrid fermentations which liberate corrosive liquids or gases.

If clay taken orally has a tendency to lightly 'constrict' it would be better to drink only the liquid in which clay has been standing.

As it stimulates the secretion of the bile, 1 teaspoon of olive oil taken with an equal part of lemon juice on an empty stomach helps the evacuations. If this does not help sufficiently, try one of the following preparations:

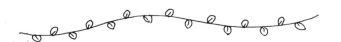

Decoction for Gastric Obstruction

Angelica	25 gr.	Sage	25 gr.
Linseeds	25 gr.	Buckthorn bark	25 gr.
Mallow flowers	25 gr.		

Put 1 or 2 tablespoons in a cup of water. Bring to a boil and simmer 2-3 minutes. Infuse 10 minutes. Add honey according to taste.

or -

1 or 2 teaspoons of psyllium with some water or broth during the evening meal.

The mucilage of seaweeds assures a good lubrication of the digestive duct. The mucilage of the leek is excellent for the liver as well; its broth helps cleanse the intestines and kidneys.

Black olives, prunes, grapes, cherries, plums and canteloupe all relieve problems of intestinal evacuation.

Swelling of the Abdomen

As we already saw in the section discussing 'aerophagia' gas is liberated in great quantity during digestion. Sometimes it accumulates in the digestive duct, expanding it enough to create a swelling of the abdomen.

The ingestion of some gas residues is normal and even helpful, it affects a useful internal massage of the intestines; however, they should not be abundant or of nauseous odor.

The excess of gas during digestion sometimes comes from an anomaly of the active intestinal flora during the last phase of the digestion of fat, flour products, cellulose. A deficiency of this intestinal flora causes the worst problems, which may persist as long as a normal flora is not reconstituted.

The composition of the flora is variable; *the flora of the vegetarian is not the same as the flora of the meat-eater,* and it is quite audacious to try to reconstitute this flora using unnatural means. Yoghurt, buttermilk, good quality cheese, and organic sauerkraut (raw) can be valuable, for their ferments contribute to rebuilding a good medium for the reconstitution of the flora.

Although clay does not bring bacteria, it still is incomparable for maintaining or re-establishing a good, normal flora, for it favors the development of useful ferments, while opposing the growth of pathogenic bacilli. In the specific case of the swelling of the abdomen, one may take it 2-3 times a day (1 teaspoon in ½ a glass of water before each meal).

Evacuation should be normal (two a day). If it is insufficient, use the same means that is prescribed for gastric trouble.

The same poultice used for aerophagia should be applied from the liver to the spleen at night before going to bed. The application of this poultice should continue as long as the annoyances persist. Keep the poultice in place 1½ hours or overnight if it does not cause any unpleasantness.

Be sure to take fruits at the beginning of meals. Never eat fruit after meals, for nothing is more propitious to putrid fermentations than fresh fruits after a meal, especially sweet ones.

Cramps and Spasms

These are usually a defense reaction of an organ whose mucous membrane is suffering irritation. A spasm is experienced when an injured area is hurt, contracting suddenly. Also the mucous membrane retracts at the passage of food particles.

Due to their anti-spasmodic properties, climbing ivy leaves, when applied as a poultice mixed with wheat bran will calm down these spasms.

In general, the treatment of spasms does not differ from the treatment of the other digestive abnormalities, especially as indicated for aerophagia.

It will be especially beneficial to take the following:

Decoction for Nerves

Orange leaves	20 gr.	Vervain	15 gr.
Green anise	15 gr.	Lime-tree	10 gr.
Melissa	15 gr.	Orange tree buds	5 gr.
Mint	15 gr.		

Put 2 tablespoons of the mixture in a cup of water. Bring to a boil and infuse 10 minutes. Honey may be added. Take this decoction after lunch and dinner for a few days, then alternate it with the infusion for stimulating the liver (p.55).

Disorders of the Intestines - Diarrhea

There are relatively few people nowadays who enjoy a normal-functioning intestines. If it is not from constipation, then they suffer from diarrhea or some other disorder.

Many cases have been observed where diarrhea alternates with constipation, showing very well the connection between these two abnormalities. An insufficient amount of bile in the intestines may be the origin of these two opposite phenomena, each of which are accompanied by putrid fermentations or abundant production of intestinal gases.

A distinction has to be made between chronic diarrhea (permanent or intermittent) and the diarrhea which occurs in short isolated attacks. The latter type often is simply a particular reaction of

the organism against toxic invasion. While diarrhea may result from a fruit cure or a decoction, it is only temporary; it is actually a positive demonstration that the body can fight well - at least in this manner.

Although the origin of diarrhea is generally caused by malfunction of the liver, it remains indispensable to purify the intestines with clay, lemon, and an herbal tea.

Do not eat any food which would be corrupted as soon as it comes in contact with the substances that are putrefying in the colon. It is advisable to fast and not run the risk of prolonging the disorder indefinitely.

Take 2 teaspoons of clay in ½ a glass of water. Mix it well and drink it in the morning or afternoon on an empty stomach. Children should drink only the clayish water and leave the sediment at the bottom of the glass.

With diarrhea it is urgently necessary to stabilize the bowel movement, at least temporarily, before starting the general cure, which aims for the re-establishment of normal functioning. In such cases there is a plant whose action is unexcelled for this particular effect. Why use dangerous medications when a pleasant fruit like *huckleberries* can do the job? This marvelous plant which grows on mountains is a small shrub that gives small deep-red spherical fruits. If you cannot find them fresh, dried ones will do. Prepare a decoction:

1 tablespoon of the dried fruit in a cup of water. Bring to a boil and simmer for 15 minutes. Strain afterwards, making sure to press the fruits in order to extract their juice. This decoction is taken 6 times in a 24 hour period, depending on the particular case; add honey if desired.

Other common plants may prove themselves very precious in times of need. Among them:

Black thornberries (wild plum)	Plantain leaves
Bramble leaves (blackberry)	Silver wood leaves
Wild geranium (alum root)	Strawberry roots and leaves

As opposed to classical medication, whose action is generally symptomatic, natural remedies may be used in cases with seemingly opposite symptoms. While a certain medication prescribed for diarrhea may constipate, this will not happen with a natural remedy. For example, lemon fluidifies the blood but yet favors its coagulation in case of external hemorrhage. Huckleberries check diarrhea but do not cause shrinkage with subsequent constipation.

They simply assure a strong disinfection of the intestines without being detrimental to them.

Many people suffering from diarrhea abstain from eating fruits, which is of course an error, since fruits are best for aiding the reconstitution of the perturbed intestinal flora.

Some vegetables, such as the carrot and the cabbage are powerful remedies for the intestines. Carrot juice has the added advantage of being well-tolerated even by those who are not accustomed to eating vegetables raw. Give two glasses a day, between or before meals -- diarrhea, even those cases accompanied by bleeding, has often been immediately diminished as a result.

Fasting is the most efficient way to cure diarrhea with the exception of carrot juice, especially for infants who have to be given food. Children and adults should take the juice after the diarrhea attack has calmed down a bit. Take it a few days more even after returning to a normal condition. Some water may be added to the juice before giving it to an infant. If the child is breast-fed the mother should take carrot juice, two glasses a day. Grated carrot should be used in vegetable dishes. A soup made with carrot will benefit babies with fragile intestines.

Drink a small amount of hot water and lemon (add honey if desired) frequently.

Apply one or several clay poultices per day on the abdomen, depending on the tolerance and only if the clay heats up in contact with the body. Be sure the applications are well out of the digestive period, at least one hour before and after meals.

Cover the abdomen with three layers of cabbage leaves for the night. Flatten them with a rolling pin and heat them rapidly (over a radiator or the like).

Introduce food gradually. First fruits and raw carrots, then cooked vegetables, and then bread and other starches.

Diarrhea may indicate a perturbation of the intestinal flora; in this case take yoghurt or buttermilk, separate or together.

It has already been mentioned how the liver is at the origin of intestinal disorders. Stimulate the functioning of this organ with the wheat bran-ivy poultice. It may alternate afterwards with a clay poultice. For children a poultice of cabbage leaves suffices to give good results.

To prevent the return of such incidents, protect the liver with the following plants: rosemary, thyme, box-wood, dandelion, chicory, marigold,

artichoke, or one of the mixtures indicated in the liver chapter.

The stimulation of the secretion of bile will be assured by the 'Decoction for Obstruction of Biliary Channels, already indicated at the end of the section of stomach acidity.

Indigestion

Excessive intake of food may lead to a major reaction of the stomach to get rid of what it does not want.

While this sudden expulsion of the contents of the stomach may not be at all favorable to the whole organism, the retention of undigested or toxic food would be even less so.

Sometimes the meal has been composed of healthy food in normal quantities, and it is the conditions of the digestion itself which are unfavorable. For example, a sudden exposure of the intestines to cold may cause a state of congestion. Because of that, food remains in the stomach or is channelled through the digestive duct incompletely transformed. In either case there might be a sensation of heaviness, nausea (sometimes vomiting), diarrhea or constipation, excess gas, swelling of the abdomen, etc.

Nothing is better for relieving the discomfort of indigestion than the juice of half a lemon taken in a cup of hot water, with or without honey. Take it in small sips.

If the indigestion is followed by epigastric pains, apply the wheat bran-ivy poultice on the sore area. Some people will find it better to use the clay poultice; it is a matter of personal tolerance.

****

DIGESTIVE TROUBLE

After two months of clay absorption, digestion has considerably improved for one of our patients. For some time he could not eat in the evening, everything remained in the stomach and he would be kept awake every night.

****

Pyrosis

This term is used to designate the upward motion of an acid liquid, sometimes reaching the mouth, with a burning sensation from the stomach to the throat.

This unpleasant phenomenon is sometimes the consequence of an intestinal obstruction which can be treated the same way as gastric troubles. It could also be used for an inflammation of the gall bladder. In either case take 1 teaspoon of olive oil mixed with the juice of ½ a lemon in the morning on an empty stomach.

After the meal take the following tea:

Infusion for Liver and Gall Bladder

Gromwell	20 gr.	Broom(Genista)	10 gr.
Horsetail	20 gr.	Dandelion	10 gr.
Licorice root	20 gr.	Fernroot	10 gr.
Woodruff	20 gr.	Marigold	10 gr.
Asparagus root	10 gr.		

2 tablespoons per boiling cup of water. Let infuse 10 minutes.

All along the epigastrium from the liver to the spleen, apply the wheat bran-ivy poultice for 1½-2 hours (or overnight if applied before retiring).

Heartburn

This burning sensation does not always have its origin in the stomach; it may very well come from the esophagus. It seems that gases or burning liquids come from the stomach and travel up the digestive tube, sometimes reaching the mouth. They are engendered by spasms in the stomach or small intestines. They reveal an obstruction in the lower parts of the digestive system, through which their normal chanelling should have taken place. The treatment is the same as for gastric trouble.

Ulcer of the Duodenum

Causes

The duodenum ulcer has added itself to the list of diseases ironically called 'diseases of civilization', such as allergies, cancer, arthritis, polio, tuberculosis and so forth. It is almost unknown in so-called 'primitive' cultures. It seems that the ulcer is mostly 'contracted' by people with heavy responsibilities. This belief coincides with what was previously written about arteriosclerosis, the 'manager's disease'. It is indisputable that nervous and anguished people develop ulcers more often than those leading a calm life.

In reality, it is not only the rhythm of life of the 'civilized' man that has to be incriminated, but also, and even more so, the type of food that he eats. It is remarkable to see the frequent increase of gastric ulcers in Soviet Russia, although only a few years ago it was practically unknown. The same is now happening in the Bavarian Alps where people used to nourish themselves exclusively with vegetables.

There are quite a lot of managerial executives and responsible people among vegetarians among whom ulcers are an unknown phenomenon. It can never be repeated enough that with a natural way of eating only a very exceptional disorder presents any resistance to cure. The ulcer that can be cured most easily is the ulcer of the duodenum. Many lesions could be avoided with just a few months of restorative measures.

Surgery is only a temporary and incomplete cure, for the cause still remains. Obviously in some situations, such as when the stomach is about to be perforated or is already so, surgery is unavoidable. These are extreme cases which should never happen if the natural treatment is started soon enough.

The origin of the gastric ulcer is to be found in the slowing down of the secretion of the bile. The first phase of digestion, in the stomach, requires an acid medium. However, when passing from the stomach to the duodenum, food must immediately undergo the neutralization of its acidity - the duodenal phase requiring an alkaline medium.

Either the stomach acidity is excessive or the secretion of the gall bladder and pancreas are not sufficient; it may also be that the mucous protecting the walls is not in a sufficient amount or missing altogether. While it is evident that over-activity, stress, fatigue and emotional problems which perturb the nervous system all contribute to the loss of the colloidal state of the tissues in the gastric wall, the medium has to be favorable to the degenerative process before these factors can have such an effect. These are indications of the extent to which various kinds of food are responsible for gastric acidity, as was seen in the section devoted to it.

The drama often starts with the first signs of

digestive difficulties. It is in order to avoid sensations of heaviness in the stomach and heartburn that artificial 'digestive aids' and 'anti-acids' are taken. Some of these expedients really do accelerate the process of digestion, others are only inhibitors that give a false impression of digestion. The former are as dangerous as the latter. Having a pepsin base, the former activate digestion so much that they often cause the digestion of the gastric mucous membrane itself! That is how deep lesions occur. The latter types of so-called 'digestives' may have alcohol as a base and thus work by inhibiting products of the gastric functions; or they may be of an alkaline base (bi-carbonate and similar products) which neutralize the digestion and acid juices of the stomach, impeding its actions. But no matter which kind, they are certainly of no help; as a result of their use, food continues its migration toward the duodenum without its elements being sufficiently transformed by the stomach.

The digestive system must make a huge effort to adapt itself to this situation. Alcohol, sweets and medication demand a considerable expenditure of energy for no productive purpose. Every antiphysiological product creates an increased amount of protective mucous secretion, which might be needed at one time or another. This may lead to the exhaustion of the organism, first because of the monopolization of the substance for this purpose, next because of the difficulties of assimilation of nutritive elements which are too impregnated with this mucous.

The Symptoms

Most often, the ulcer manifests itself with diffuse pain in all epigastric regions with irradiations under the shoulder blade. This pain almost always occurs 3-4 hours after eating, which is during the duodenal phase of digestion. Vomiting sometimes accompanies the ulcer, which indicates the obstruction of the liver.

Repeated vomiting of blood indicates an aggravation of the condition; it is the same with the presence of black blood in the stools. This may mean a possible perforation which will have to be immediately treated by surgery.

The Cure

It is useless to treat an ulcer directly without first changing the way of eating. Nor is it wise to

fast in periods of crucial attacks. Disordered secretions of acids and proteolytic ferments may be the body's reaction to the fast and this can irritate or degenerate the already ulcered wall. On the other hand, taking solid food attracts juices and digestive ferments and will alleviate, if not completely get rid of the pains.

It is necessary to gradually modify food intake, eliminating meat and all other harmful products such as alcoholic drink, coffee and milk, white bread and sugar, although one may continue to eat eggs and some dairy products in very small quantities. These 'tolerated' foods will help sustain the body and provide energy until the liver is restored sufficiently to be able to tolerate natural foods. At this stage, gradually introduce raw vegetables. However, carrot juice may be taken without restriction (1 or 2 glasses per day).

Here is an example of treatment which generally gives rapid and satisfying results:

In the morning, on an empty stomach, 1 teaspoon of olive oil with the juice of ½ a lemon. Wait at least 15 minutes before having breakfast which will include a cup of rosemary or thyme tea.

Before the meal, a teaspoon of clay in ½ a glass of water. Prepare in the morning to be taken before lunch and dinner.

After the meal, take 1 cup of the infusion indicated for gastric acidity (p. 83).

Between meals, in case of intense pains, take this tea:

Decoction for Gastric Pains

Absinth	Marjoram
Beteny	Sage
Calamint	Scolopendrium
Germander	officinale
Ground ivy	Scordium
Hyssop	Veronica
	Wintergreen

Combine equal parts of the above. Use a full tablespoon in a cup of water. Bring to a boil; simmer gently for about 2 minutes and infuse 5 minutes.

Before going to bed, apply the wheat bran-ivy poultice on the stomach and liver.

If the preceding treatment is well-tolerated, and does not tire the patient too much, then have him take a cold hip bath every morning, for 4-5 minutes. At this stage, the clay poultice can be alternated nightly with the wheat bran-ivy poultice. Be sure to apply it at least 1 hour before and after meals.

****

STOMACH ULCER AFTER TWO GASTRECTOMIES

In 1938 a priest aged 35 years was operated on for a stomach perforation produced by a pylorus ulcer, with a complication of peritonitis. Two years later, the ulcer reappeared with hemorrhages and greater pains, necessitating a second operation in 1942. Pain and hemorrhages again reappeared at the end of November 1952. Appetite diminished, strength declined, sleep became more difficult and more pain was felt. A third operation was foreseen.

At this time, the patient became aware of clay treatment through reading the original French edition of M. Dextreit's work and decided to try it. Clay absorption began at the end of September, 1953. At the end of January, 1954, an improvement was felt; and by the end of February, pains disappeared, and the ulcer healed. Healing was complete and positive.

****

Sometimes it is necessary to have a decoction of buckthorn before retiring if the stools are not sufficient. Mix 1 tablespoon of buckthorn bark with 1 teaspoon of green anise in a cup of water. Boil 2-3 minutes.

It may happen that even the best kind of food will not be well-tolerated by an injured digestive system. Then it is necessary to be very prudent in the attempt to change the diet. It may even require periodically halting and resuming treatment. Eventually, when health is restored, reactions to food may be very different.

Once the ulcer is healed, which may take 3-6 months, it would be wise to remember past mistakes so as to avoid falling into the same bad habits which were the origin of so much misery.

Routine for one day

In the morning Upon waking up take a cold hip bath (60°-68°), for 3-5 minutes and 1 teaspoon of clay in ½ a glass of water which has been prepared the previous night. Or alternate it with a teaspoon of olive oil mixed with the juice of ½ a lemon, using each one for a week at a time. If possible, do some breathing and physical exercises (p.116); this will help tremendously in the cure.

Breakfast Fruit in season or wheat cream or thick vegetable broth, or whole wheat bread and honey. Have a cup of thyme or rosemary tea.

Before the two main meals A cup of the decoction for the liver, to be taken before the meal if lemon-water is to be taken after, or if anything liquid is not well-tolerated at the end of the meal. When it is necessary to take clay before these two meals, take a decoction for the liver after the meal. The olive oil and lemon mixture may be alternated with clay weekly.

Lunch Fresh fruits, various raw vegetables, cereals, or cooked vegetables. Cheese or buttermilk; dried fruits or home-made pastry or honey. One egg, 2-3 times a week.

Before the evening meal A foot bath with red-grape vine leaves in case the circulation is defective or if the body needs to be warmed up. It is desirable to follow this with some physical exercises.

Evening meal Fresh fruits, various raw vegetables, thick vegetable broth or cooked vegetables or cereals; yoghurt or dried fruits, or honey.

The evening meal should be lighter than the one taken at lunch, if possible; if there is not enough free time, eat lightly at noon and reserve the big meal for the night. This is not ideal but it is better to organize in this manner than to eat too fast at noon. Eat calmly and chew well. Drink as little as possible during the meals and then only water mixed with lemon juice or a decoction.

After the meal Either a decoction for the liver or stomach, or the juice of half a lemon in a cup of hot water (honey is optional); or a decoction of thyme or mint, vervain, rosemary, hyssop, or chamomile.

Before going to bed A poultice of clay or wheat bran-ivy leaves on the area to be treated (liver, stomach, or both at the same time).

In case of fatigue or depression, massage the spine with a mixture of 1 part grated garlic and 2 parts of camphor oil. Take a laxative tea when there is constipation. In a case when a decoction for the liver has been taken after the evening meal, omit the laxative tea that night.

THE ELIMINATION CHANNELS

Their Obstruction and Relief

Most diseases have no other source than constipation. The accumulation of matters in the colon promotes an unhealthy medium which permits all sorts of undesirable phenomena. Intestinal putrefactions soil the humors they enter and badly affect neighboring organs.

How many inflammations or infections of internal or genital organs have no other origin than the neighboring presence of a persistent accumulation of putrefactions in the colon?

This continual obstruction encourages parasites such as worms and mushrooms, and the appearance of lesions against which the intestines will attempt to protect themselves by secreting mucous in great quantity until finally the walls dry up.

When intestinal matter reaches the lesion a spasm of defense is produced. The intestinal wall contracts every time the slightest irritation of the injured area occurs. These spasms, which are sometimes very painful, prevent the normal passage of matter, and even worse, they cause them to back up. This is what is called *spasmodic constipation.* The stools are in the form of ribbons, fractioned and always insufficient.

These accumulated toxins go to the liver and contaminate the bile, which in turn goes to the intestines and aggravates the state of corruption there even more.

Constipation may be accompanied by neuralgia, migraine, depression, anguish, anemia, loss of weight, hemorrhoids, cracks in the anus caused by the harshness of the feces, nausea, heartburn, vertigo, palpitations, insomnia, nightmares, hives, swelling of the abdomen, colitis, flatulence, bad breath. This should not be a surprise. Even cardiac troubles may occur when the intestinal expansion reaches to the diaphragm and presses on the heart and lungs. In the case of congestive conditions, the constipation adds a risk of brain hemorrhage, skull compression or cardiac afflictions.

The forms of constipation

There are two main forms of constipation:
1-'revealed' constipation which results from an obstruction of the passage of fecal matter; here a mechanical obstacle such as a tumor, malfunction, inertia or atony is probably responsible. The stools are rare and hard and are channelled much too slowly towards the colon. This obstruction is usually temporary.
2- 'masked' constipation which can be present even

in people whose bowels move regularly every day. However, the stools are insufficient and do not represent the normal elimination of all the waste products. *This constipation is more dangerous.* It suffices to take a laxative decoction to soon find out to what degree non-evacuated waste products have accumulated.

The stools do not only contain food wastes, but also half-used blood globules, peelings of the mucous membrane of the intestines, parasites, microbes, etc., so not eating is not adequate explanation for a temporary suspension of evacuations.

Many people are fooled by 'false diarrhea' which makes them think that they are not constipated. They should know that constipation is not a state of consistency but of amount - these stools of false diarrhea are always followed by a hard stool which serves as a cork, to obstruct further elimination.

Soft and separated stools may sometimes alternate with shaped - or even hard stools. This happens when the passage of fecal matter is too slow, leading to a drying up in the left colon, whose role is to absorb the liquids. With this drying up, it is evident that the expulsion of matter is not easy.

Mechanism of evacuation

Understanding the mechanism of evacuation makes it possible to clearly discern the causes of constipation. The terminal part of the small intestines is the seat of secretions of an intestinal juice which comprises many ferments. This phase of digestion is mostly localized in the small intestines where very important microbian flora normally live, including the *bacillus amylobacter,* whose main role is to break down previously undigested starch, and the *bacillus cellulosal,* which succeeds in digesting 60-70% of the cellulose contained in food.

During a 24 hour period, there are three to seven great movements of propulsion in the colon to assure the migration of matter. First liquid and then more and more doughy, the stools start becoming solid at the level of the sigmoid colon (end part of the large intestines). It is the filling up of the sigmoid plus the fact that the stools are nearing the rectum that creates the urge to evacuate.

Being consciously controlled, defecation, which is the last phase of evacuation, is caused by the sigmoid, which pushes the stools toward the rectum. It acts as a syringe - the sigmoid acts as a piston, the rectum as the cylinder. Normally the rectum is traversed instantaneously and the evacuation is easy.

Causes of constipation

The conditions accompanying constipation and the phenomena which end it show that the intestines are almost totally dependent upon the liver. It is the bile which lubricates the intestinal walls, regulates the level of the bacterial flora, opposes dangerous proliferations, stirs up the peristaltic movements and dissolves and eliminates fatigued tissue, contributing to its renewal. Incontestably, the conductor of the intestinal functions is the liver.

Proteins and starches are transformed in the portion of the small intestines called the duodenum by the combined action of the pancreatic and biliary juices which also assure the emulsion of fats. A deficiency of the liver and pancreas leads to phenomena of putrefaction occurring when substances enter the intestinal duct without being completely transformed.

If liver insufficiency can be the cause of two such apparently different phenomena as diarrhea and constipation, factors such as chemical products, toxic food and irritating drinks make the situation even worse.

RELATED DISEASES

Colitis

Accumulated matter provokes the inflammation of the mucous membrane of the intestines. They adhere there, impeding the removal of degraded cells, causing atrophy of the wall and weakening of the defenses; lesions are possible. These irritations have repercussions on the entire nervous system; not only will there be intestinal spasms, but irritability and all sorts of nervous troubles are likely throughout the body.

Because of this acute nervous condition, foods are swallowed too rapidly. Insufficiently chewed and salivated, they will be badly digested and will cause the colon to ferment. The fermentations and eventual putrefactions liberate all sorts of gases which are absorbed together with carbohydrates in the right colon. The abundance of these gases is an obstacle to the evacuation of these carbohydrates and to the passage of the stools.

Constipation, born in the ascending colon, is often accompanied by pains at the right side of the

Other factors of perturbation

In addition to bile, other factors contribute to constipation; both physical and psychological. That is why it could be dangerous not to immediately answer the urge to evacuate; if this is not satisfied in time, matter which was previously soft will harden, adhering to the intestinal wall which rapidly absorbs their liquid. A nervous phenomenon may also occur, pushing the stools back. The entire mechanism of defecation will be disturbed if these incidents occur too often.

The constipation of breast-fed babies is a normal extension of the constipation of the mother. Thus it is the mother that has to be treated. The artificially nourished baby also sometimes becomes constipated, either because this false food does not agree with him, or because his liver was deficient at birth. In all cases, constipation may also occur when the baby is either over or undernourished.

Later on the child may become the victim of constipation if his environment opposes his needs. Sitting in classroom or busy playing, he sometimes neglects to answer his need. A little carelessness is enough to lead to the hardening of the stools; then the situation will become even worse, for fearing difficulties, he may more often fail to respond.

abdomen. As the caecal phase of digestion takes place between 5-6 hours after the meal, the pains usually attain their paroxysm at that moment. Fatigue or prolonged standing contributes to the sensation of the pain. The colon is often disturbed by the gases which form large pockets in the intestines, or a twisting of the intestines because of its elongation. In order to renew the damaged mucous membrane, the organism makes great efforts of protection and large peelings of the intestinal tissue are eliminated at this time. These are the 'skins' which the person suffering from colitis sees in his stool, along with, at times, blood, pus caused by lesions, and mucous.

Appendicitis and constipation

Appendicitis is the inflammation of the vernicular appendix. This may occur because of a prolonged state of obstruction in the ascending colon. Resulting putrefactions reach the appendix where they create first an inflammation and then an infection.

The removal of the appendix accentuates the imbalance of the intestinal functions, for the appendix is not a superfluous organ. It secretes juices which act on the peristaltis and promote the good balance of the bacterial flora. Being a lymphoid organ, the appendix is without a doubt an organ of protection. Note the frequent recurrence of constipation following the removal of the appendix and also the similar appearance of colds after the removal of the tonsils, which is also a lymphoid organ.

Constipating and harmful effects of certain foods

Experience has proven that the abandoning of meat and white bread suffices at least to greatly ameliorate the situation if not to re-establish normal functioning.

Not only are meat and white bread lacking the cellulose necessary to give shape to the feces, they also do not contain the living elements necessary to help maintain intestinal flora. In addition, meat contains a great amount of dangerous toxins which trigger putrid fermentations. The effort to neutralize these toxins harms the liver.

Meat is the origin of putrefactions in the intestines, along with alcohol, chemical medications and all toxic substances which prevent the formation of bile, thus causing the irritation of the walls of the digestive system.

Animal fats and all margarines contribute to the maintenance of the putrefactions. Canned food and pressure-cooked food do their share, too. These foods no longer contain their ferments, the auxiliaries indispensable to a normal digestion, for they are destroyed by excessive heat; this alone is enough to produce putrefactions.

TREATMENT OF CONSTIPATION

Suppositories and enemas

Suppositories are dangerous; first of all they are habit-forming, and also their continual irritation of the rectal walls can cause ulcerations and scleroses.

Enemas constitute an emergency measure which should be used only in cases demanding an urgent solution (prolonged constipation, fever, congestive state, etc.). Enemas do some good in that they soften the hardened matter and stimulate the nervous centers due to the light excitation produced by water on the mucous membrane - however, they may dilate the rectum and habituate the nervous mechanisms through this excitation.

If an enema becomes necessary, here is the simplest and most efficient way:

To ½ a quart of water add 1 tablespoon of sea salt, 2 tablespoons for a quart, etc. Proceed slowly and carefully without pressure, placing the recipient where the water is, 20 inches above the flow of water.

For children use olive oil, either pure or mixed with lukewarm water. Put 1 or 2 tablespoons of olive oil in each glass of water. In this case it would be wise to emulsify the oil with an egg yolk so that it may incorporate in the water.

Some natural laxatives

Medical laxatives operate by exciting the mucous membranes of the intestines or of the gall bladder. Their usage is dangerous since they bring about a disturbance in the intestinal flora. They may stimulate, but these artificial laxatives cannot bring about a return to normal functioning; they have no value whatsoever in terms of a lasting cure.

Mucilages cause the intestines to swell, by keeping water in the stools, which increases their volume while at the same time opposes their drying out. They lubricate the intestinal wall and help prevent colitis but sometimes may create gases; a hot drink suffices to limit this - a light decoction of buckthorn and green anise will work even better. Put a pinch of each in a cup of water.

Agar-agar is derived from seaweeds, it comes in the form of bars or powder. Use 1-3 teaspoons (depending on age and condition) in soup or broth. Cook for a few minutes.

Althea is rich in mucilage. In order to make it palatable, mix it with some licorice root. In a quart of water put 2 tablespoons of althea root and 1 tablespoon of licorice root. Boil gently for approximately 10 minutes. Drink lukewarm whenever desired.

Note: Althea may also be used for enemas. Boil 2 oz. in a quart of water.

Flax seeds may be added to other plants or used alone. Use 3 full tablespoons in a quart of boiling water. Let soften overnight. Take 3 or 4 cups during the day.

Note: The seeds can also be used for enemas. Add 2 oz. to 1 quart of boiling water and let simmer 2 minutes. The solution will give a soft enema.

White mustard seeds are taken with soup, 1 or more teaspoons. It has a softening and a stimulating effect at the same time.

2 or 3 tablespoons of *wheat bran* cooked in soup contribute to the good functioning of the intestines. However, it seems senseless to take bran to make up for the constipating effect of white bread. It is preferable to leave the bran in its original state, in bread, with the elements which normally accompany it in nature. Whole wheat bread, which contains all the bran of the wheat kernels, brings important living elements and increases the volume of the stools.

Cold-pressed olive oil is the best and sweetest of curatives. It helps to lubricate the mucous membranes of the intestines, and yet does not seal it off and prevent nutritive elements from being absorbed. Olive oil also helps the secretion of hepatic and pancreatic juices.

The best time to take olive oil, if desired for its laxative effect, is in the morning on an empty stomach, 1-3 teaspoons (depending on the age and case) will be quite effective. Olive oil will be better digested if one emulsifies it with an equal quantity of lemon juice. Olive oil may also serve as a gentle enema for children, either pure, or mixed with luke-warm water.

HELPFUL PLANTS

BUCKTHORN

This plant is mostly recommended for constipation accompanied by liver insufficiency and intestinal spasms. As it does not cause exaggerated peristaltis, it is generally well-tolerated even by pregnant women.

Use 1 or 2 teaspoons (depending on the individual) per cup of water. Bring to a boil and simmer gently for 15 minutes. A pinch of green anise may be added to prevent a gas formation. 1 cup of this decoction before going to bed should be enough to give good results. However, if it is not sufficient, another cup may be taken in the morning on an empty stomach.

BINDWEED (Convolvulus)

This acts on the liver and the intestines at the same time. 1 teaspoon of leaves are used per cup of water. Dosage may be changed depending on individual taste. Boil water, lower the flame, add the plant, remove from fire after a minute or two and let infuse 10 minutes. Take a cup before each meal or one before retiring.

CASCARA(sacred bark)

This variety of buckthorn stimulates the contractibility of the intestines. It is sometimes used by people who wish to lose weight.

Put a teaspoon of it in a cup of boiling water. Infuse 10 minutes. Take before retiring.

JUNIPER BERRIES

These berries tonify, disinfect, and bring an end to the putrefactions in the intestines. Add them to dishes or eat as is. For a decoction, infuse a teaspoon in a cup of boiling water for 10 minutes. Drink 3 times a day.

CASSIA FISTULES

Sucking this is very pleasant and gives a sweet laxative effect. Especially recommended for children. For a stronger effect, boil ½ a quart of water and add 1½-2 oz. of the crushed pod. Take a cup of this drink before retiring and, if need be, in the morning on an empty stomach.

PEACH-TREE

The flower is mostly recommended for nervous children who are constipated often.

Use 30 gr. in 2 cups of water. Infuse 10 minutes. Take 1 teaspoon or tablespoon depending on the age and case.

RHUBARB

It acts by a stimulation of the nervous network in the intestines. Avoid a continual use of it, for constipation may return.

In order to stimulate the intestines and liver, take a cup before each meal or in the morning on an empty stomach and another before retiring. Infuse a pinch in a cup of boiling water for 10 minutes.

WILD SENNA

Acting like rhubarb on the nervous network of the intestines, senna is indicated in case of atonia. its action is very energetic, so it would be wise to temper it with plants having calming effects such as mint, calamint, lime-tree. Pregnant women should abstain from it.

Senna may precipitate colitis if the intestines are fragile. In such a case use the follicle, which acts more softly than the leaves. Children will like the follicle for its pleasant taste and sweet effect.

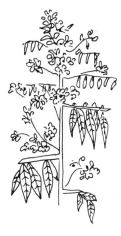

senna

For adults - put a teaspoon of senna (5-10 follicles) in a decoction of thyme or rosemary. *Do not boil.* Infuse 10 minutes. Take before retiring.

For children - put 1 follicle for each year of age up to 10, in a cup of cold water. Let soften overnight. Strain in the morning and take as it is or with some honey.

HERBAL RECIPES

Decoction for Light Constipation

Buckthorn bark	25 gr.	Angelica root	20 gr.
Sage leaves	20 gr.	Althea flowers	20 gr.
Linseeds	20 gr.		

Mix well and use a tablespoonful per cup. Boil 3 minutes and infuse 10. Drink 1 or 2 cups a day, on an empty stomach in the morning or before retiring.

Decoction for Obstinate Constipation

Bittersweet stem	20 gr.	Nettle root	20 gr.
Buckthorn bark	20 gr.	Wild chicory	
Althea flowers	20 gr.	leaves	20 gr.
Gooseberry		Rhubarb	
leaves	20 gr.	(rhizome)	10 gr.
Lime tree			
flowers	20 gr.		

Mix well. Use 1 tablespoon per cup. Boil 2 minutes. Afterwards, add to this a teaspoon of wild senna (or 5-10 follicles). Let infuse 10 minutes. Drink a cup before going to bed. Honey may be added.

Infusion for Fragile Intestines

Elder-tree bark		Linseeds	15 gr.
(the 2nd layer)	30 gr.	Sticklewort	
Rhubarb	25 gr.	(agrimony)	15 gr.
Female fern		Buckthorn	10 gr.
root	15 gr.	Iris	10 gr.

Use 1 tablespoon for a cup of boiling water. Put the plant in the water, remove from fire, and infuse 10 minutes. Take once before retiring, or in the morning on an empty stomach.

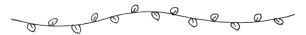

Decoction for Atonic Intestines

Cassia pulp	30 gr.	Rhubarb root	20 gr.
Licorice root	20 gr.	Juniper berries	10 gr.

Put a teaspoon in a cup of water, boil gently on low flame for 5 minutes. Remove from fire and add a teaspoon of senna pods (or 5-10 follicles). Infuse 10 minutes and strain. Take a cup before retiring at night.

Note: In case of constipation caused by deficiency of the liver, take a decoction for stimulating the liver.

PHYSIOTHERAPY OF CONSTIPATION

Exercise and sunlight

Physical exercise is very helpful, and should be done every day. This is very important, the daily period may be quite brief.

Whenever possible, the abdomen should be exposed to light and to the sun, in order to revitalize the tissues. A 'bath' of fresh air is equally recommended for the light massage which acts on the peripheral nervous endings.

Baths

Take a cold hip bath daily. This acts simultaneously on the nervous system and blood circulation, stimulating the peristaltic movements while calming down the spasms. The relaxation thus created will often bring about urine or stool emission just after the bath. The technique is simple:

Sit for 4-5 minutes in cold water which should reach the level of the groin. For a more soothing effect, throw some of this water over the abdomen. See p.57.

Compresses and massages

Cold compresses on the abdomen, ablutions on the back of the legs, tramplings in cold water and massages of the abdomen with olive oil and garlic have given good results in particular cases. Experiment to find out which of these therapies is most appropriate.

In case of painful and prolonged spasms use the wheat bran-ivy poultice.

Clay

Application of clay is useful in all cases, even including such diseases as appendicitis and colitis; apply a poultice on the lower abdomen and keep on for 2 hours or overnight if no unpleasant feeling is sensed.

As has already been said, be prudent about taking clay orally. Some constipations are cured by clay, however some constipations worsen temporarily because of it. In this case, take only the water in which clay has stood. If, on the contrary, there is no bad effect, take it every other week, 1 teaspoon in ½ a glass of water.

Water

When taken in the right time water helps cure constipation. Some people take a glass of cold water every morning and do not feel any discomfort; others prefer room-temperature or hot water.

In the United States, there is a tendency to advise drinking a lot of water (3 glasses during each meal). Given the dilution of the gastric juices from a too-large amount of water, there is a lot of gas produced.

Breathing exercises and relaxation

The influence of abdominal and respiratory movements facilitates the evacuation of the bile while increasing the strength and the intensity of the intestinal contractions.

Proceed with a breathing exercise acting on the diaphragm and the viscera. Breathe in slowly while forcing out the abdomen. Fill up the lower part of the lungs. Then, extending the chest, let air enter in the middle and then the upper part of the lungs, getting air via the distension of the upper part of the chest and the raising up of the shoulders. Breathe out after this, pulling in the abdomen slowly while relaxing the chest; let down the middle ribs first and then the upper ones; then let down the shoulders. When proficient with this exercise, try the one on p.116.

TEN GOOD EXERCISES FOR THE INTESTINES

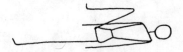

1. Lying down on the back with the arms close to the body, bring each leg alternately towards the abdomen by bending the knees and pulling them near the chest. Repeat this exercise for a minute or so. The same exercise can be practiced in a standing position.

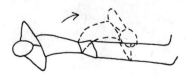

2. Lying down on the back, hands at the nape of the neck, the feet, if possible under a piece of furniture, bring the upper part of the body towards the legs, trying to touch them with the head.

3. Lying down on the back, the arms stretched out, the legs up, forming a right angle, bring the feet first to the right and then the left side. This revolving should stem from the hips, the upper part of the body remaining flat on the floor.

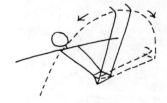

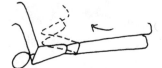

4. Lying down on the back, the arms remaining in a vertical position, bring both legs towards the chest, bending the knees.

5. Sit on the heels, keep the trunk straight and the arms close to the body. Elevate the arms to a vertical position and then bend the trunk so that the arms touch the floor. Also stretch the neck backwards and forwards.

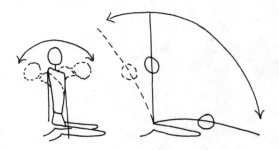

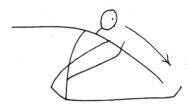

6. Sitting on the floor, the legs stretched apart, the arms stretched out parallel to the floor. Touch the left foot with the right hand and the right foot with the left hand. Between each bending movement come back to the original position.

7. Standing up, knees straight, the arms in horizontal position in front of you, bend from the waist and try to touch the feet with the finger tips.

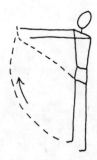

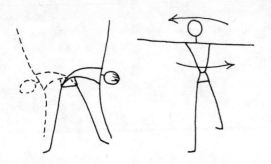

8. Standing up, knees straight, the legs stretched apart, arms stretched out parallel to the floor. Touch the right foot with the left hand and the left foot with the right hand. Between each bending movement come back to the original position.

9. Standing up, the body straight, the legs far apart, the arm in a vertical position, the hands touching each other, bend the trunk towards the right side, then the left side, trying to touch the ground. Come back to the standing position after each movement.

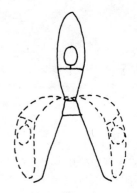

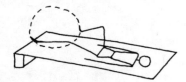

10. Lying down on something slanted (head in the lower position) keeping the hands close to the body, make pedaling and criss-crossing movements with the legs.

* *

THE FOOD REMEDIES

The recommended foods are, for the most part, the same as those indicated in earlier chapters. However, there are some specifications to be given concerning this particular disease which are very helpful.

WHOLE WHEAT BREAD

The part of cellulose contained in the bran which is not assimilated by the intermediary of the intestinal flora gives consistency to the fecal matters and acts as a strong brush. The germ embryo itself contains an oil which has a sweet laxative effect. Bran and germ constitute the most vitalizing elements of the wheat bread. On the other hand, it is quite possible that some intestines tolerate whole wheat bread poorly. *These are the people whose mucous membranes are seriously injured or whose intestinal flora have been impaired.* We know that it is this bacterial flora that completes the digestion of a great part of the cellulose and the starch that adheres to it. In case of an imbalance in the composition of this flora, there remains too much non-assimilated cellulose and an irritation may follow. It would be premature to conclude from this that cellulose is harmful to the intestines. In the beginning, use a partially sifted flour, removing 15% of the bran, and simply proceed in healing with different means, such as clay and decoctions. Later introduce cellulose gradually.

The quality of the bread is of capital importance, for the transformation of cellulose starts at the moment the flour is combined with leaven (sour dough). It is thus possible that a whole wheat bread with yeast may not be tolerated, while another made with natural leaven is well accepted. It is easy to incriminate cellulose in the irritation of the intestines, until one observes that a cookie or a sauce made with fresh whole wheat flour is generally salutary. Whole wheat bread has been accused of being a decalcifying agent, due to the presence of phytic acid in the bran, an acid which prevents calcium from being assimilated. It should be known that this acid is neutralized at the time of fermentation with natural leaven, thanks to a ferment, phystase, which hydrolizes phytic acid. It remains only if the leavening is with yeast.

OATS

Oats are soothing for irritated intestines and combat constipation. However, they should only be used in the cold season. They can be added to soups, desserts, or eaten as porridge.

HULLED BARLEY

Barley is a soft grain which may be added to soups in case of irritation of the digestive duct. It may be used the whole year.

FRUITS AND VEGETABLES

All fruits and vegetables are usually good for the intestines. Here are some which are particularly favorable.

Plums (preferably green-gage)

They stimulate peristalsis, and do an excellent work when taken in the morning on an empty stomach, not eating anything else until lunch. Best results may be hoped for by eating plums exclusively for a few days, abstaining from any other kind of food.

Plum-juice is also recommended, but eat some whole plums with it. Take a glass of juice before lunch and dinner while eating only plums for breakfast. Or the opposite might be done - juice in the morning and plums before the other meals.

Prunes

Prunes are famous for their work against constipation. They are even more active in the morning on an empty stomach, either as is or soaked in lukewarm water. To increase their action soak them overnight in a decoction of buckthorn. Boil a pint of water with 1 teaspoon of buckthorn depending on the age and case. Strain and add 10-20 prunes; soak overnight.

Grapes

Grapes are excellent for secretions of bile, to promote peristalsis, stimulate the mucous membrane and prevent putrefaction at the same time. Their cellulose, pectin, mucilages, vitamins, ferments and aromatic essences make them an irreplaceable remedy for constipation.

The grape cure will be similar to the plum cure. However, if you wish to extend the time (to more than a week) take only the juice, in order to avoid the possible accumulation of tannin, which might create another form of constipation by astringency. But this concerns only the integral cure, for grapes may be taken in the morning on an empty stomach, throughout the season.

Figs

The fresh fig cure is recommended for it does not make the organism overwork with an excess of nitrogen. The dry fig is nutritive and rich in nitrogenous substances; consume it moderately (10-15 a day). Choose sun-dried figs.

A laxative broth may be prepared by putting 12 figs and 4 tablespoons of hulled barley in a quart of water. Bring to a boil and simmer a ½ hour.

Apples

This fruit is recommended for both constipation and diarrhea, thanks to its purifying action. It also contributes to the healing of ulcers. Avoid peeling it in order to conserve its epicarp. It should be eaten raw. If a stomach cannot accept it, grate it and add a small amount of honey. Cooked and baked apples also give good results.

The apple or apple juice cure will be similar to the plum cure.

Pears

Pears are useful for lazy intestines. Thanks to their sulphur, they prevent putrefactions. Their natural sugar stimulates the mucous membranes. Their cellulose gives consistency to the feces and stimulates the peristaltic movement.

Oranges

Cooked in a small amount of water and eaten with the meals and especially in the morning, orange peel acts like agar-agar; it exercises a mechanical action on the intestines and stimulates the secretion of the bile.

Raspberries

The juice of this fruit is precious in case of gastro-intestinal troubles. Take a few glasses of the juice every day.

Carrots

Since it fluidifies the bile, the carrot is particularly recommended for the constipation linked with liver insufficiency. Use this vegetable raw as often as possible, grated and seasoned with lemon and olive oil.

It is good to drink carrot juice from time to time, in the morning on an empty stomach.

Lemon

The lemon rind may be used like the orange rind. The juice is a strong cleansing agent which destroys the bacilli of typhoid cholera and dysentery.

Tomato

Its grains are covered with a mucilage which lubricates the intestinal walls, helping in the elimination. The skin also contributes to elimination by giving consistency to food wastes.

Use it ripe during its season in the region where you live. Take it alone in the morning on an empty stomach.

Garlic and Onion

They are good cleansing agents which prevent putrefactions and fight worms. Always add to raw salads.

Spinach

It is rich in mucilages. Its saponin facilitates the secretions of the digestive juices and stimulates the mucous membrane of the intestines. Its chlorophyll vitalizes the intestines and its cellulose participates in their cleansing.

Lettuce

Cooked lettuce acts like spinach. Choose it as green as possible. *Chicory* and *dandelion* are also recommended, for they help in the secretion of the bile.

Leek

Leeks contain a lot of mucilages. They are a good cleanser of the intestines. Being rich in alkaline salts, this vegetable stimulates the liver and by repercussion, the intestines.

AROMATIC PLANTS

Aromatic plants should be widely used, for they have anti-putrid qualities. It is better to add them after cooking. Sprinkle some in raw vegetable dishes. Be careful not to confuse aromatic plants with spices which are irritating.

Use plenty of garlic, welsh onion, chives, chervil, parsley, sage, savory, tarragon, burnet, mustard, shallots. Sprinkle salad with garlic, cumin, caper, parsley, chervil, saffron, bay leaves, thyme, rosemary, nutmeg, onion, horseradish, etc. For cooked meals use vanilla, anise, ginger, angelica, cinnamon.

HONEY

Honey is good for constipation in children. It should be used in small amounts. Rosemary honey stimulates a congested liver. All the types of honey prevent putrefaction due to their natural formic acid.

****

RECIPES FOR RELIEF OF CONSTIPATION

COOKIES

Mix 10 tablespoons of wheat, freshly and roughly ground, with 2 tablespoons of olive oil, 2 tablespoon of honey and just enough water to make it easier to handle.

Place in an oiled frying pan, either in the form of cookies or a flat cake. Prunes or slices of apple or pear may be added to the dough. Serve hot or cold according to taste.

WHOLE WHEAT PLUM CAKE

For four people:

2½ cups fresh whole wheat flour	1 egg
1 oz. olive oil	1 cup honey
1 lemon	1 cup water
2½ cups plums or prunes soaked for 12 hours	2 oz. chopped almonds

Mix the water with the flour, add egg, oil, ½ cup of the honey, the juice of the lemon, 1 oz. almonds. Mix. Put in an oiled glass or earthenware baking dish. Cover with a layer of pitted plums (or prunes). Spread remaining honey on top and sprinkle with remainder of chopped almonds. Bake 30 minutes in a medium oven (325°-375°).
Note: Be careful that prunes have soaked up enough water, otherwise the cake will not hold its shape.

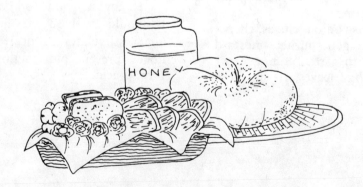

CRACKERS

For 20 crackers, mix 2 or 3 eggs, 1 cup honey, 1 tablespoon of orange blossom water, 3 cups of whole wheat flour and 6 oz. of crushed almonds. Beat for 5 minutes. Place on an oiled dish. The thickness should not exceed 1/8". Cook 10 minutes in a 300° oven.

STUFFED CUCUMBER

For one person:

1 cucumber	1 carrot, grated
2 olives, chopped	1 garlic clove, crushed
2 tablespoons olive oil	2 parsley stems
1 large red radish	2 pinches of salt
a few leaves of cabbage	

Choose a small but fat cucumber 4"-5" long. Peel, then from one end, pull out the seeds and the pulp. Mix this chopped pulp and seeds with the carrot and olives. Season with garlic and finely chopped parsley, oil and salt. Fill the cucumber with this mixture, stuffing it in well. Fill up the hole with the radish. Put aside in a fresh place for 15 minutes. Serve on cabbage leaves. Sprinkle with lemon juice. Some fine herbs may also be added.

SPINACH ASPIC

For 3 or 4 people:

1 lb. of spinach	1 carrot
½ oz. agar-agar	1 pinch of sea salt
1 very small pinch nutmeg	Bouquet of fresh herbs, thyme, parsley, etc.

Cook the spinach and carrot (previously roughly grated) in a quart of boiling water together with the bouquet. Drain and remove the herbs. Crush the spinach with the back of a fork, add salt and nutmeg.
Dilute the agar-agar in the water where the vegetables were cooked. Let simmer for awhile until some evaporation takes place. Mix agar-agar with the rest of the ingredients. Pour in a bowl or any kind of mold slightly oiled. Let it cool off completely. Unmold with the point of a knife. Serve surrounded with parsley, slices of tomatoes or onions.

LET US BREATHE

Respiratory Ailments and Their Cure

THE FLU

Before discussing the symptom of this or any particular disease, it is better to investigate its cause. Modern medicine takes the position that the flu is caused by a virus. They have discovered a different virus for every kind of influenza, which makes it hard to prescribe a uniform medical treatment. With a new virus the situation becomes even more complicated; treatment proceeds by chance and usually calls for today's ubiquitous panacea, the aspirin pill, and other such products. Various antiseptics are injected in the nose and other such things, all of which weaken the organism, on account of the serious imbalance engendered to the bacterial flora.

In modern medicine one mostly blames the germs which would spread throughout certain parts of the organism and would proliferate to the point of invading the whole body. The influenza would then be caused either by the microbe itself or by its toxic secretions.

Before accepting this hypothesis, it is necessary to ask why other subjects in contact with these pathogenic germs at the same time do not experience the same troubles. Scientists have discovered in the cell a pro-virus which ultimately will give birth to the virus itself when there is stimulation of any sort. This stimulation can be created by various factors: toxic substances, food or muscular wastes, incompletely formed proteins, chemical medications, harmful germs. Thus, it is now admitted that contagion would mostly indicate the re-activation of germs already present in the organism, becoming virulent under the stimulation of pathogenic microbes coming from another individual.

It seems that medical theories are getting somewhat closer to the naturist thesis. It is quite possible that what happens in a period of epidemic is a 'virulation' of germs which had been until now inactive, caused by other pathogenic germs coming from a subject already sick. These are the points on which naturists and modern medicine agree to a certain extent; however, on the rest they diverge completely.

It is commonly thought that the flu and other similar diseases have as their origin an outside agent, and it is not possible to define in advance the nature of the particular agent. Thus no preventive measure can be envisaged; instead it is necessary to passively wait for the aggression so as to then be able to fight back the perturbing and now 'identified' agent, and the pills and injections, etc. casually employed, make even this fight passive as far as the patient is concerned.

Again, though, contrary to this, is the fact that there are many subjects who come in contact with the same germs and are not affected, and therefore, wouldn't it be logical to think that these people are physically more resistant? This proves that when any particular person contacts diseases, it is at *least* as much due to his internal condition as to any outside agent.

The virus theory has been and is being explored in every way by the scientific world; they have observed virus embryos in the cells which become virulent only under the effect of some sort of stimulation, intoxification from food, muscular, chemical waste, etc. This stimulation may be created also by contact with other pathogenic germs coming from inside (endogenous production) or from outside (exogenous production). This is how the word 'contagion' should be understood:

not that a disease is introduced into the organism, but that it may result from the saprophytic germs (normal bodies in the organism). The trouble may originate from some perturbation in this protective flora, which becomes harmful if some of its constituents have been destroyed by foreign substances, such as antiseptics, antibiotics, etc. As the normal balanced medium is no longer present, the varieties that have survived may then proliferate and become virulent.

The role of natural food in the preservation of health is not yet sufficiently recognized. It is no wonder that disease is so prevalent considering all the refining foods go through nowadays.

For example, to take away the complete outside layer of wheat and other grains is dangerous; for it is there that vital protective elements are contained. Silica guarantees the defense of the lungs against infection and this precious mineral is present in the outside layer of cereals; yet in the sifting process silica is lost, along with B vitamins which collaborate in the nervous equilibrium. For more on this vital mineral, see p.155.

Every industrialized food is imbalanced; because of that, it must take from the reserves of the organism the substances it is lacking and which are necessary for its assimilation. Thus industrial sugar leads to a great loss of vitamins, ferments and mineral salts (mostly calcium), while helping in the production of some residual acids (such as oxalic, lactic, etc.) at the time of its transformation.

On the other hand, the breaking down of animal food in the body liberates toxic products that are difficult to neutralize. One of these products, indol, drains the sulphur found in the organic tissues; for only in combination with sulphur can indol be eliminated. What usually happens is either the organism does not have enough sulphur in storage and the indol residue will seriously toxify the whole organism, or there will be enough sulphur to neutralize the animal food wastes but the organism will then no longer have enough of it to assure its protection, especially in case of influenza.

The wrong type of food may also have indirect consequences. A normal cell contains the enzyme catalase which has a polyvalent defense mechanism. Bad nutrition weakens the cell, as it cannot secure sufficient catalase. As a consequence some bacteria may possibly become pathogenic. This is how infection may start from the intervention of exterior agents.

Knowing that bad food is the main source of disease, it makes sense to stay away from it. Abstain from alcohol and every imbalanced type of food.

Anything refined, bleached, denatured, or even enriched should be excluded, as well as sugar in all its forms. The foods which really protect against diseases are those which have not gone through any transformation processes. All sorts of advice concerning food are given in previous chapters; it suffices to rapidly read through this book to acquire all that is needed to remain on the safe side of health.

The Cure

In terms of nutrition, the quality of food is not the only consideration, what is most important is that food be able to be utilized by the digestive organs, for if it is not well-transformed, even the healthiest type of food can be toxic. Preparation is therefore important. *Cooked cereal will be used as often as possible.* All kinds of cereals can be widely used for they play a major part in restoring deficiencies and establishing organic balance.

The use of such products as eggs and cheese, yoghurt and other dairy products remains a matter of personal fitness. It is best to try to eat less of them, eliminating one after the other.

These considerations will only work at *pre* or *post* flu periods. If the flu could not be totally prevented (especially in big cities where toxic emanations are rather abundant) it becomes no longer a question of food, no matter how healthy, especially if there is temperature, for then it is preferable to fast and drink a lot (decoctions, hot water with lemon, and clay-water).

In cases with fever, try to induce perspiration with a decoction of either borage, elder-tree flowers, or box-tree leaves. In case of fever and difficulty in breathing, try to produce revulsions with mustard plaster or something similar. See also "In Case of Fever", p.192.

It would be a mistake in judgment to pass up this opportunity by forcibly suppressing the symptoms, for these reactions show that the organism is taking advantage of this crisis to liberate itself of all sorts of wastes and toxins. This crisis will be curative only if the interventions follow nature's direction. It is quite obvious that no medication of a chemical nature should be given.

Plants play an important role by drawing the toxins towards the intestines, kidneys, bladder, skin and upper respiratory channels. Accelerate the intestinal evacuations with buckthorn, senna, rhubarb, cassia fistules; the urinary evacuations with couch-grass, corn, rest-harrow, bearberry, ash-tree, cherry stems, etc., and the elimination through the skin with borage, linden flowers, elder-tree, box-tree, lavender, elecampane, etc. and the respiratory channels with mallow(althea), hyssop, agar-agar, thyme, ground-ivy leaves.

Of all plants, thyme is the best for the flu. Make a concentrated decoction of it, and take 5-6 cups a day, whether the flu is already there or coming. Lemon juice in hot water with honey is also excellent.

As a preventive in time of epidemic, do the following: eat some lemon peel (1 inch square) in the morning just before going out. A second piece, after lunch, just before going out, for people working in offices where co-workers have the flu.

As a curative: 1) take some peel as soon as the first symptoms begin to show (fever, sore throat, migraine, tinglings in the nose). 2) take another piece 1 hour later. Then 3 times a day for 48 hours.

This peel must be well-chewed and kept in the mouth a long time. Swallow it after 10-15 minutes when it is in a liquid form.

Clay will be of great help; apply it on the lower abdomen and on the affected area, such as lungs, throat, and liver. The poultices can be alternated, placing one first on the abdomen and then on the lungs, the throat, etc., each one remaining in place 2-3 hours. At night, put a poultice on the abdomen and keep overnight, except if there is discomfort.

Never try to 'cut off' the fever; when the temperature is lowered by artificial means, it enforces an interruption of the process of defense and elimination. The result could be an abnormal state which is a harbinger of the worse calamities, such as arteriosclerosis, diabetes, cancer, and other degenerative diseases. Nevertheless, too high a fever should be feared; however, it suffices to apply clay poultices on the abdomen and to take a few cold hip baths (5 minutes each) to witness an instantaneous lowering of the temperature. See 'fever'.

Once the fever and other inconveniences are gone, solid food may be introduced gradually. Avoid starches (cereals, potatoes and such things as beans and peas) for a few days, taking first fruits and then raw vegetables.

SORE THROAT INFLAMMATIONS AND INFECTIONS

Many people mistakenly believe that a sore throat which has not been properly 'treated', i.e. medicated, can be the origin of an acute rheumatism of the joints, with cardiac complications. This is reversing the causality, for a sore throat is already a rheumatic manifestation; it is more exactly a rheumatism of soft tissues. The sore throat is not the cause of the cardiac seizure, it is its corollary. So a sore throat must be taken very seriously for what it is, and treated as carefully as possible, with all the active means that we possess. Acting on the general condition at the same time as the local problem insures against complications, and is an exemplary method of taking advantage of this salutary crisis to eliminate a latent abnormality.

All sore throats present themselves as inflammatory manifestations of the isthmus of the throat and of the pharynx, accompanied by temperature, headache, stiffness in the back and limbs, gastric troubles. The inflammation may then reach the Eustachian tube and create temporary deafness.

It is best to stay away from food, while drinking as much as possible; lemon juice mixed with water and honey, clay-water, thyme decoctions, and at night, the following decoction:

Laxative Decoction for Inflamed Glands

Buckthorn bark	60 gr.	Couch-grass	
Ash-tree leaves	30 gr.	root	30 gr.
Barley (hulled)	30 gr.	Hyssop	30 gr.
Licorice root	30 gr.		

2 tablespoons in a cup of water. Bring to a boil and remove from the fire.

It would also be advisable to take a decoction for the liver functions, found on p.55.

Cold hip baths, 5-10 minutes long, taken every 2 hours, during the whole day will contribute to keeping the temperature at a tolerable limit. In the meantime, clay should be applied on the lower abdomen and the throat, alternately. The clay poultices should be almost 1" thick and left in place for the 2 hours between the cold hip baths. At night place the poultice on the liver and leave it overnight, unless the elevation of temperature again necessitates a poultice on the lower abdomen.

Gargling with salted water (sea salt) will help quite a bit; water with a strong concentration of lemon juice will also help greatly. It is even possible to 'paint' the tonsils with a mixture of half-honey and half lemon juice.

After the crisis, once the temperature is back to normal, gradually return to solid food, starting with fruits, then vegetables (grated in the form of salads), then cooked vegetables, some buttermilk. Wait a few days before the introduction of bread and cereals, cheese and eggs.

Continue the clay poultice on the liver every night, together with the cold hip bath in the morning and the decoction for the liver.

ASTHMA AND HAY FEVER

The belief that it suffices to keep away from the substances that provoke the allergies is another example of the symptomatic limited outlook of modern medical thinking. Allergies and other inconveniences will subsist as long as the internal cause is not uprooted.

Allergic troubles may arise whenever the liver is forced to make poisons from certain substances due to their stimulation, inhalation or absorption, or when the liver cannot neutralize the toxins, because of a deficiency in some of its functions. The toxins thus produced or preserved reach the nervous or endocrine centers, provoking a response; allergic troubles are the outcome of this response. Other hormonal manifestations may decrease or increase these troubles. Thus, among women, problems during the menstrual period may be accompanied by asthma attacks, while pregnancy may cause either the disappearance or the aggravation of the attacks.

As with most forms of eczema, asthma and hay fever are manifestations of arthritic dispositions. Even though the attacks mostly occur in conjunction with a particular exterior agent, it is but a secondary cause. Examination always reveals a liver disorder in asthmatics.

Effects

These afflictions can be very dangerous, for the heart may tire of trying to keep up with these frequent attacks. Even if the body successfully resists the repeated assaults, the life of the asthmatic is that of a real martyr. He becomes obsessed; the slightest difficulty in breathing immediately causes anxiety. Even when he is on his way to be cured the asthmatic experiences great difficulties in freeing himself from his apprehensions. Thus asthma has both physical and psychological roots.

Asthma attacks can be violent and intense, and nearly always are unpredictable. Difficulty in breathing is experienced when the subject tries to breathe in, so he attempts to restrict these phases by caving in the chest, bending forward and bringing the shoulders together. A malformation of the body may result with a modification in the way of walking. Asthma often starts with a crisis similar to that of hay fever, with sneezing, tears and other signs.

The bad attacks generally start at night. The person is suddenly taken by an anguished feeling and a need for air. He sits bent forward, his face is puffed. This may last long or end quickly. Very often after the attack, the subject experiences a thick kind of a cough, accompanied by expectorations. These periods may last long and take a chronic character. Also the repetition of asthma attacks may lead to the distension of the alveoli of the lungs and the diminution of their elasticity, manifested as continuous breathing difficulty and a predisposition to bronchitis and other pulmonary afflictions, even to heart failure.

Emergency care for Asthma attacks

At the approach of the first sign of the attacks, seat the patient, put pillows around and behind his back, and give him a cup of the following decoction:

Decoction for Asthma

Hyssop	30 gr.	Elecampane root	10 gr.
Marjoram	30 gr.	Narcissus	10 gr.
Mint	30 gr.	Scurvy grass	10 gr.
Pennyroyal	30 gr.	Water lily	10 gr.
Birthwort	10 gr.		

Take 2 tablespoons of the mixture per cup of water. Bring to a boil and infuse 10 minutes. Take 3-4 cups a day.

If these plants are not available, other plants whose effect, while not so noticeable, but will still do much good, may be used. Aside from some of the plants included in the previously indicated decoction, use separately, thyme, rosemary, lavender, mistletoe, cornpoppy, St. John's wort. Sweeten the decoctions with honey, especially lavender, thyme, origanum, rosemary, pine-tree honey.

During the attacks, the back of the asthmatic becomes as hard as wood. Contributing to the 'release' of the back with a soft and prolonged massage (15-20 minutes) will be an appreciable help. Search carefully for the part that is particularly sore, and concentrate there, either with the thumb if the pain is deep, or with the whole hand if the soreness is on the surface. Try to roll the skin between the thumb and the index-finger in a soft manner. End with a broad massage, keeping a circular movement, starting from the spine, the hands flat.

If this does not bring a sufficient release, complete the treatment with *fomentations:*

Heat water in a large pot. Plunge a large towel in the hot water, squeeze it a bit, and apply it on the back of the patient (use rubber gloves not to burn yourself) as hot as possible. Leave the compress and prepare another towel which will follow the previous one, and so on for 20-30 minutes.

The Cure

No matter how advanced the case, the complete cure of asthma is what should be aimed for. However, this implies a severe reform of lifestyle, particularly eating habits. Rigorously exclude everything toxic, unnatural, stimulating or adulterated (meat, fats, industrial oils, alcohol, sugar, canned food, coffee, tea, chocolate, etc.) and, of course, tobacco. Raw vegetables should be introduced and all whole cereals, as well as olive oil, lemon and aromatic plants such as thyme, rosemary, garlic, parsley, chervil, fennel, celery, etc.

As the role of the liver is crucial, its functions should be re-established. Use the following tea:

Infusion for Liver and Gall Bladder

Gromwell	20 gr.	Broom(genista)	10 gr.
Horsetail	20 gr.	Dandelion	10 gr.
Licorice root	20 gr.	Fernroot	10 gr.
Woodruff	20 gr.	Marigold	10 gr.
Asparagus root	20 gr.		

A full tablespoon in a cup of boiling water. Let infuse 10 minutes.

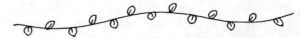

Complete treatment with lukewarm clay poultices on the liver which will be prepared before retiring and kept overnight. The wheat bran-ivy leaf poultice can also be used. It will act on the solar plexus and will relax the diaphragm and muscles connected with breathing.

Every morning on an empty stomach, take a tablespoon of clay diluted in ½ a glass of water, on alternate weeks. The week clay is not taken, have every morning, also on an empty stomach, a teaspoon of olive oil mixed with the juice of ½ a lemon.

Develop the habit of having a daily cold hip bath, preferably in the morning. See p.57.

As an additional aid, try boiling the stem of a cabbage with almonds for a long time. Add cane sugar and simmer until a syrup is obtained, of which a small glass is drunk in the morning and evening.

BRONCHITIS

Acute bronchitis generally happens after a sudden change of temperature in an organ from hot to cold. Under the effect of this abrupt cooling, the capillaries are blocked; because of that, the blood, not circulating properly, leaves in these capillaries the toxins and other wastes it was carrying along. A defense reaction is started, and the cough, which is necessary for the elimination of accumulated toxins, begins. Elements of defense and protection enter into play to assure the neutralization and elimination of the toxic substances. All these symptoms are accompanied by a fever which is always useful and beneficient.

The Cure

Revulsions will be necessary in this case, for they will free the capillaries of black toxic blood which is stationed there, thus establishing a normal circulation; this will secure the movement of the toxic substances toward natural channels. Apply a mustard plaster twice a day. It suffices to powder a cheesecloth (soaked in cold water which has been squeezed and laid on a table) with mustard flour. Apply the powdered side on the skin. When it starts tickling, count 10-15 minutes and remove.

While it would be a mistake to 'cut' the fever with artificial means, it will be necessary to bring it down to a tolerable limit. The cold hip bath proves itself excellent for this purpose, together with applications of clay poultices on the lower abdomen.

It is sometimes difficult to make people understand that there is no risk whatsoever in taking cold hip baths at the time of bronchitis or any other inflammatory state. It suffices to take some simple precautions: the body must remain well-covered (legs and trunk), during and after the bath. The room must be kept warm. The tub should be large enough to be comfortable, the water reaching the groin. In general the bath lasts 3-5 minutes, however, in time of fever, it may last up to 10 minutes. One may take up to 5 baths a day, depending on the individual reaction, i.e. if the cold is not felt throughout the body.

Clay poultices should be added to the hip baths if the patient can tolerate them.

No solid food should be eaten during the feverish period, for above normal body temperature (98.6°) the digestive ferments are in part destroyed or unable to act. As these ferments are indispensable to the integral transformation of food, it follows that their destruction implies an interruption of transformation, leaving it incomplete, and therefore toxic elements are products which prolong the fever.

When the temperature returns to normal, replace the mustard plasters with light massages, sometimes called frictions. Mix 2 parts of camphor oil with 1 part crushed garlic and rub the chest with it, while at the same time, reducing the number of hip baths.

To help the expectorations, boil a pinch of agar-agar for a few minutes. Strain and add thyme (1 stem or 1 teaspoon) and let infuse 10 minutes. Take 2 or 3 cups a day. You may also use the following tea:

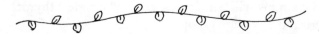

Infusion for Bronchial Cough

Agrimony	30 gr.	Althea	10 gr.
Ground ivy	30 gr.	Colt's foot	10 gr.
Hedge mustard	30 gr.	Mullein	10 gr.

Put a full tablespoon of the mixture in a cup of boiling water and let infuse 10 minutes. Add honey if desired.

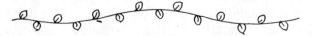

When the cough is very bad, a poultice of wheat bran-ivy should be applied.

The after-effects of the bronchitis can be eliminated by taking clay orally, 1 teaspoon diluted in ½ a glass of water, in the morning on an empty stomach. A decoction for liver functions should also be taken.

Solid food can be introduced gradually. First carrot juice and carrots, then the next day, for example, whole fruits, raw vegetables, vegetable soups, etc. Wait a few days before introducing starchy food such as cereals, bread, potatoes.

EMPHYSEMA AND CHRONIC BRONCHITIS

Hay fever and asthma result most of all from functional trouble while chronic bronchitis and emphysema may be accompanied by lesions and the persistent dilation of pulmonary alveoli, with the caliber increase of the bronchia and the inflammation of their mucous membranes.

These are, of course, the after-effects of an acute form of affliction which has been treated with palliatives. It is always dangerous to interrupt a natural manifestation of defense, such as stopping the cough abruptly by bringing the fever down. Thanks to the cough, the organism gets rid of mucosities which it had secreted to play a protective role. The cough also exercises a role of decompression. Fever allows the destruction of harmful germs. Interrupting such natural phenomena serves only to modify the nature of the disease, thus temporarily displacing it and making it chronic.

The Cure

The treatment in depth will vary depending on the general condition of the subject. However, here is the normal procedure -

In the morning - take 1 teaspoon of olive oil mixed with the juice of ½ a lemon on an empty stomach.
Before one of the meals - 1 teaspoon of clay in ½ a glass of water.

After meals - 1 cup of the following decoction:

Infusion for Obstruction of Biliary Channels

Woodruff	40 gr.	Marigold	20 gr.
Boldo	30 gr.	Rosemary leaves	20 gr.
Licorice root	30 gr.	Yellow bedstraw	20 gr.
Horsetail	25 gr.	Mint	15 gr.
Asparagus root	20 gr.		

Mix 2 tablespoons in a cup of boiling water. Infuse 10 minutes.

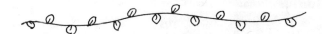

Change food until it gradually becomes vegetarian, giving predominance to raw fruits and vegetables and cereals. Every morning a short hip bath of 3-5 minutes should be taken.

In the evening a clay poultice should be applied on the liver, kept on overnight, if well-tolerated.

To temper the attacks of coughing or breathlessness, take one of the decoctions indicated for asthma or acute bronchitis. Frictions with a mixture of 2 parts camphor oil and 1 part crushed garlic; afterwards apply a hot wheat bran-ivy poultice (see p.143).

TUBERCULOSIS

In all properly functioning organisms with normal defense mechanisms and reactions, all invasions of germs, whatever they are, are immediately neutralized - any perturbation which may result will only be minor. "Contagion" is possible only if the organism is weakened.

People following the harmonist method have powerful and numerous protective agents, diffused throughout the body; it may be saliva, gastric, biliary, or pancreatic juices, intestinal secretions, perspiration, mother's milk, even urine. Very few germs can resist such secretions.

The most difficult handicap to overcome is a distorted conception of disease. It is often harder to get rid of such ideas than of the disease itself. It is even harder for people who have a medical training to abandon the conception of the exogenous origin of diseases.

The role of heredity in tuberculosis cannot be ignored, for weak constitutions as well as bad habits can be transmitted from generation to generation. However, the physiological misery which generates tuberculosis is not exclusively relegated to poor family conditions; wealthy people can develop and nurture it by their excesses.

One common factor quickly emerges from the various stories and case histories of tubercular people; that the injury to the lungs was preceded by long periods of liver disorder together with intestinal troubles.

What happened is clear; since food was not tolerated in its 'living' state (raw fruits and vegetables) it was eaten overcooked and denatured in part, or else unnatural and unhealthy to begin with. The inevitable result is difficulty in the processes of digestion, transformation and fixation. It is in the wake of this malnutrition that tuberculosis may appear, for the weakened cells give birth to the famous bacilli. *The latter do not come from outside, but are internally produced.* Due to a deficiency of the protective silica, these corrupted cells - the bacilli - are going to be able to attack the pulmonary walls at the points where silica is missing.

It is evident that if a sick person already treated medically suffers a relapse, it would be imprudent to suddenly cease medical treatment and follow the natural method. Natural methods require a certain amount of minimum reserves and a defensive system capable of some degree of functioning and normal reactions. It is advisable to wait for a period of calm, in terms of the evolution of the disease and the prescription and application of the medical care before attempting a gradual reform of the treatment and the patient's habits.

When this becomes possible the first step to be taken care of is the restoration of the digestive system. Nothing is more favorable for this than clay taken orally; it should be taken once or twice a day before meals (1 teaspoon in ½ a glass of water), every day for a few weeks.

The gall bladder functions should be strengthened by taking 1 teaspoon of olive oil mixed with the juice of ½ a lemon in the morning, every other week. The alternate week take fenugreek (1 tablespoon in 2 cups of water; boil and reduce liquid to half). Fenugreek acts on the liver and pancreas, and therefore will improve assimilation of food.

The liver should be gently stimulated with the following infusion:

Infusion for the Liver

Gromwell	30 gr.	Yellow bedstraw	30 gr.
Licorice	30 gr.	Marigold	20 gr.
Rosemary	30 gr.	Mint	20 gr.
Woodruff	30 gr.		

2 tablespoons per cup of boiling water; infuse 15 minutes. Drink hot, 1 cup, after meals. Honey is optional.

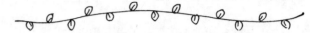

Every night apply a poultice of wheat bran-ivy leaves on the stomach and liver. Leave it on all night if there is no discomfort.

It is also good to treat the diseased areas locally; this will help stop the evolution of the disease in periods of acute suffering.

An infusion of elder-tree flowers (1 handful per quart of boiling water; infuse 15 minutes; drink when desired) will help regularize the functions. Frictions with a mixture of camphor oil and grated garlic (2:1) and clay poultices on the lung area (especially in all affected areas) will all help re-establish the functions.

In the beginning clay should be applied not too cold. In any case, when clay is applied, give great attention to finding out if the poultice warms up after application; if not, it is advisable to remove it. Clay is supposed to create warmth and become warm itself in this case.

Some people who still have vital reserves can take the cold hip bath. This should be taken in a temperature-controlled room and last 3-5 minutes. It should not be taken if it causes a cold feeling. Wait one, two or three weeks before trying it again.

When the digestive functions are better, aim to favor remineralization by taking the egg-lemon juice preparation (p.113).

The following tea should also be taken:

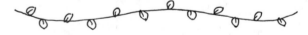

Decoction for Remineralization

Blind nettle	25 gr.	Lavender	20 gr.
Horsetail	25 gr.	Wild celery root	30 gr.
Rosemary	25 gr.	Germander	15 gr.
Small centaury	25 gr.	Hops	15 gr.

A tablespoon per cup of water. Bring to a boil and simmer 5 minutes. Take 1 cup during or just before each meal.

The progression toward a natural way of eating and of healing oneself must be prudent. It is not at all advisable to give up at once all the old bad habits, even the worst ones. It is better to gradually cease having such products as alcohol, meat and animal fat, canned foods, white bread, oil and industrial fats, alkaloids, such as coffee and tea. Fruits and fresh vegetables should be introduced, raw as often as possible; whole-grain cereals, dried fruits, fresh white cheese and yoghurt, organic eggs, honey.

Since a tubercular person lacks silica he should eat whole wheat bread (homemade with sour dough).

Sprouted wheat has many re-constitutive ele-ments. Add it to raw dishes, soups, etc. - take 3 tablespoons of it a day.

Carrot, cabbage and beet juice will be extremely helpful; have 2 or 3 glasses a day, preferably between meals.

Add plenty of garlic to raw dishes. It is the most efficient antiseptic in the natural kingdom. Do not neglect the lemon, whose citric acid is necessary to the transformation and fixation of calcium.

SINUSITIS

This disease refers to an infection in the cavities and nasal recesses. Sometimes there is no suppura-tion, only inflammation; this is the 'dry' sinusitis. It is generally the most painful and localized in the frontal region.

Those who are subject to sinusitis fear to catch any head cold, knowing that the coming out of pus - generally from one nostril - is the beginning of a long and painful period of disease. Sometimes there are complications. Towards the end there may be blood mixed with the pus.

When sinusitis takes a chronic form, the suppura-tion persists; the digestive system will be affected by the pus swallowed while sleeping.

The Cure

It goes without saying that sinusitis is truly cured only by taking care of the liver. However, since the period of crisis is painful and dangerous at the same time, a double effect treatment is required. First take care of what is most urgent by exercising a sedative action on the painful area that favors collection of the pus, so that it does not infect other areas. One should then start the treat-ment in depth by accelerating the function of neutralization and elimination of toxins.

Proceed the following way:
Several times a day have a nose cleansing with clay-water:

In a cup of lukewarm water, put a heaping tablespoon of clay; mix; plunge the nose into it, keeping on nostril closed with the finger; breathe in slowly so that the water rises, coming through the throat. Repeat 5 or 6 times, alternating nostrils. Complete the treatment by putting some drops of lemon in each nostril.

When the sinuses are very irritated, clayish water may not be well-tolerated; instead use a concentrated decoction of thyme.

Thyme should be used both in infusions which will be taken several times a day and also in inhalations. These inhalations are prepared in the following manner:

Boil a few stems (or 3 teaspoons of dried thyme) in a small pot containing ¾ of its volume in water. Just before using it, squeeze the juice of a lemon into the pot, then quickly place the face above the pot, covering the head with a towel.

Remain in this position as long as the liquid is hot enough to liberate steam. Breathe deeply, as much as possible. Afterward, wash the face with cold water and dry rapidly with a towel.

If the pain is acute, apply clay poultices on the forehead or wherever the pain is. The poultice must be approximately ¾"-1" thick, kept on for 2 hours. Re-apply a new one, if necessary.

Take a teaspoon of clay in ½ a glass of water, in the morning on an empty stomach, and take the following before the two main meals:

Decoction for Liver Congestion

Licorice root	30 gr.	Horsetail	10 gr.
Woodruff	30 gr.	Marigold	10 gr.
Artichoke leaves	20 gr.	Rosemary	
Bearberry leaves	10 gr.	(flowered tops)	10 gr.
Black currant		Small centaury	10 gr.
(or gooseberry		Yellow bedstraw	10 gr.
leaves)	10 gr.		

1 or 2 tablespoons per cup of water. Bring to a boil and let infuse 10 minutes.

Do not eat anything during fever, not even fruit or carrot juices or vegetable broth. Drink only infusions, lemon-water and clay-water. The infusion normally taken before the meal may be taken any time during the day. See 'fever', p.192.

When the fever is gone, food can be introduced starting with fruit and carrot juices, then vegetable broth, later on continuing with raw fruits and vegetables. Wait a few days before having starches such as bread, brown rice and other cereals, potatoes, etc.

Once the crisis is gone, be careful to maintain the basic treatment, i.e. eating the right foods, drinking infusions good for the liver and having cold hip baths once in a while.

RHINO-PHARYNGITIS

The pollution is so bad in the big cities that it has become more and more difficult to keep the superior breathing organ from getting inflamed. We already learned that the afflictions of the respiratory tubes are the consequence of a failure of the liver functions. Toxic substances are not neutralized, the ingested foods do not reach the final stage of their transformation, protective elements are not produced in sufficient amount. Because of that, the smallest irritation of the respiratory tubes becomes an inflammation, if not an infection.

When this inflammatory manifestation affects most especially the mucous membrane of the pharynx, at the level of the nasal duct, that particular inflammation is called rhino-pharyngitis; which, like tonsilitis and adenoid infection, affects mostly young people.

The symptoms of rhino-pharyngitis are subtle, that is the reason it is difficult to identify it. The temperature may go as high as 102°-104° and last more than a week.

Here is the important clue for diagnosis. In general, its accompanying fever is higher in the morning than in the evening, which is not a usual thing in comparison to most other inflammations and infections.

Due to the length of the period of fever, it would not be possible to observe the general rules normally followed in the time of fever. The patient should not go on fasting for too long - not because there is a danger from not eating solid food for 1, 2, or 3 weeks, but because not many people can resist the temptation of food. If the patient does not ask for food, do not offer it to him, however, if he is very hungry, give him fruits, then raw vegetables (the next day, for example), then cooked vegetables especially in the form of soups. Even after the fever is gone, wait a few days before giving cereals. In time, introduce whole wheat bread, brown rice, wheat in all forms and other cereals.

The Cure

Start with liquids which are not nutritive, such as lemon-water, clay water, decoctions for the liver and infusion of thyme. Avoid fruit and carrot juices and even vegetable broths - these help maintain the fever. When the fever passes the 100.4° mark, the digestive ferments are neutralized in part and the digestion of food cannot take place normally. Still, the liquids indicated above should be drunk in order to accelerate the elimination of the toxins.

If the stools are insufficient, take a laxative decoction such as buckthorn, senna follicles, etc. Do not hesitate to give an enema with salted water if necessary if the patient had no bowel movement that day. There is always a lowering of temperature after abundant stools. Even when fasting, one should have bowel movements, for there are always wastes to be evacuated.

If the patient is not too sick and can get out of bed, give him a cold hip bath for 5-10 minutes every 2 or 3 hours.

Between the baths apply clay poultices on the lower abdomen and on the back of the neck, alternately. Replace the poultice on the back of the neck with one on the throat. All three poultices remain in place for 2 hours.

In the evening put 3 or 4 layers of raw cabbage leaves on the abdomen and liver. Bandage and leave in place overnight.

Morning and evening put a few drops of salted water (sea salt) in the nose or else follow the procedure for nasal washing, recommended for sinusitis.

If it is possible to spend a few days in the good air, do not miss the opportunity, at the same time continuing the indicated treatment, of course.

CLAY TREATMENT FOR THE LUNGS

Either for the treatment of rheumatism and bronchitis or for that of a tuberculous consumption, the use of heated clay is preferable to that of a cold or tepid one. In Davos, Switzerland, tuberculosis specialists used very well-heated clay. They coated the patient's thorax, leaving it for twelve hours or more and obtained marvelous results.

As clay provokes reactions of some significance, it will be impossible to continue these massive applications to an organism which is already fatigued and which may become exhausted after a long time. Such important treatment must be administered under the surveillance of experienced parctitioners.

It should be pointed out that bronchitis, rheumatism, laryngitis, measles, etc. should be treated with a daily clay poultice on the chest, and occasionally another on the side (a tepid poultice 2 cms. thick). Before arriving at the frequency of two poultices a day, it is advisable to put the nutritive organs in order, reserving the first applications for the lower abdomen, then for the liver. Those of the lungs will start later in the treatment.

More serious illnesses (tuberculosis, consumption) that have the effect of curtailing one's usual activities will justify 2 poultices a day; a cold one on the lower abdomen and a hot one on the lungs (one day on the chest, the next on the back). Complete the treatment with frictions of clay mud mixed with chopped garlic.

MENU FOR A DAY
(to prevent respiratory ailments)

Breakfast

1 - *fresh or dried fruits*   -or
2 - *wheat cream (freshly ground kernels)*   -or
3 - *thick vegetable broth*   -or
4 - *whole wheat bread with honey or fresh butter*
Infusion of thyme or rosemary

Lunch

fresh fruits
raw vegetable salad
cooked vegetables or cereal
cheese or buttermilk
dried fruits or homemade pastry

Dinner

fresh fruits
raw vegetable salad
vegetable soup
dried fruits

Always drink lemon-water and infusions.

THE NERVOUS SYSTEM

Physical and Emotional Problems

Although terms for categorizing nervous troubles are becoming increasingly numerous and various, the true cause and corresponding treatment remain but one. Asthenia, neurosis, insomnia, nervous depression, neurasthenia, troubles of the sympathetic system, or neuro-vegetative, vaso-motor, all grow from the same root.

The imbalance basically originates from a weakness in the nervous cell; either this cell does not receive the necessary elements for its own needs, or it is degraded by wastes and other toxic substances such as alcohol, tobacco, coffee, tea, etc.

The brain races like a car engine, as if the accelerator is stuck. It is not at those moments of exaltation or depression that the person can take upon himself the decision to remedy these abnormalities; this should be taken care of during the calmer periods. During the critical times he can only have recourse to specific remedies of natural or modern medicine. However, in times of rest he may develop the good sense of using a more

permanent treatment.

The harmonist is not granted the best life, for he has to accept the conditions of life common to everyone. However, his personal efforts bear him such fruits that he has a wide security margin to work within. Thanks to this margin he can better tolerate these problems, which, even if too big for him, he can still withstand and deal with longer than most people, due to his foundation of solid physiological health. It is always possible that such a person can be struck by nervous depression, but this is very exceptional, and if so, he will be able to take care of it with a natural treatment.

To say that a nervous trouble is of nervous origin corresponds to a confession of ignorance. There is no trouble without a deep cause. For the nervous functions to work harmoniously, it is indispensable that the cells receive the proper nutritive elements, that the vital energy be correctly channelled and wastes normally discharged.

The presently practiced medicine is generally not

of great help to a psychologically disturbed person. The various examinations to which he is submitted do not reveal anything abnormal, so he is classified as an imaginary sick person and channelled to a psychotherapist. Now the focus is on his neurosis; the psychotherapist does not seem in the least concerned about any organic disorder. The patient will be treated as if he had no body.

Whatever the source is, it remains in our will and ability to locate that source - whether it be found that the cause is psychological or that it is physiological, we will act accordingly.

A NATURAL TREATMENT

Technically, it can be said that every disease is of nervous origin, since it is the nerves that transmit the communicating impulses of the organic functions. In the same way, it can be said that every nervous sickness proceeds from organic trouble, bad nutrition and intoxification of the nervous paths or nervous centers.

Each nervous duct contains two vessels, one vein and one artery; it is understandable that if the blood is not pure, if it contains crystals and other similar rough substances, an irritation and eventually even a lesion in these vessels can occur. These wastes carried by the blood may also pollute the nervous centers, eventually injuring them. This can be compared to a non-functioning electric appliance, that when first taken apart, does not reveal anything abnormal, while closer examination shows that the contact points are oxidized or carbonized. A similar phenomenon is the origin of many nervous troubles. Organic deposits which could not be eliminated have accumulated at the point of contact and the current no longer passes through.

A vicious cycle may begin if the command is badly transmitted, the organic exchanges are slowed down or are interrupted. The evacuations become worse and worse and the toxic condition will worsen in the organism, which will in turn have a corresponding effect on the nervous system. Here is another cycle that may start: the blood analysis of a depressed person may reveal a low level of elements such as calcium, iron and phosphorus. Since phosphates are being carried out by the urine as shown by urinalysis, the use of medications containing phosphates will only increase these losses.

The treatment must follow two parallel routes: taking care of what is most urgent by acting directly or indirectly on the nervous cells, and putting into order digestive, assimilative and eliminative functions, in order to help repair the nervous cells.

The Cure

Three mornings a week, take the following preparation:

In the evening put a whole egg with its shell well cleaned in a cup. Fill up the cup with lemon juice, let soften overnight. In the morning, remove the egg, setting it aside for future cooking purposes and drink the liquid. The calcium absorbed from the shell will stimulate the functions of assimilation and aid the fixation of calcium. For best results it should be continued for three months, and repeated several times during the year, if necessary.

The other days of the week, take a decoction of fenugreek:

1 tablespoon in 2 cups of water; cook until it reduces to 1 cup.

Since the taste of fenugreek is not always appreciated, it may be prepared the evening before and taken cool or lukewarm the next morning. Cooled off the taste will not be as strong.

As it acts on the liver and the pancreas, fenugreek can greatly stimulate the assimilation process, that is why people say that fenugreek 'fattens'; however, it will only add weight to those needing to gain some.

Before one of the meals (lunch or dinner) take 1 teaspoon of clay in ½ a glass of water

After lunch have the following tea which favors the liver functions:

Infusion for Stimulation of the Liver

Horsetail	30 gr.	Yellow bedstraw	30 gr.
Licorice root	30 gr.	Marigold	20 gr.
Rosemary	30 gr.	Mint	20 gr.
Woodruff	30 gr.		

2 tablespoons of the mixture in a cup of boiling water. Infuse for 15 minutes.

After dinner take the same infusion, or the following, which is good for sleeping:

Decoction for Nerves

Orange tree leaves 20 gr.		Vervain	15 gr.
Green anise	15 gr.	Lime-tree(linden)	10 gr.
Melissa	15 gr.	Orange tree buds	5 gr.
Mint	15 gr.		

2 tablespoons of the mixture in a cup of water. Bring to a boil and let infuse 10 minutes.

When it becomes necessary to act more rapidly and more specifically on the nerves, use the following, which is very efficient in different cases, such as depression, overexcitation, or insomnia:

Decoction for Nervousness and Insomnia

Calamint	20 gr.	Valerian	20 gr.
Melissa	20 gr.	Woodruff	20 gr.
Wild thyme	20 gr.	Hawthorn	10 gr.
Peppermint	20 gr.	Passion flower	10 gr.

2 tablespoons of the mixture in a cup of water. Bring to a boil and let infuse 5 minutes. 2 cups a day, between meals, and 1 before going to bed, in case of insomnia. Continue for 8 successive days or every other day.

Do not hesitate to take this inoffensive decoction, for a good night's sleep is an important element of health and equilibrium.

A plant can have a calming effect on one person, and a stimulating one with another; that is why it is good to first make a few experiments with weak doses, before mixing it with other plants. Two main effects are sought for asthenia and other abnormalities of that order; a tonic action and a non-exciting but non-depressing calming action. Here are the plants which answer to this double requirement.

Non-depressing Sedatives

Basil (3-5%)	*Bird's foot trefoil (3-5%)*
Corn-poppy (2-3%)	*Daffodil (3%)*
***Fumitory (2-3%)**	*Green anise (3-5%)*
Hawthorn (5%)	*Lime-tree(linden) (5%)*
Passion flower (5%)	*Sweet marjoram (2-5%)*
Thyme (5%)	*Valerian (10%, macerated*
Water lily (2-5%)	*for a long time)*
Willow (3-5%)	*White melilot (5%)*
Yellow bedstraw (2-3%)	*Woodruff (5%)*

Non-exciting Tonics

Blind nettle (3-5%)	**Lavender (4-5%)*
Calamint (2-3%)	**Lily-of-the-valley (2-3%)*
Elecampane (3-5%)	*Matricaria chamomilla (5%)*
Germander (3-4%)	*Madder (1-2%)*
Hawthorn (5%, tonic	**Melissa (2-5%)*
and moderator of the	**Milfoil (3-5%)*
heart)	*Sage (2-3%)*
Hops (2-4%)	*Tormentil (1-3%)*
Horsetail (10%)	*Wild thyme (5%)*
Large centaury (3-4%)	

These plants are to be used individually or in mixture, choosing a few of them and being careful with the proportions. The percentage in parentheses is the volume in grams per quart.

If the depression is accompanied by physical fatigue or exhaustion, take the following decoction during meals:

Decoction for Remineralization

Blind nettle	25 gr.	Lavender	20 gr.
Horsetail	25 gr.	Wild celery root	20 gr.
Rosemary	25 gr.	Germander	15 gr.
Small centaury	25 gr.	Hop	15 gr.
Elecampane	20 gr.		

1 tablespoonful per cup of water. Bring gently to a boil and simmer 5 minutes. Take 1 cup during each meal or just before the meal.

Every morning a cold hip bath which should last 3-5 minutes should be taken. During nervous depression, it is preferable to take the bath very cold, not lasting longer than 2 or 3 minutes. If there is over-excitation, have the water slightly lukewarm and then lasting for 5-10 minutes. For complete directions, see p.157.

Apply clay on the back of the neck, but only after a few preliminary days of treatment on the liver, using either the clay or wheat bran-ivy poultice, applied on the liver and stomach.

----

*These plants are tonic and antispasmodic at the same time. They could, like hawthorn, figure in the list of sedatives or on that of the tonic plants
**Taken for a short while is a tonic; for a long one, a sedative.

Even the serious hereditary nervous troubles of one patient totally disappeared after a year and a half of clay poultices on the nape of the neck.

A foot bath with a decoction of red-grape vine leaves will accelerate the circulation and stimulate the exchanges. If, instead of red-grape vine leaves 2 handfuls of bran and 2 of walnut-tree leaves are used, the nervous system is calmed and strengthened at the same time. *For it would be out of the question to 'calm' in the medical sense of the word, which means to weaken, but on the contrary to strengthen in order to be really calm.* Do not jump from a calming plant to a stimulating one, and back again; act carefully, focusing on the return to equilibrium, which is to be found between the accelerating and the restraining forces.

It would also be good to take a complete bath in the following solution:

> Fill the tub with hot water. Put seaweed and 5-7 pounds of wheat bran and 3-12 oz. of walnut-tree leaves (put bran and leaves in a cheesecloth) in a basin, add 1 gallon of water, bring to a boil and pour in the bathtub, where hot water for the bath is ready.

Massage the spine lightly with camphor oil or a mixture of camphor oil and crushed garlic(2:1). This is important for the nervous functions.

RECOMMENDED FOODS

In the beginning of the treatment the food should be light. The goal is to give the organism the maximum of nutritive elements without tiring it - best for this is vegetable juices. Every day take, between meals, 1 or 2 glasses of carrot or beet juice, or ½ a glass of cabbage juice, or 1-2 glasses of the following combinations: carrot-turnip, carrot-cabbage, carrot-cabbage-onion, carrot-turnip-leek, etc.

The most important place in the menus should be reserved for raw vegetables in the form of salads, grated vegetables and fruits. Just after that come all the cereals, especially wheat, brown rice, hulled barley, buckwheat and millet. A combination of cereals and cooked vegetables is a good one. The dishes should be well-seasoned with aromatic plants.

It is possible to have a dish of brown rice and vegetables for example, and alternate it daily with a heavy soup containing vegetables and grains in the form of noodles, semolina, etc.).

Whole wheat or buckwheat noodles may sometimes replace the cereal dish. Such items as beans, lentils and peas may be given once a week, during the cold season, if they are tolerated.

The meal may be ended with yoghurt or some cheese (if one is used to having dairy food) or perhaps apple sauce, or a homemade pastry.

Two or three times a week it is all right to have an egg (choosing the most pleasant preparation) and homemade pastry, even if made with eggs.

Dried fruits may also be consumed; they must be used prudently, due to their concentration of nutritive elements. For example, such fruits as almonds or walnuts, if taken in excess may give liver problems. On the other hand, dried sweet fruits may be consumed without apprehension. Take dates, raisins, figs, dried bananas, apricots, peaches, apples, prunes, etc. *at a favorable moment, a time that seems propitious for their digestion.* This may be at the beginning of a meal, with fresh fruits, or as a dessert, or at breakfast. Everyone should experiment and discern what is best for him.

There is a relationship between acute anguished moments and the presence of lactic acid in the tissues. It is evident that foods which produce lactic acid favor this situation; this happens at the time of their degradation, especially with such a product as sugar. The organism is not able to eliminate this acid, caused by adrenalin gland discharges which activate the combustion of sugars, producing an excess of lactic acid. That is why it is important to stay away from alcohol, meat, animal fats, white bread and all bleached cereals, for they all lead to

the same problem.

Wheat germ is a good help, for it brings precious elements to the nervous cells. Season dishes with it (1, 2, or 3 teaspoons).

GOOD BREATHING, BETTER NERVOUS SYSTEM

Breathing well normally eliminates gaseous wastes in the blood; red blood cells are charged with oxygen which they then bring to all the cells. Besides impoverishing the blood, improper breathing can cause an imbalance in the glandular system. This can be seen in children, who, because of improper breathing - using the mouth instead of the nose - often show signs of mental retardation. Simply to teach good breathing to these children will allow them to grow normally.

A change in life conditions brings the most improvement, but still a few simple measures should also be taken: cleanse the nose with clay-water, salt-water solution or a decoction of thyme (plunge the nose in the liquid, maintaining one nostril closed; breathe in with one nostril at a time);

Be particularly careful with the appearance of the table and the presentations of the dishes so that the meal is as joyous as possible.

drops of lemon do a good cleansing (adding some olive oil makes a softer solution); fumigations of thyme are also excellent.

The nostrils are full of hair which act as an air filter. The hair is also responsible for heating the air before its introduction into the bronchia. In breathing out through the nose, the hair is moistened, thanks to the humid air coming out of the lungs.

We seldom breathe with both nostrils at the same time, therefore, practice letting the air enter through one while closing the other, alternately. It should be done several times. Do this sitting in a comfortable position or go out in the fresh air. Take off tie, belt and any other confining clothes. Make an effort to relax, eliminating all kinds of preoccupations.

Breathing Exercises

Proceed with one nostril first, and then with both. Breathe out slowly, counting mentally until 4, until the breath is completely out. If, for example, the breathing out process takes 4 seconds, when 4 is reached, make a stop, count 2 seconds and start breathing in, counting up to 4. Make a stop. Hold the air, counting 2 seconds.

Eventually increase the breathing time, always stopping between in and out stages. These exercises should of course be practiced in the open air or close to an open window. Some arm movements make these exercises easier; it suffices to lift up the arms when breathing in and lower them when breathing out.

THE TREE OF LIFE

Healing The Spine

It cannot be denied that the spine suffers the consequences of our daily impositions on it, often-repeated gestures, competitive sports, overuse of mechanical means of locomotion (using the car for one hundred yards instead of going by foot), and bad food.

In most cases, people having spine trouble will attempt to attenuate the symptoms without searching for how to eliminate the cause. Upon discovering decalcification calcium is taken directly. It seems so elementary! They do not think for an instant that if the spine lacks calcium it probably is because of an imbalance in the distribution of the various nutritive substances rather than a lack of supply.

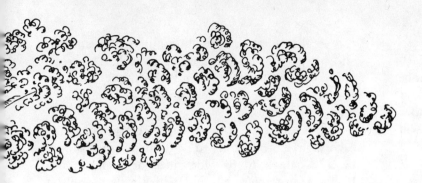

Calcification is not simply a matter of calcium; chemists have seen this and now speak of a phosphorus/calcium complex. This is still an oversimplification, for in reality it is a whole group of substances which are necessary to secure the assimilation of calcium and its fixation. It is not enough to introduce a useful substance in the body, it yet remains for the substances to be properly fixed and assimilated.

Medicinal calcium acts first as a stimulant of diverse functions; this stimulation always leads to an eventual depression after a period of euphoria.

This chemical calcium is unknown to the organism. It is practically inassimilable. It leaves deposits around the bones. This imitation of real calcification is done in an anarchic manner and contributes to the premature hardening of the spine ligaments.

The spine constitutes the reserve of calcium of the organism; from it the latter draws what it needs. If this drawing exceeds a certain limit, a deficiency in calcium follows. Things worsen when chemical calcium is introduced, for that extra element only contributes in obstructing the organism.

Calcium is often introduced through the rectum or by injection in the veins; this causes a relative state of sclerosis both in the rectum and vessel walls.

By examining the profile of the spine one notices two clear curves. These two curves serve the purpose of absorbing shocks; without them our brain would not be able to withstand even the simple movement of walking.

The spine sometimes has other curves of abnormal origin - cyphosis, for example. This dorsal deformation may be situated in the lumbar region. This is called the lumbar cyphosis. From being convex in the front, the curve becomes abnormally convex in the back. The exaggeration of this curve, its too accentuated projection in front, constitutes lordosis. If curves are present when facing the spine this is called scoliosis.

In most cases these deformations are caused by malnutrition; it may be that not enough different kinds of food are being eaten, also it may be that non-eliminated wastes accumulating on the same vertebrae contribute to putting them out of place. Malformation may be caused by ray treatment which has encouraged the growth of one face of the spine only.

All the weight of the spine is on five massive vertebrae, the lumbar vertebrae, the fifth one (situated above the sacrum) carrying the bulk of the weight. *Discal hernia* occurs when the fibrous disc between the 4th and 5th vertebrae is out of place. This often happens at the end of the winter, since with the unavailability of fresh and alive food, the spinal system becomes devitalized.

We have personally supervised enough natural treatments of various afflictions of the spine to be in a position to state that there are very few people who cannot find a solution to their trouble. Many people who were condemned to an orthopedic corset, bone surgery or immobilization have now been able to resume normal activities after a few months of natural treatment.

The Cure

So much has been written about the importance of proper eating that it is not necessary to write it again. Nevertheless, there are specifications that ought to be given to make sure that the food will be a healer as well.

Lemon is excellent when taken in proper quantity. Four lemons should be taken daily, each one diluted in ½ a glass of water, without sugar.

Food shall be alive and varied. It is not in vain that nature gives us such diversity of food. All the fruits, vegetables, salads and aromatic plants have their role and necessity. Eat raw food as often as possible and take advantage of its vital energy. Also bear in mind that in all bone afflictions a deficiency in silica is revealed which is found in the outer layer of vegetables in general and cereals in particular.

It would be beneficial to take a cold hip bath every day. It stimulates processes in the organism such as assimilation and elimination.

In periods of painful attacks, massage the whole spine with a mixture of 2 parts camphor oil and 1 part grated garlic.

A person suffering from a spinal affliction will find relief in the massages, stretchings and other manipulations practiced by a masseur; however, this is only treating the symptoms and therefore will bring only temporary relief. Exercises of rotation and mobilization of the joints are effective when accompanied by proper food; both will correct any defect of the spine.

Every day certain movements which aim at moving the vertebrae in all directions should be done. Walking, biking, gardening, etc., are excellent exercises which help strengthen the spine. These exercises should be done gently, being careful not to prolong them more than necessary.

Sometimes the tendons weaken. They can be likened to the ropes on a mast - as long as they all are strong they maintain the pole, the vertebrae imbricated one in the other. If only one should weaken, the vertebrae can all slip away.

The most efficient of all remedies, to our knowledge, is clay. Although some afflictions necessitate a longer treatment, six months of daily applications will usually take very good care of the most tenacious afflictions.

For example, there was a case of a boy 11 years old with cervical adenitis and decalcification of the vertebral column. Clay poultices were applied on the spleen and ganglions and the boy also took clay orally. First one ganglion burst, then another and his general state improved as well. The treatment had begun at the end of October and the parents considered the boy quite healed the following spring.

In most cases it would suffice to apply clay each night before going to bed; the poultice should be ¾"-1" thick, 6"-8" wide and as long as necessary. If clay is not tolerated cold, which is best, apply it slightly lukewarm, heating it with steam in a double boiler. Keep the poultice on overnight if possible. It should be removed immediately, if it causes any feeling of cold inside the body.

Clay should be prepared in such a manner as to remain flexible so that it conforms to the body. It should be compact, neither too liquid nor too dry.

If two different places ought to be treated (for example in case of a double scoliosis, or a cyphosis associated with a lordosis), alternate the applications, one evening on one place, and the next on the other.

The already mentioned massage with camphor oil and garlic should be administered every night. Proceed from the base of the spine upwards, using a clockwise movement which starts at a point on the spine itself and extends out a few inches. This can last 10-15 minutes.

The back of the person receiving the frictions should be maintained curved. Place a thick pillow under his abdomen in order for the penetration to be more efficient. After the massage apply the clay, being careful to remove all traces of the remaining oil.

Wearing a corset should be reserved for serious cases when the spine cannot maintain itself by its own strength. In the other cases avoid it, for any mechanical means to help the spine often leads to the atrophy of the muscles.

If, previous to the start of a natural treatment, a corset had been adopted, be careful to remove it only in periods when there is not much effort to be made. These removals should be prolonged until the corset becomes no longer necessary.

In one case, a patient with an affliction in the vertebral column had been wearing a strong lombo-state (dorsal corset) grasping the whole chest. He had previously submitted himself to numerous treatments (graft, immobilization on a table, plaster mold, etc.), but improvement was delayed due to continuous appearances of abscesses in the armpits. The abscesses rapidly disappeared under clay treatment by oral route and poultices were then applied on the vertebral column. After four months of treatment the patient began to discard the corset for one hour every day. At the end of the seventh month, the corset was abandoned completely and the 'ex-patient' recommenced his activities as a farmer.

Sometimes an imbalance of the pelvis accompanying a malformation of the spine is compensated for by wearing an extra heel in one of the shoes. This is not recommended except for some cases - for it is putting oneself in an abnormal situation. If the wearing of the extra piece of leather is judged unavoidable, nevertheless it should be considered as temporary.

Sleeping on something hard is not recommended either, for it presupposes that the person will always remain on his back. The hard surface will cause the patient to experience some troubles in trying to sleep, pain in the body and other discomfort. Perhaps a plank can be put under the mattress; but we prefer a firm mattress to anything else, flexible enough to adjust to the forms of the body.

Some doctors advise sleeping without a pillow at all. Here again we do not agree, unless lying down on the back or on the stomach. Sleeping on the side is preferable, for it helps relax the muscles, using of course a pillow neither too flat nor too thick.

Very often a discal hernia is accompanied by a sciatica; in this case, add hot foot baths to the clay poultices:

> Boil 1 gallon of water together with 3 handfuls of wheat bran and 2 handfuls of walnut-tree leaves.

A cold hip bath calms a sciatic attack, however, the cure will not be effective if the lumbar region is not taken care of properly.

The cervical part of the spine is often the seat of an arthrosis which can end up in a blockage of the vertebrae in that area and cause persisting violent headaches. In such a case clay poultices should be regularly applied on the back of the neck until the troubles disappear. Camphor oil and garlic (2:1) massages are also indicated for this.

The person should not move much during a crisis; he should above all stay away from lifting up any weight. However, it is important to remember that ankylosis may occur if there is no movement at all. To prevent such a thing exercise should be done with the help of another person. The patient should lie down and a friend should gently pull his hands until he brings him to a sitting position; he will then help him to rotate his body to the right and left side.

When improvement is shown, try to climb a ladder using the arms only. This will fortify the muscles. Eventually fortify other muscles by carrying some weight on the head.

All these external treatments can be administered and will give good results as long as a proper type of eating accompanies them.

DECALCIFICATION OF THE SPINE

There is only one sort of calcium that can be absorbed by the organism and that is the calcium that exists naturally in food where it is in combination with other elements!

Everyone acknowledges the fact that excretions contain more calcium at the time of a cure containing calcium in medicinal form. The organism recognizes a period of stimulation because of the effort it needs to make to get rid of the non-physiological calcium. This period of euphoria is afterwards followed by an aggravated condition of depression. The habit of getting rid of calcium is so well learnt by the organism that it automatically rids itself of the calcium which is part of the constitution of its reserves.

It is remarkable that in diseased tissues, whether it be of tuberculous lungs, an artery with arteriosclerosis or an injured intestine, two symptoms are always found: a deficiency in silica and an excess of calcium, the excess calcium being brought about by an exaggerated intake.

Before searching for the cause of silica deficiency it is important to keep in mind that excess and deficiency always come together, one leading inevitably to the other. The increase of food substances leads to the overworking of the organism which should elaborate these substances. From this comes a slowing down of the functions of assimilation and fixation. Therefore it is impossible to declare that the condition is *only* plethoric (elements in excess) or *only* deficient. These afflictions always occur because of demineralization. However, it is erroneous to speak only of 'decalcification' or even of 'demineralization', for it is not only mineral salts that are missing but also enzymes, ferments, and vitamins.

The Italian professors Rossi and Gremoncini published a report in which they bring the proof of the efficiency of citric acid in the re-calcification process. A natural element, lemon contributes at the same time to the dissolution of the calcic, oxalic and other concretions and to the utilization of calcium and phosphorus. Associating citric acid, phosphorus, calcium and Vitamin D, Rossi and Gremoncini brought about several remarkable results, especially among infants.

These two professors observed that citric acid, which is present in all the tissues, is the essential element of mineralization. It ameliorates a rachitic condition by activating the calcification process of the cartilages. Its actions also reinforce the proliferations of the proteinic complex in which calcification takes place. Just by adding citric acid to the diet Rossi and Gremoncini obtained regular increase in weight in the infants. This is justified by the fact that calcium, when in the presence of citric acid, does not combine with the fatty acids present in the digestive tube and therefore is more easily absorbed.

It is thus a great error which is committed when it is asserted that the phytic acid in whole wheat bread opposes the good use of calcium. Proof is that in children following the natural rules of living and eating complete cereals, no signs of decalcification are shown; it is the other children who are saturated with white bread, sweets and other unnatural food who suffer from this disease.

Only food of the vegetable kingdom and cheese, eggs, and honey favor calcification because they are acceptable and usable by the organism. Virgin olive oil and greens bring in the elements which are necessary for the production of the D vitamins, which are gained from sunbaths and from the transformation of sterols. Exposure to the sun allows a rational use of cholesterol, which becomes dangerous only when there is no exposure to the sun or when there is a deficiency of silica.

In order to help recalcification - especially for those who are new to the natural harmonist way of life - vegetable juices (mostly cabbage, turnip, carrot) are greatly useful because of their richness in living elements (ferments, vitamins). To this add lemon and a few grated almonds so that the citric acid and phosphorus combine with the calcium of the vegetables used. To this a few green leaves (cabbage or lettuce), which have been liquified in a blender, may be added.

Unrefined cereals should be given every day in all forms - sprouted wheat especially, as it accelerates recalcification.

Since this suffering represents years of malnutrition and incorrect eating, it would be proper before doing anything else to start by draining and stimulating the organism.

For that purpose take clay (1 teaspoon in ½ a glass of water) every day, on an empty stomach, or before one of the meals. It can be alternated with fenugreek, one week clay, the next week fenugreek and so on. To prepare fenugreek, see above.

Also take the infusion on p.55, which is good for the liver and gall bladder.

The following is part of the basic treatment: short cold hip baths, clay poultices or cabbage leaves on the liver.

Any painful or injured part, (such as the spine, for example) should be treated with overnight clay applications; do this for weeks if necessary.

A significant decrease in the calcium content of the blood may cause troubles of the nervous system(depression, insomnia, neurasthenia, etc.). In order to obtain rapid stimulation, prepare the egg-lemon juice mixture, p.113. Twice a week, break the egg in the morning, mix it with the juice and drink everything.

Since there are few people who do not exhibit some sign of decalcification, however small, it would be beneficial to all to experiment with these methods.

****

DISLOCATED VERTEBRAE

Clay treatment succeeded in correcting dislocated cervical vertebrae of one patient. She can now turn her head from right to left easily and periodical trips to the doctor to put them in place are no longer necessary.

****

GETTING RID OF PAIN

Treating Rheumatism and Arthritis

Among widely varying manifestations such as hay fever and hemorrhoids, or stiff neck and cellulite, is found an identical origin, an abnormal rate of increase of blood density due to the retention of metabolic wastes and many other toxic substances such as urea, uric acid, cholesterol, acetone, ammonia, and phosphates and residues of cellular activity such as oxalic acid, and lactic acid.

This predominance of acidic wastes is understandable, on one hand because of the transformation of nitrogenous excesses coming from food into acids, and on the other hand because of acidic residues of the muscular activity. To this add acids coming directly from food, alcohol and coffee, for example.

The invasion by uric acid and other toxins is often revealed before the appearance of the related troubles by a procession of small spots in the eye, resembling snowflakes.

Perturbation of the digestive flora is equally important in arthritic manifestations. There are some types of intestinal bacteria which destroy significant quantities of uric acid. Serious danger arises when this is not accomplished. Most of the medicaments prescribed for arthritic conditions only bring more trouble to the intestinal flora,

creating a weakening of the functions of defense. The famous classical remedy for rheumatism, salicylate of soda, prevents the reproduction of bacteria, including the bacteria that take care of uric acid.

Recent remedies, such as cortisone and its derivatives exercise the same disastrous influence on the intestinal flora, plus many additional harmful effects in other directions.

THE PAIN

Rheumatic and arthritic pains are so painful mostly because of the muscular contraction created by the local asphyxia of the tissues; the circulation being considerably slowed down. This slowing down comes from an overcharge of the blood and from some nervous inhibitions of toxic origin. The result is poor blood and lack of oxygen in the tissues; that is why revulsions, massages and frictions are sometimes very helpful; they activate the circulation by channeling the wastes toward the proper exits.

An over-exposure to cold may sometimes be at the origin of a rheumatic attack, as it can lead to

obstruction of the capillaries, and consequently the reduction of the speed of the metabolism. Spasms may also occur because of a slowing down of the circulation, thus a reduction of nutrition.

Cramps may also be caused by an accumulation of toxins from the muscle tissues. These toxins are the real cause of stiffness in the back after exertion. Someone eating properly does not experience these pains, even after intensive work.

A UNIQUE DISEASE

Arthritis is mostly an inflammatory affliction of the joints. The synovial lesions reach the cartilages, then the bones, and may eventually end up in deformation or ankylosis.

It may happen in the case of synovial inflammation that liquid accumulates in the articular cavity and dilates the serous membrane, which creates a swelling. At this moment one can distinctly feel the serous membrane being pushed forward because of this overflow. This overflow may mix with blood when there is a fracture in the knee-cap.

A diminution of synovial secretions creates pains and cracking in what is called *dry arthritis*.

Arthritis may take a tuberculous form which can be localized either in the articular extremities or on the synovial membrane. That is precisely when great pain starts, followed by limping, and eventually limitation of certain movements and deformation of the pelvic bones. Suppuration occurs generally at the hollow of the groin. This cold abscess causes the destruction of the femur's head which becomes dislocated.

When localized in the knee the tuberculous arthritis forms the 'white tumor;' when localized in the spine it forms what is called *Pott's disease.*

Recent scientific discoveries have revealed that for latent virus embryos in the cells to become actively virulent there must be stimulation from endogenous or exogenous agents; this can occur only when body defenses are weak and toxic bodies are present.

The trouble may have come about as a result of an imbalance in the intestinal flora, of which many important varieties are easily destroyed by foreign substances, including antibiotics and antiseptics as well as the chemicals in certain commercially available foods.

Arthrosis is mostly a manifestation of degeneracy affecting the same areas as arthritis; while arthritis may affect very young people, arthrosis usually happens to people over forty. It is characterized by the degeneracy of the cartilage, which ends up with the premature wearing of the bone extremities.

The name *rheumatism* generally refers to the acute manifestations of arthritis and arthrosis. It is commonly believed that a virus is the origin of rheumatism attacks. Or else, the toxins may come from a fault in the transformation of proteins and as they are not eliminated by the neutralizing agents which are normally present in the bacterial flora, they find good ground to thrive and spread in these weak areas.

The digestion process may sometimes create fermentations of secondary order, which are necessary for the transformation of nutritive elements. These secondary fermentations occur when food is unnatural or when deficient liver functions do not allow the proper transformation of products of digestion. Poisons may result from this, even if the food is of a healthy nature; *excess eating is not only useless but dangerous, for it brings too great an amount of amino acids and substances of proteic nature into the blood.*
What is to be done?

It is of primary importance to stay away from any food that generates acids or contains acidifying poisons. Meat, alcohol and alkaloids must be banished without delay. Continuing to eat harmful food may have the most terrible consequences. Having caused the inflammation of the joints and their neighboring parts (sometimes lesions of the bones, cartilages, muscles) the crystals of sodium urate, uric or oxalic acid are going to attack next the kidneys and cause a nephritis with lesions or kidney stones.

The accumulation of these toxic substances can lessen the normal elimination process of the kidney, do harm to the permeability of its filter, and end in albuminuria and other troubles.

Because of the presence of oxalic acid in the residues of muscular actions and the degradation of some nutritive elements it is sometimes advised to stay away from this acid. There is a vast difference between vegetal acid and mineral acid; the former is assimilable and keeps in balance with its alkaline counterpart while the latter is unassimilable and therefore should be eliminated immediately.

Given that muscles' movements lead to the production of lactic acid, there is the problem of whether buttermilk or yoghurt can be used. Here, it is important to know how to differentiate between the *new* lactic acid, of buttermilk and yoghurt, and the *used* lactic acid. Besides, buttermilk and yoghurt help maintain a normal intestinal flora; they include the bacteria which secure the neutralization of purine. In virtue of this fact, these two are of value. However, *the rest of the food should be of a vegetarian nature,* otherwise eating buttermilk and yoghurt might increase the danger of acidifying the humors.

The salubrity of the intestines demands the presence of natural sulphur; only then can poisons resulting from the digestion of proteins be neutralized. It takes a long while before these poisons disappear completely, even with intensive care and a good vegetarian diet. It all depends on whether the liver functions have become normal or not. That is why it is wise to stress garlic, onion and cabbage, as will be seen later. There is no manifestation of obstruction without demineralization. This is easy to understand once aware of the fact that *elimination precedes assimilation.* If the elimination is imperfect, which is the case in arthritis, the assimilation will also be imperfect. It suffices to accelerate elimination in order to have the remineralization process take place in the best conditions. This remineralization will be favored by eating raw food (fruit and vegetables) and cereals (sprouted wheat, whole wheat bread, hulled barley, brown rice, couscous, millet, oats, rye, buckwheat). Cures of vegetable juices (carrot, cabbage, turnip, etc.) allow the easy absorption of elements good for the reconstitution of the organism.

The presence of toxic bodies in certain foods renders them particularly dangerous for arthritic people, not only because of the near obstructions they create, but also because of the waste of the mineral substances they cause. For example, in order to be neutralized, indol, one of the products of degradation of the animal cell, requires all the available sulphur that could be found in the organism. Considering the importance of sulphur in the fixation of calcium, it is immediately clear that its use for sanitation ends is catastrophic for nutrition in general and for calcification in particular.

Prescribing medication containing sulphur only adds to the efforts. To try to make up for deficiencies by stuffing in excesses is to commit a most dangerous mistake. A fatigued organism has to be gently and lightly nourished at first. It is only through these means that it is possible to envisage a lasting re-establishment of health.

NATURAL TREATMENTS FOR RHEUMATISMS AND ARTHRITIS

Chronic Rheumatism

The presence of toxic substances around the joints causes the obstruction of the capillaries, leading to an accumulation of residues of metabolic wastes which hinder the entrance of new elements such as food and oxygen. The result is an inflammatory condition, then lesions of the cartilage and later of the bone and neighboring parts. A fibrous tissue will replace the destroyed cartilage. This modification of the surfaces of the joints limits the movements. The limited motion, the thickening and hypertrophy of the synovial pocket, with an increase of the secreted liquid creates a strain in the joints where this liquid is.

When touched by the inflammation, the ligaments do not maintain parts in their correct place, and they themselves may easily come out of place. The tendons may calcify, harden and lose their flexibility. With acute rheumatism, this is the risk of having the bones soldered together. Or else, knobs may appear on the tendon of a finger.

All forms of arthritis or rheumatism have this in common, they always manifest themselves by a constriction, which is in part responsible for the pain. That is why it is sometimes necessary to use fomentations. It is very simple:

Plunge a towel in very hot water, almost boiling, squeeze it a bit so that the water does not run out and apply it folded in four or eight on the painful area. The hotter it is, the better. Renew every 2 or 3 minutes, using 2 towels, alternately, for 20-30 minutes. These applications soothe the pain by inducing relaxation.

In addition to a strict reform of eating habits, the treatment in depth must include use of an appropriate mixture of plants to cleanse the liver (p. 55), and a cure with the sapwood of the wild lime-tree:

Put 1 handful in a quart of water; boil down to ¾ its volume; drink it all in 1 or 2 days, during crisis, and again when desired over the next 10 days. It can be repeated for another 10 days in following months.

Clay poultices, an efficient and irreplaceable remedy, should be applied on the affected areas. In acute crisis with fever, when joints are inflamed or congested, relieve them by applying large poultices of cold clay. On the other hand, chronic states need frequent hot applications. There are no general rules; simply begin by testing with treatment of cold clay and heating them later if they do not become hot or become in any way disagreeable after application. It is necessary to apply clay directly onto the painful parts. Each application may be left on for 2-4 hours; however, the poultices should be most often applied before going to bed and left in place overnight. In normal treatment, a daily poultice is sufficient. Cover with a thick material to protect against cooling and maintain firmly in place with a good bandage.

In the rare cases when clay is not tolerated, producing sensations of cold or nervousness, replace the applications by a cabbage poultice:

Break the raw cabbage leaf spines with a rolling pin. After having crushed the large cabbage leaves, heat them by dipping them in boiling water (with pot removed from the fire) for 1 or 2 minutes and then draining them, or else by exposing the leaves to a source of heat (frying pan, stove, radiator, etc.). While still hot, apply a layer of three leaves on the affected area. Cover with a piece of woolen cloth to retain heat and bandage. Leave on a few hours or overnight.

Complete with massages with camphor oil and grated garlic (2:1) or equal parts of clay mud and garlic.

Thyme baths can also be used for the treatment of rheumatism, gout, arthritis, nervous or general weakness. For a complete bath of 15 minutes:

Boil 1 pound of thyme in 2 quarts of water and add it to the hot bath water. For local baths (foot, hand) or local dressing, boil a handful of thyme in a gallon or so of water for 10 minutes.

Thyme poultices may be used for rheumatic pains, crooked neck, lumbago, etc. Crush thyme, boil it dry in any container, put it in muslin or gauze and apply directly while hot. Crushed thyme, mixed with wheat bran and a little water and then well heated, makes a very active poultice.

Increase the elimination through the kidneys by applying a poultice of wheat bran-ivy or bran-cabbage-onion on them.

Chronic Polyarthritis

This is one of the most serious and dramatic

forms of rheumatism. Not only is it at the origin of extreme pain, but it develops gradually towards bone deformation and fusion and stiffening of the joints. Women are more frequently afflicted than men, and mostly after menopause (in 90% of the cases.). Even children are not spared.

A chronic disease, polyarthritis also manifests itself by acute attacks in the joints, such as the fingers, for example. These pains are more acute in the morning than at night. The person feels very tired, plagued with a stiff back - his complexion is pale, his temperature above normal. The painful joints are swollen. Sometimes the swelling in the joints is preceded by an eruption of psoriasis.

After the attack, the swelling is reduced, but the joints are stiffer; that is when the muscular atrophy begins, accompanied by the emaciation of the limbs. Other articulations may in turn be touched, wrists, the area around the ankle, elbows, knees.

The fingers curve in towards the opposite side of the thumb; they remain half-bent, extension impossible. Even the toes are affected and deformed.

The acute attacks demonstrate that the organism is desperately trying to get rid of toxic and residual substances that have gathered around the joints. Sometimes the obstruction is so great that the energetic reserves of the organism cannot succeed in elimination. There is a decrease of the solid bodies normally eliminated through the urine: urea, uric and oxalic acid, phosphates.

In the case of poly-arthritis these harmful substances injure bones, cartilages, tissues, nerves, vessels and muscular insertions.

The Cure

The only way to drain these harmful substances is to stimulate the liver. This in itself will secure the transformation and distribution of the nutritive elements in food. Food of course will be carefully chosen; no acidifying agents should be taken, such as meat, alcohol and alkaloids.

Take the active decoction on p. 55 for the congestion of the liver functions.

Treatment will include clay taken orally, cold hip baths, foot and hand baths in red-grape vine leaf solution, clay poultices on the lower abdomen, and sunbaths in the summer or in warm climates.

For local treatment begin with clay applications

on the most affected joint (the poultice can be kept on for 2-3 hours or overnight). Cabbage leaves crushed with a rolling pin should also be applied. The two may be alternated. Frictions with a mixture of olive oil and grated garlic (2:1) may be given on very sore areas.

In certain cases, it will be necessary to apply the following remedy:

Chip some cloves of garlic, and apply them directly on the skin; some hours later, a water sac will be formed which will burst. Remove the poultice and replace it with another of clay.

To accelerate the evacuations at the level of the kidneys, apply a hot wheat bran-ivy poultice.

Make sure that the intestines function normally. If need be, stimulate them with an appropriate decoction of senna, buckthorn, or cassia, etc. See also the laxative decoctions in the section on constipation .

Arthritis of the Hip

Cavities and nodes result from a defective metabolism and the accumulation of waste and other toxic substances. The end of the femur (thigh bone) is deformed or crushed, sometimes even completely destroyed. Often there is such bone growth in the cavity receiving the femur's head that the bone is pushed out.

The length of the cure depends on how serious the injury is. Improvement is always possible, even in the most serious cases, especially if the patient keeps rested.

The Cure

Here, too, the liver plays a great part; for the transformation of food and the synthesis and neutralization of wastes and toxins will all be taken care of if this organ is functioning well. Being a regulator of the hormonal secretions, the liver will re-establish the endocrinian equilibrium which had been perturbed by arthritis and rheumatism.

Clay applications should be as frequent as possible. The poultices should be one inch thick and wide, covering the whole hip. Bandage and leave in place for 3-4 hours or overnight. A cold poultice is best; however, if it is not tolerated, use it slightly lukewarm; simply put it over a pot or anything hot. . Apply one poultice a day. As was previously mentioned, when it comes to serious cases, the patient will have to remain in bed. However, immobility may lead to ankylosis. In order to avoid this, the patient should move his leg(s) several times a day, with another person's help if necessary. Various movements, such as pedaling, should be done gently.

These activities should go on throughout the treatment, however, frequent periods of rest in bed should alternate with any kind of activity, standing or lying down. If no progress at all has been made after 3 or 4 months of treatment, this means the injury is quite serious and for the time being only rest will help -- in combination with the right kind of food, of course.

Rheumatism of the Spine

There are many young people, barely thirty, suffering from a prenatural hardening of their spine.

Many forms of rheumatism affect the spine, but there are two that are particularly serious: the spondylarthritis and deforming rheumatism of the spine. Spondylarthritis is an important change of the bone tissue because of demineralization and residual calcification occurring at the same time. In short, it is a sclerosis of the bone, preceding necrosis, which takes place after the aggravation of the condition.

The pains are intermittent, but sharp, mostly at night; they irradiate throughout the neck, shoulders and thighs. After each attack some after-effects remain, consisting in the loss of flexibility of the spine, with progressive limitation of movement. Eventually, pains diminish and give way to ankylosis. The whole spine may be frozen, because now the vertebrae are soldered one to another -- this happens when there is no more cartilage between the vertebrae. The patient cannot bend down or even turn his head if the vertebrae of his neck are touched by ankylosis.

The situation is no better with the deforming rheumatism of the spine. This results from compressed vertebrae and worn-out cartilage. The vertebrae themselves take the form of a parrot's beak. The lumbar and cervical vertebrae may be particularly touched.

The treatment is the same as for chronic polyarthritis, applying clay to the affected areas of the spine. The whole body should be exposed to sunlight (See also the chapter on the spine).

Cervico-brachial Neuralgia

Arthritis of the shoulder may create complications. Pain coming from the back of the neck and irradiating toward the shoulder reaches even the arms and the fingers. If the situation is not taken care of in time, lesions develop in the nerves themselves. The pains are very sharp and even sharper when at rest. Sometimes the limbs are atrophied.

The treatment in depth is the one used for arthritis in general. However, the sharp pains are not always easy to deal with. The cabbage applications may be added to the clay poultices, and also frictions with camphor oil, bran-cabbage-onion poultices. Fomentations give the best results for immediate sedation of the pain. See p.105.

Once the pain has gone, continue daily clay applications on the shoulder and the neck, alternately, for several weeks.

Lumbago

Added to the initial cause, which is any of the forms of arthritis, is a second cause: displacement of the vertebrae, a forming of a fibrous layer and inflammation of the muscles, tendons and nerves.

The pain of lumbago is extremely sharp, a simple small movement may start it off, even though subsequent movements remain inconsequential. The person finds it urgent to lie down, remaining motionless. If he cannot lie down, he will search for the best position to relax himself, such as sitting astride a chair, arms resting on the back of the chair.

The return to normal condition may take time; for the torn ligaments must heal. It would be wise to prolong the clay applications for it may be that the lumbago is caused by a compressing of the disc which is placed between the 4th and 5th lumbar vertebrae or by chronic rheumatism of the spine.

Sciatica

Sometimes it may be just a simple irritation of a nerve by accumulated toxins in that area which creates the all-too-common neuralgic sciatica. The situation becomes more serious when these toxins cause more damage in that region, creating serious lesions. In many cases of sciatica, irritation was started by causes directly localized in the spine duct at the beginning of the sciatic nerve. This may be a tumor or disease of the bone tissue, but it is most often a rheumatism or a hernia of the disc placed between the 4th and 5th vertebrae. In any case the nerve is evidently 'pinched' at its beginning, the painful point being situated far away from the real seat of the affliction. All sorts of direct actions on the spine will sometimes bring a release; a corset might help somewhat, but only as a palliative. Even putting the disc in place through surgery or with a stretching exercise will probably not have a permanent effect. The obvious cure lies in correcting the cause of the abnormal situation.

The Cure

Whatever is the origin of sciatica, the treatment is the same. The patient, even if he is ready and willing to go along with the treatment in depth, still aspires above all to have his pains sedated. In order to accomplish this, it would be wise to give massages, baths, fomentations, fumigations. Massage the painful area with a mixture of garlic and camphor oil (2:1). Apply hot poultices of wheat bran-climbing ivy or give foot baths and hot compresses on the legs using 2 or 3 handfuls of these leaves. Hot compresses may also be used prepared with a decoction of wild marjoram; fumigations (steam-bathing specific areas) with a mixture of thyme, mint, verbena and woodruff are also excellent pain-relievers:

> Use 2 oz. of each plant for 2-3 quarts of water. Boil everything 10-15 minutes. Expose the painful part to steam as long as possible, being careful to cover the area touched by the steam with a thick material.
> Sometimes raw cabbage leaves do a good job, when maintained in place several hours.

Drink infusion of chamomile and meadowsweet.
Clay poultices should be applied on the painful area; with these as a complement to the previously mentioned practices, it is possible to cure a bad neuralgic sciatica. However, for a real guarantee, it would be necessary to follow a *genuine total treatment* which involves a complete change in one's way of eating.
Take clay orally (1 teaspoon in ½ a glass of water). Eat fresh fruits and especially lemons in the form of juice mixed with water.
Do not hesitate to take cold hip baths. The pains will calm down and toxins will discharge. If

the cold water seems imposing, warm up the part of the body to be immersed beforehand, massage it energetically after immersion and then cover it immediately with warm blankets. While it might seem that heat is most suited for this purpose, it is with cold baths and cold clay applications that the best results are obtained. Nevertheless, if it cannot be tolerated, slightly heat up the water to a tolerable temperature. In the same manner, clay may also be slightly heated up. The poultice should be placed on the most painful area or on the base of the spine. If the poultice becomes cold or if the treated part does not warm up, then heat the clay in a double boiler.

In case of weakenings of the vertebrae apply clay daily for several months on the lumbar region. The poultice should be left in place overnight, and the treatment completed by cold hip baths and massages with camphor oil and garlic. Gradually start doing a few physical exercises which are good for fortifying the ligaments and tendons of the weak area. Proceed gently. For example, see the exercises in the chapter on constipation.

Dupuytren Disease

This is recognized by the shrinking of the fibrous layer of the palm. The hand and fingers are shriveled and give the impression of a claw. Soon it becomes impossible to stretch out the fingers.

To the basic natural treatment add clay poultices on the wrist, massages with camphor oil and grated garlic (2:1); bathe the forearm in hot water or a decoction of wheat bran and walnut tree leaves (2 handfuls of each; boil 10-15 minutes in 2-3 quarts of water).

Gout

Gout attack occurs when there is an excessive amount of crystals in the synovial liquid and on the surface of the cartilage. Sharp pains are experienced together with inflammation of the neighboring tissues.

The increase of uric acid is considerable. A person suffering from gout has 10-15 times more uric acid in his blood than normal.

Polyarthritis is more frequent in women, while gout more often afflicts men. Women who happen to have it are usually those who underwent a surgical removal of their female organs.

It is remarkable how a gout attack starts with the same symptoms as that of a liver attack: furred tongue, nausea, vomiting, constipation occurring alternately with diarrhea, hemorrhoids, aerophagia, depressed state and bloody urine. Also breathlessness, cramps, and swelling in the touched areas.

After that, though, there is a sudden attack with violent pain in the toe. The person experiences chills, slight elevation of temperature, swelling and red coloration of the joints, accentuation of breathlessness and palpitations.

Joints other than the toe may be touched. Gout rheumatism affects all the joints while visceral gout affects all body organs.

Gout differentiates itself from other rheumatic attacks mostly by the dilation of the veins - probably caused by excess waste in the blood - and by the sensitivity of the whole epidermis.

If gout is not taken care of in time, nephritis, albuminuria, hypertension, and urea follow.

Although the local manifestations differ somewhat, the origin of rheumatic and arthritic attacks is almost the same in all cases; that is why the treatment must be the same.

To activate the elimination of the residuary substances in the blood, proceed to a cleansing of the kidneys with the following decoction:

Decoction for Arteriosclerosis

Meadowsweet	30 gr.	Rest harrow root	15 gr.
Bearberry	25 gr.	Shepherd's purse	15 gr.
Couch-grass root	25 gr.	Stinging nettle	15 gr.
Eryngium	15 gr.	Cherry stems	10 gr.
Heath flowers	15 gr.		

Put 2 full tablespoons of this mixture in a quart of water. Bring to a boil; let simmer 2 minutes and infuse for 20 minutes. Drink when desired.

Do not forget the helpful cold clay poultices which calm great pains. Apply them one after the other on the affected area, if necessary, each one remaining in place for 2-3 hours.

Acute Rheumatism of the Joints

This is first manifested by a stiffness in the back and limbs, chills and even shivering, and an agitated sleep. When the person wakes up, fever and feelings

* *

RHEUMATISM OF THE HIP

Thanks to clay, one patient was given an alternative to surgery of the hips, already envisaged by the rheumatologist. He was 37 at the first attack. The doctors could not understand that he could be struck with this arthrosis at his young age, but they did not propose any treatment. All he could do was wait while the disease took greater proportions and approached the stage of surgery. Then he heard of clay and other natural remedies. The clay poultices were applied every night.

Thirty months later, when he had not been suffering for a long time already, he returned for an X-ray. The results were such that the doctors, instead of becoming interested in his treatment, doubted the worth of the X-rays and all the previous examinations as well!

* *

****

DISCAL HERNIA

Mr. J. was suffering from sciatica so painful that he could barely get up. He consulted an acupuncturist and two osteopaths, who said surgery was necessary.

He decided to apply clay, two poultices a day, and one at night. He also took cold hip baths, lemon and clay orally and a recalcifying decoction. He did this for two months, very steadily.

By the third month, there was marked steady improvement and after this the condition became normal. Nevertheless, he kept continuing the treatment on a slower pace for some time to ensure the cure.

****

of numbness are experienced. The throat is red and painful (sore throat is a manifestation of rheumatism), the tonsils are swollen; the inflammation reaches the palate; the swallowing, even of saliva is difficult.

The person experiences sharp pains in the joints (knees, wrists, ankles and shoulders) during certain periods. All movement becomes impossible - sometimes the person cannot tolerate any clothes, not even a shirt or sheets on his skin, which is red, shiny and very warm. The person perspires and his urine is rare and colored.

The attacks may last 4-8 days, sometimes even more, coming back frequently.

The cardiac complications are *endocarditis* with lesions of the mitral and aortic valves (the blood can flow back); *pericarditis*, which is an inflammation of the external envelope of the heart, accompanied by a great difficulty in breathing and a slowing down of the cardiac flow; and *myocarditis*, where the cardiac muscle is injured by rheumatism; it is the most serious of all the complications and can be fatal.

The Treatment

Any kind of solid food is inopportune due to the feverish state. The least amount of food will become poison on account of the perturbation in the production of ferments. On the other hand, it is advisable to drink a good deal. Although some think it proper to stay away from liquids, fearing edema due to obstruction of the kidneys, this is not correct; it is better to give liquids in order to 'wash' the blood and liver. Give water with a strong concentration of lemon juice in it (up to 6, 8, or even 10 lemons a day), water with grated garlic (prepare in the evening by putting 4 or 5 garlic cloves in a glass of water; strain and drink in the morning on an empty stomach), the following decoction may be taken with or between meals for stimulating the liver, sustaining the heart and activating the circulation:

Decoction for the Heart and Circulation

Red-grape vine		Goosegrass	15 gr.
leaves	25 gr.	Germander	10 gr.
Mistletoe	20 gr.	Hawthorn	10 gr.
Shepherd's purse	20 gr.	Woodruff	5 gr.
Barberry bark	15 gr.	Dandelion	15 gr.

Put 5 tablespoons of the mixture in a quart of water. Bring to a boil and let simmer gently 2 or 3 minutes. Let infuse 15 mintues, or, even better, let macerate overnight. Drink when desired with or without honey.

Alternate this decoction with an infusion of meadowsweet - 1 tablespoon per cup of boiling water; infuse 10 minutes.

The clay poultices should be long and thick (1") and remain in place approximately two hours. Renew them as often as possible, applying them, for example, on the lower abdomen first, then on the joints, the liver, again on the joints, and again on the lower abdomen, etc.

Give a cold hip bath between clay applications, if it is well-tolerated. Remain in the water for 3-5 minutes. One should not experience chills while taking the bath; if you do, stop the bath, and instead, apply three layers of cabbage leaves.

For a precaution, massage the chest gently - especially the left side of the thorax - with oil of camphor. If pains are felt in the heart area, prepare a bran-climbing ivy poultice (p. 64) and apply very hot; first on the left part of the thorax and then on the whole chest.

If there is not enough urine, act on the kidneys by applying the same poultice there, however, the ivy leaves may be replaced by two cabbage leaves and two chopped onions.

In order to release the heart and activate circulation add foot and hand baths to the treatment:

> Put 2 or 3 handfuls of red-grape vine leaves in a gallon of water, bring to a boil and let simmer 15 minutes. The bath should be as hot as possible and last 15-20 minutes, adding some hot water periodically to keep a constant temperature.

These baths should be given if the patient can get up, otherwise hand baths will do for the moment.

Make sure that the patient has regular bowel movements; if he is constipated, do not hesitate to give him an enema (1 quart of lukewarm water and 1 tablespoon of sea salt) and a decoction of buckthorn (1 tablespoon in a cup of water).

Pyorrhea: Arthritis of the Gums

When arthritis affects the gums it creates what is commonly known as *pyorrhea,* where the teeth loosen in their sockets. Because of this shaking, food particles penetrate between root and gum, creating a state of inflammation and putrefaction which allows harmful germs to proliferate.

Teeth that are too loose can seldom be saved; however, before having them pulled out, it would be worthwhile to try to improve the situation with some special measures.

Twice a week, clay (in powdered form) should be used as a toothpaste*, while the other days of the week, use either salt-water or lemon-water. Dry thyme, ground or powdered, can also be mixed with clay powder. A person following the harmonist method does not use a chemical toothpaste, which by itself is an open door to perturbating agents, for it neutralizes the saliva's ferments.

A tooth brush should be used which is neither too hard nor too soft. Brush the gums vigorously, vertically. Never brush across, but use an up-and-down movement for the upper row and the contrary for the lower row. Brush the inside surface of the teeth as well as the outside, giving the latter more attention. Do not fear causing the gums to bleed. After brushing the teeth, massage the gums with the thumbs, in an upward movement for the lower jaw and a downward movement for the upper jaw. This massage,
1) brings back the flesh on the teeth
2) gets rid of food wastes which may have penetrated the gums and the root
3) frees the gums from the infectious products of putrefaction
4) firms the tissues.

This should be done once, twice, even three times a day, depending on the seriousness of the condition. To that one should add mouth baths with salted water (sea salt, 1 teaspoon in a glass of water). Suck small pieces of clay, especially before going to bed. Of course, no sugar in any form should be taken, such as candies, which help maintain a pathogenic bacterial flora. Stay away from chemical toothpaste which perturbs the protective flora.

If the bitter taste in the mouth is too unpleasant, press some cotton soaked with lavender essence on the gums, or else the clay powder may be mixed with a little bit of dried and ground leaves of mint or anise. In case of extreme pain, such as an abscess, apply the cut part of a fig (that has been cooked a few minutes in some milk) on the gums. Clay poultices may be applied on the cheek and renewed every two hours while the figs, applied hot, should be renewed every hour. The fig may also be left on overnight.

By the way, chopped garlic may be put on a cavity or aching tooth. This does not excuse one from going to the dentist, though.

---

*Clay toothpaste is now available commercially in the U.S.
See Buyer's Guide.

A MOST BASIC TREATMENT

We are not dealing here with an 'exclusive' or 'special' treatment: it is rather a way of life adapted to natural laws. If clay and decoctions will not be taken continuously, they should at least be part of a cure for approximately three weeks, especially in the spring and the autumn. However, before arriving at this stage, do not hesitate to use natural remedies as long as the situation demands it.

Since all arthritic manifestations are of a common origin, the basic treatment also is common to all of them:

In the morning on an empty stomach, alternate:
One week: 1 teaspoon of powdered clay in ½ a glass of water. Prepare the previous night.
One week: 1 teaspoon of olive oil with an equal quantity of lemon juice.

Before the meals: a decoction for the liver
After the meals: The juice of ½ a lemon in a cup of hot water. Add honey if necessary.

Before going to bed: Take a sedative decoction if you are nervous or unable to sleep, or a laxative decoction in case of constipation. Either of the gentle laxative preparations on p. 91 , or the following:

Decoction for Rheumatism

Soapwort	30 gr.	Elder tree leaves	15 gr.
Licorice root	20 gr.	Horsetail	15 gr.
Meadowsweet	20 gr.	Huckleberry leaves	15 gr.
Broom(genista)	15 gr.	Mint	15 gr.

Put a handful of the mixture in a quart of water. Bring to a boil and let infuse until cooling. Drink any time of the day.

As there is always decalcification accompanying arthritis and rheumatism, it would be opportune, after a month of basic treatment, to introduce the egg shell-lemon juice preparation in place of the olive oil-lemon mixture.

Moreover, the decoction for the liver should be replaced by the remineralizing decoction indicated on p.108.

Important note: The reader should refer to the sections on food in 'The Liver' and 'The Elimination Channels' to get a general picture of what he should and should not eat.

THE SUGAR DISEASE

Curing Ourselves of Diabetes

Everyone is a potential diabetic. At any moment of our life, because of improper eating, prolonged fatigue, problems and responsibilities or emotional stress, we can find ourselves in a state of malnutrition, with all the troubles that come from it. That is one way diabetes begins.

There are many forms of diabetes, as there are many forms of other diseases; they are isolated and classified, differentiated with distinct terms and treated accordingly. This is a mistake. Basically, there is one cause and the fundamental treatment should be the same for all the forms, whether it be for the fat, the thin, the sweet, or the nervous person.

It is generally agreed that diabetes occurs when there is an alteration in the pancreas (in the isles of Langerhans, more exactly); although some authorities have pointed out the fact that autopsies on diabetics do not always show abnormalities in the pancreas, this is not significant. It is already known that mental troubles may occur without any anatomic changes in the brain; the same is true with the liver functions, which are often disturbed, although the examination of the liver does not reveal anything abnormal.

Stimulating the pancreatic functions lessens diabetes, so it would seem that the perturbation of these functions is the source of the trouble. Still, the pancreas alone cannot take care of all the carbohydrates; other glands must contribute to this process, starting with the salivary glands and the parathyroids, continuing with the glands present in the mucous membrane of the stomach, the spleen, and of course, the liver and gall bladder.

On the other hand, certain endocrine glands exercise an influence on the biological balance in general and the regulation of glycerine in particular. Thus, the adrenalin, a secretion of the suprarenals, increases the glycemia rate, while the cortex of the same glands contributes to the storage of reserves of glycogen by the production of various substances, including cortisone. The thyroxine emitted by the thyroid also increases the glycemia rate. A disorder of the hypophysis can create secretions which neutralize the insulin coming from the pancreas.

THE DIABETIC CONDITION

Modern medicine relies on analyses to reveal diabetes, mainly by checking for excess glucose in the blood and in the urine. These methods, while quite precise, do not provide for diagnosis of the

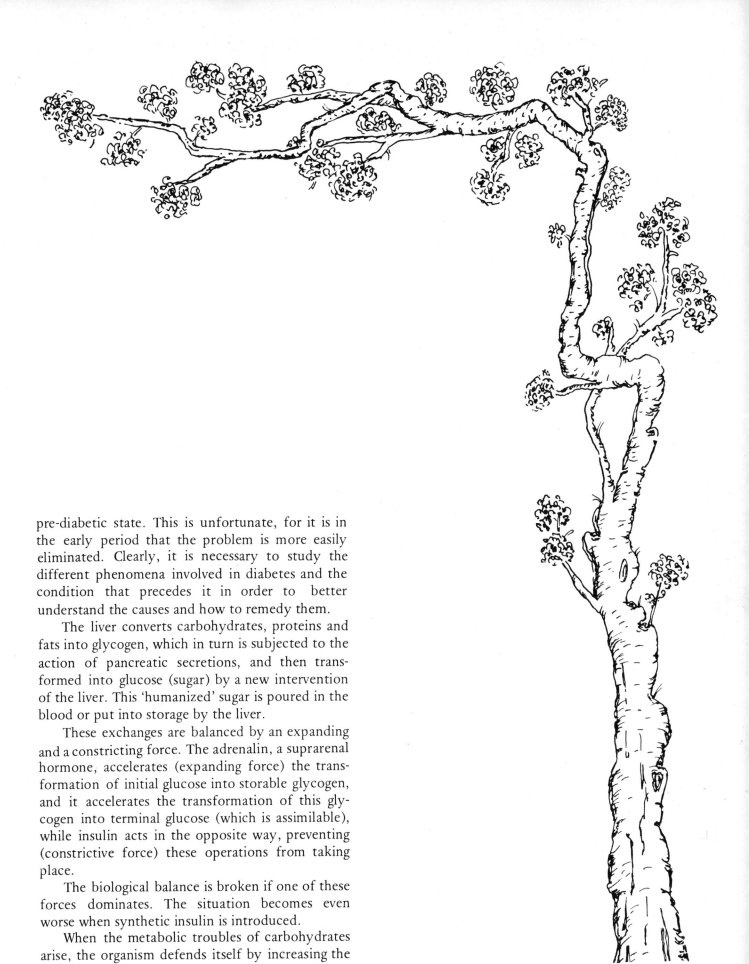

pre-diabetic state. This is unfortunate, for it is in the early period that the problem is more easily eliminated. Clearly, it is necessary to study the different phenomena involved in diabetes and the condition that precedes it in order to better understand the causes and how to remedy them.

The liver converts carbohydrates, proteins and fats into glycogen, which in turn is subjected to the action of pancreatic secretions, and then transformed into glucose (sugar) by a new intervention of the liver. This 'humanized' sugar is poured in the blood or put into storage by the liver.

These exchanges are balanced by an expanding and a constricting force. The adrenalin, a suprarenal hormone, accelerates (expanding force) the transformation of initial glucose into storable glycogen, and it accelerates the transformation of this glycogen into terminal glucose (which is assimilable), while insulin acts in the opposite way, preventing (constrictive force) these operations from taking place.

The biological balance is broken if one of these forces dominates. The situation becomes even worse when synthetic insulin is introduced.

When the metabolic troubles of carbohydrates arise, the organism defends itself by increasing the glucose content of the blood, which temporarily makes up for the malnutrition of the tissues. However, this excess glucose eventually must break the biological balance, provoking the kidneys to eliminate it in the urine. Thus what actually happens is that there is a heavy loss of carbohydrates provided by food. This phenomenon of the elimination of the excess glucose necessitates the increase of the volume of urine. It may increase from 1½ quarts (in 24 hours) to 3, 4, 5 quarts and even more. The person has a great thirst, while the deficiency in glucose increases appetite excessively. Such troubles as trembling of the hands, fatigue, headaches, depression, pale complexion, feeling of hunger or thirst have already preceded these phenomena. Later on these troubles will amplify and others will arise, such as perspiration or wet hands and forehead, incoherence, loss of consciousness. The appearance of acidic waste (acetone) will give the urine a sharp odor.

If they should persist, the metabolic troubles of the carbohydrates may cause arterial, kidney and retinal lesions. The situation is even more serious with the smoker; in fact, tobacco accentuates the danger of arteritis, and even worse, it can be at the origin of a 'hypoglycemia attack', for tobacco prevents the metabolism of sugars.

With the slackening of the defenses, the kidneys become less able to eliminate the excess glucose from the blood. The accumulation of this glucose in the tissues is in part responsible for the obesity of many diabetics, whose urine is obviously less abundant and thirst less intense.

Obesity often precedes diabetes of the adult, overeating being one of the factors which most favors this imbalance. Fat in excess prevents glucose from being stored or being used for a good purpose. Furthermore, the abundance of fats in food obliges the pancreas to intensify the production of the juices which will break them down, to the detriment of the secretion of other juices and hormones, one of them being insulin.

THE CONSEQUENCES

As he has to make sugar from his own cells (fat, muscle cells, etc.) the patient can suffer loss of weight and muscle atrophy. The extent of this usually depends on the initial conditions.

Furthermore, the increasing need for glucose -

and the efforts made at the same time for its production and elimination, the presence of excess glucose in the tissues, the deficiency resulting from elimination troubles, and the increase of the acid content of the humors all put the organism in a state of lowest resistance. These disorders cause an imbalance in the bacterial flora, of which certain species are going to proliferate, causing such problems as boils, anthraxes, pyorrhea, etc. Not only that, this condition of low resistance and imbalance in the bacterial flora will have already manifested itself by such phenomena as sores and ulcers taking a long time to heal. All the organs and especially the lungs cannot defend themselves properly because of the persistence of this abnormal state.

Acidosis

The organism of a diabetic - like all deficient organisms - cannot satisfy its needs except by having an excessive amount of food. The effort attempted by the organism to transform these food elements into nutritious elements produces large amounts of acid wastes. While the kidney will eliminate part, the remaining excess will obstruct the humors by acidifying them.

This acidosis is characterized by bad breath (acetone odor) together with mental and physical fatigue, dizziness, headaches and anxiety. Although usually a big eater, the diabetic loses his appetite during an attack of acidosis. Even his respiratory rhythm could be affected. The acid wastes going through the tissues reach the skin, causing eczema and other eruptive manifestations with itching, especially in the genital area. If the acidification of the humors persists and becomes more serious, a diabetic coma may occur.

Injuries in the vessels

One deficiency leads to another and goes hand in hand with the accumulation of the dangerous substances which prevent proper assimilation. Thus the diabetic person will suffer a deficiency of silica, which leads to the fragilization of the vessels. Aside from this, since the diabetic person often replaces sugars by fats and animal proteins - which create several sorts of toxic wastes - there is a thickening and obstruction of the humors by these wastes (cholesterol, acetonic bodies, etc.).

The vessels are not being well defended because of the absence of the protective layer of silica, so toxins are able to settle, thus diminishing the inside diameter of the vessels and creating lesions in the internal wall. It is in these places that clots will be formed, obstructing the vessels. This stage of malnutrition due to obstruction by waste products creates a premature aging of the vessels with all the troubles that accompany it: sclerosis of the eye, arteritis, gangrene, etc.

The 'Diets'

The diets usually imposed on diabetics focus on abnormality rather than aiming to create a normal balanced condition. In any case, the notion of 'regimen' and 'diet' is usually based on misunderstanding. Food cannot be evaluated by name alone, ignoring important variables of quality, and then rigidly prescribed or banned. *In cases of diabetes, one should not be so quick to condemn sugars and starches.* It is evident that there are exceptions to this; it would be out of the question to go on imposing on the deficient organism a type of food which could not be transformed and assimilated in the actual state of things. For example, if the diabetic person cannot properly utilize food rich in starches, their reduction would be understandable.

The sugars

People with diabetic conditions are told to stay away from sugar. What is really meant here is industrial sugar, which increases the glycemia rate, without bringing the nourishment of natural sugar.

In the case of diabetics, the abnormal and urgent need for sugar leads the organism to produce a glucose of inferior quality which the kidneys cannot retain and which is consequently found in the urine.

Thus it would seem illogical to completely suppress the ingestion of natural sugar, which is assimilable, such as found in fresh or dried fruits, carrots, beets, etc. These natural sugars answer the urgent needs of the organism; they possess, among other things, the power of stimulating the pancreas and the secretion of its hormone, insulin; they also avoid the risk of a diabetic coma. These diets which exclude natural sugars cause an atrophy of the pancreas.

The starches

The rarefaction of the pancreatic secretions perturbs the transformation of some carbohydrates. Foods that are rich in starches are not well elaborated, that is the reason why people have the tendency to eliminate bread and cereals. Here, too, the facts are not presented clearly - no distinction is made between a complete cereal and an unrefined one. It is quite sure that the ferments contained in the removed parts contribute to the digestion and assimilation of the remaining parts, when the integrity of the cereal has been preserved.

Diabetics are at the mercy of vascular accidents of a more serious nature, such as arteritis. The 'restrictive' diets and also the so-called 'normal' way of eating weaken the arterial defenses against toxic wastes in the blood by creating a deficiency of silica, which is generally located in the outer layer of cereals.

Meat

The dangerous influence of meat on the hypothalamic functions is now well-known - the nervous and glandular cells being literally 'forced' by the animal protein.

The danger of animal protein is two-fold: first because they acidify - we know the lethal danger that the diabetic runs on account of the acidification of the humors, and second because they can be transformed into primary glucose, which, when not utilized by the organism at this stage increases the rate of glycosuria (glucose in the urine). The diabetic runs another danger in eating meat in that the urea rate in the blood increases.

Alcohol and Alkaloids

The harmful role of alcohol in all its forms is too obvious to be mentioned here. The same is true of coffee and tea which are harmful to the nervous cell. Alcohol and alkaloids precipitate the cholesterol present in the humors, favoring its deposit in the internal surface of the vessels or its concretion in the gall bladder.

Fats

The diabetic is advised to stay away from

carbohydrates (mostly those rich in starches and sugars). He is oriented towards eating such things as butter, which is exactly what he should not be eating.

It has been noticed that there are more diabetics among people in a higher economic group, this in exact proportion with the consumption of animal fats. In every country, death caused by diabetes corresponds proportionally to the consumption of these fats. As soon as periods of restricted intake occur, the number of deaths regresses.

Fats, like alcohol, can very well lead to cirrhosis of the liver, a condition which often accompanies diabetes.

There is one type of fat which is not bad for the organism and that is olive oil. The presence of cholesterol in olive oil must be clarified, for there is not only 'one' cholesterol, but many kinds: and the cholesterol of olive oil, which is a protective and constitutive substance of the cell, has nothing in common with the all-too-famous cholesterol present in animal tissues.

However, given the fact that fat matters of all origin are more or less acidifying, it is preferable to restrict their usage to avoid acidosis and acetonemia. Still, keep in mind that the better and the fresher the olive oil, the smaller its percentage of acidity. In fact, olive oil, when mixed with lemon juice, is one of the best remedies for acetonemia.

ADVICE ON EATING

A person with a diabetic condition must be exceptionally prudent in choosing food, for a diseased organism lacks flexibility. Previous prohibitions and caloric counting will have left such scars on him that he will now have very great difficulty seeing things clearly when it comes to deciding by himself what to do in terms of healing and eating. He will have to grant himself a period of adaptation to gradually introduce and get used to the food he needs.

Some foods are natural remedies, thanks to the stimulation they exercise on certain functions. Thus, onion and chicory stimulate the functions of the pancreas, while artichoke contains inulin, an inverted sugar which does not require pancreatic juices. Salsify and Jerusalem artichoke have almost the same qualities. Asparagus contributes to the diminution of glycosuria; the same is true for beets,

which, thanks to their magnesium, act favorably on the kidneys. Since experience has shown that diabetic people tolerate levulose better than glucose, fruits such as strawberry and peach are highly recommended. Watercress, cherries, lemon, orange, and grapefruit are also well-accepted. Not being rich in carbohydrates, walnuts and hazelnuts can be rapidly assimilated. Black olives are excellent for they act favorably on the liver, being a natural fat together with other useful elements. Potato is acceptable if it is not saturated with potassic fertilizer. Barley is highly recommended, and not only because its germ contributes to decreasing the glucose content.

The lack of precision has made the problem of cereals insoluble. We know that the pancreas finds it difficult to transform starches, which can create acidic and toxic wastes so it would seem reasonable to tell the diabetic to stay away from cereals. However, as has been said previously, this is only true for refined cereals. It is evident that it would not be appropriate to introduce the patient to a normal healthy regimen too rapidly, especially if he has been eating very differently all his life. It would be better to gradually introduce brown rice, hulled barley and whole wheat bread (80% complete) made with natural leaven (sourdough), all of which must be chewed very well to ensure proper salivary digestion.

Temporarily, it would be preferable not to use peas, beans, lentils; primarily because assimilating them is difficult for a diabetic person, and also because they are acidifying. Chestnuts also should be avoided until normal functioning is re-established.

Vegetables and fruits should be eaten raw as often as possible, and unpeeled as well, in order to make use of the precious silica contained in the peels.

It is very difficult to say how much of a particular food can be absorbed; this depends on the individual; his condition, his social life, and so on. The change from one food to another, one period to another, should be slow and prudent; one period will follow another only if the previous one has been accepted.

Some Precious Foods

Fresh fruits in season, sweet or acid, taken in the morning on an empty stomach or before meals.

All kinds of fresh vegetables, preferably raw, occasionally cooked. Soups, vegetable broth. Stress green vegetables such as cabbage, spinach, watercress, etc., raw if possible, seasoned with olive oil, lemon juice, sea salt, garlic, parsley.

Aromatic plants, to be used freely: chervil, parsley, garlic, onion, thyme, bay leaves, tarragon, rosemary, sage, walnut, nutmeg, cumin, saffron, chive, vanilla, clove, basil, cinnamon, etc. exercise a most important activity on the salivary glands, stomach, pancreas and liver functions.

Fruits such as black olives, almonds, hazelnuts, peanuts, are also excellent (peanuts and walnuts in moderate quantities as they are acidifying).

Use olive oil, cold-pressed, for seasoning and cooking.

Whole wheat bread made with natural leaven (sour dough).

Cheeses may be used - in small quantities, of course - for their fermenting qualities. Buttermilk also, but no milk, as it is not good for the liver. Egg yolk is good once in a while, but not the white which is too acidifying.

Dates, figs, grapes, raisins, prunes, apricots are excellent for stimulating the pancreatic secretions - they should be introduced gradually in moderate quantities.

* *

MENU FOR A DAY

Breakfast
—fresh fruits (e.g. 1 or 2 apples or pears) -or
—black olives, hazelnuts, etc.   -or
—vegetable soup
An infusion of thyme or rosemary to end the meal.

Lunch and Dinner
—a fresh fruit
—a salad (see Basconnaise, p.51)
—cooked vegetables (in season), brown rice or barley
—buttermilk (take away the acid liquid)
— 2 slices of whole wheat bread
—2 or 3 times a week, an egg yolk.

See p.143 for some suggested daily menus.

* *

THE NATURAL TREATMENT

The Plants

Their action is diverse; some favor the decrease of glycemia, others on the contrary, aid against glycosuria. We also must bear in mind their power of strengthening the functions of synthesis and assimilation.

The real remedy specific to diabetes is the one which will bring the body into such a condition that it can properly utilize nutritive elements. *It is more important to properly nourish a diabetic organism than to neutralize the sugar produced by that organism.*

In this case, mixtures of plants are preferable to a plant used by itself, but single herbs should not be overlooked.

One of the most useful plants, not only for diabetes but for all kinds of digestive troubles, is fenugreek. Acting on the pancreas and the gall bladder at the same time, it stimulates the secretions. Prepare it the following way:

> Put 1 tablespoonful of fenugreek seeds in 2 cups of water. Bring to a boil and let simmer until water is reduced to 1 cup. Take a cup in the morning on an empty stomach, every other week, for several months.

The thin person will gain weight if he will use it for a long while; its action is slow but effective.

Some other plants are also good when taken separately: wild geranium(alum root), eucalyptus, huckleberry leaves, polygonum, valerian, kidney bean (pod), agrimony.
For each one:

> Use 1 handful per quart of water. Bring to a boil. Simmer gently for 2-3 minutes and let infuse a few more minutes. May be used as a table drink.

Here are two mixtures which can be used as table drinks or between meals, warm or cold.

Decoction for Diabetes

Black Currants	Wild geranium(alum root)
Green hop	Blind nettle
Wild thyme	

—or—

Galega	Huckleberry leaves
Hops	Wild geranium(alum root)
Polygonum	

Put 1 tablespoon of each plant, or 5 tablespoons of the mixture of equal parts in a quart of water. Bring to a boil, simmer for a few minutes. infuse and strain. Each mixture should be used for 1 month, and the other the following month, or else alternate weekly, according to preference.

CLAY

The reader should go over the chapter on clay to familiarize himself with its properties. This also will teach him how to prepare the clay poultice which he will be using here. Aside from its absorbent and revitalizing properties, clay is also a catalyst when taken orally, for it favors the transformation of foods into nutritive elements. On the other hand it prevents the acidification of the humors by neutralizing a part of the acid wastes.

Take it on alternate mornings on an empty

For those who cannot take the bitter taste of these two drinks, it will be helpful to rest one week per month and substitute the following infusion for the liver:

Infusion for the Liver

Gromwell	30 gr.	Yellow bedstraw	30 gr.
Licorice	30 gr.	Marigold	20 gr.
Rosemary	30 gr.	Mint	20 gr.
Woodruff	30 gr.		

2 tablespoons per cup of boiling water, infuse 10-15 minutes. Drink hot. Add honey if necessary.

There are yet more plants that ought not to be neglected; they have a beneficial effect on the liver. The following mixture, which is very efficient, may be used in three week cures, two or three times a year:

Decoction for Congestion of the Liver

Woodruff	30 gr.	Horsetail	10 gr.
Licorice	30 gr.	Marigold	10 gr.
Artichoke	20 gr.	Rosemary	10 gr.
Bearberry	10 gr.	Small centaury	10 gr.
Black currants	10 gr.	Yellow bedstraw	10 gr.

A tablespoonful of this mixture in a cup of water; bring to a boil, simmer 2 minutes; infuse 10 minutes. 1 cup before each of the two main meals, cold or warm.

stomach (1 teaspoon in ½ a glass of water) in conjunction with fenugreek. Clay can be taken 15 minutes before the evening meal if it is not tolerated in the morning.

The action of clay on the liver has great effects on the digestive system, and also influences the glandular system and nervous centers. Apply it as a poultice every night; one on the liver to be kept on overnight if well tolerated. Twice a week apply the same poultice on the pancreas instead of the liver, unless one can take baths at the same time. Later on, apply poultices on the back of the neck, which is good for the nervous centers.

If the effect of clay is too tiring when used once a day, alternate it with a poultice of wheat bran and climbing ivy leaves:

5 handfuls of wheat bran   2 handfuls of ivy leaves

Cook in some water for 10 minutes. When all the water has evaporated, place in a cheesecloth, fold, and apply hot.

Use daily applications of clay three weeks each month. In some cases the treatment may last several months. Do not hesitate to interrupt it if there are signs of fatigue; resume after having gained some strength.

Hip Baths

The diversity and depth of the perturbation of the nutritive functions in the diabetic is such that any helpful measure should not be neglected.

The hip bath must be part of the treatment of the diabetic person. Done properly, (see p. 57), it will stimulate and strengthen the functions and leave the organism in a state of alertness.

MENUS

BREAKFAST

1 or 2 apples
4 or 5 olives
Thyme infusion

LUNCH

2 peaches or 2 oranges (depending on season)
salad of season with minced raw onion
salsify (cooked in earthenware or cast iron pot)
cheese

DINNER

some fruits as for breakfast
grated carrots
salad of season
vegetable soup (optional)
yoghurt

BREAKFAST

    Vegetable-barley soup

LUNCH

    ½ a pound or so of cherries, or 3 tangerines in season
    raw cabbage (green or red) shredded
    escarole, endive, or any lettuce with a hard-boiled egg
    potatoes
    a few hazel nuts

DINNER

    fruits as for lunch
    tomato salad or kohlrabi(grated) in season
    vegetable soup
    cheese

BREAKFAST

    2 apples and 10 hazelnuts
    hot water and lemon juice

LUNCH

    ½ a pound of strawberries or 2 grapefruit in season
    raw onions seasoned with sea salt, olive oil and lemon
    salad in season
    asparagus
    cheese

DINNER

    fruit as for lunch
    watercress salad, potatoes, hard egg and black olives
    yoghurt
    5 almonds

BREAKFAST

    vegetable soup

LUNCH

    ½ a pound or so of strawberries, or 2 grapefruit
    Basconnaise (see p.51)
    brown rice with black olives
    yoghurt or buttermilk

DINNER

    Fruits as for lunch
    raw artichoke, with olive oil, lemon juice, sea salt
    vegetable soup (optional)
    cheese

BREAKFAST

    10-20 olives with a small amount of bread and garlic
    infusion of thyme

LUNCH

    2 pears
    beet salad, raw
    Jerusalem articokes, cooked in water, seasoned
    boiled egg
    seaweed

DINNER

    fruit as for lunch
    raw salsify, grated
    Belgian endive salad
    cabbage soup (optional)
    cheese

" AND THOU SHALT EAT

    AND BE SATISFIED........................."

                        Deuteronomy 6:11

THREE MANIFESTATIONS OF DEFICIENCY

Fatigue — Anemia — Demineralization

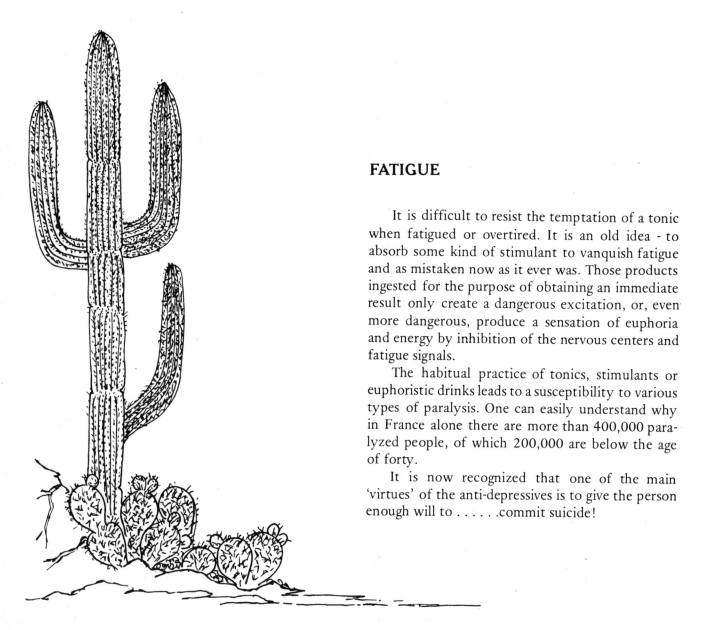

FATIGUE

It is difficult to resist the temptation of a tonic when fatigued or overtired. It is an old idea - to absorb some kind of stimulant to vanquish fatigue and as mistaken now as it ever was. Those products ingested for the purpose of obtaining an immediate result only create a dangerous excitation, or, even more dangerous, produce a sensation of euphoria and energy by inhibition of the nervous centers and fatigue signals.

The habitual practice of tonics, stimulants or euphoristic drinks leads to a susceptibility to various types of paralysis. One can easily understand why in France alone there are more than 400,000 paralyzed people, of which 200,000 are below the age of forty.

It is now recognized that one of the main 'virtues' of the anti-depressives is to give the person enough will to . . . . . .commit suicide!

The simple cup of coffee, without which "I wouldn't be able to get going" is deadly to the nervous system, the same is true with common tea and other alkaloids.

Temporary fatigues can be taken care of with a few glasses of carrot or cabbage juice and a few teaspoons of germinated wheat. It should be mentioned, however, that the nutritive elements of the carrot, cabbage and sprouted wheat must first be neutralized in order to liberate their energy and give it to the ailing organism. In a more serious case where the fatigue lingers for a longer time, it would be advisable to use green vegetables, which are rich in chlorophyll, store solar energy and liberate it at the first contact with the mouth.

In other words, there are two main kinds of fatigue, that which comes after a long effort and finds its cure in simple rest or some kind of a tonic; and the fatigue which even after a night's sleep has not disappeared. This last one betrays a deep trouble in the faculties of assimilation of food. These troubles may be worsened by a nervous or endocrinian imbalance. It is often an improper biological transmutation* that is taking place.

————————————————————————————

*For more information on this important phenomenon, see p. 151.

Organic functions must be re-established at full potential and 'living' food must become the major source of nourishment.

The Cure

To help the metabolism of calcium and other possibly deficient elements, it suffices to take the lemon and egg preparation 3 times a week (p.113).

On the other mornings, take a decoction of fenugreek seeds (1 tablespoon in 2 cups of water: bring to a boil and simmer to ½ its volume).

Take the clay drink: 1 teaspoon in ½ a glass of water; either in the morning on an empty stomach or before retiring at night (best for lazy intestines).

Take the decoction for aiding assimilation on p.159.

Take 1 glass of carrot or cabbage juice between meals.

Every morning a short cold hip bath lasting no more than 3-5 minutes should be taken.

Take a hot foot bath during the day. Both hip and foot baths will help accelerate the organic exchanges. It should be prepared either with 2 handfuls of red-grape vine leaves (for the blood

circulation) or 2 handfuls of sea salt to work as a stimulant, or with a handful of wheat bran and another handful of walnut tree leaves to tonify the nervous system.

Once or twice a week a *complete* hot bath with 4-5 pounds of sea salt and also a few handfuls of seaweed, put in a few hours before.

At night, before going to bed, massage the spine. A mixture of 2 parts camphor oil and 1 part grated garlic may be used. This will activate the circulation.

Eat fruits and vegetables with their peels if they have not been sprayed with chemicals.

Also eat whole wheat bread made with leaven, wheat sprouts (in salads, soups) and all kinds of green vegetables.

Cereal should be as complete and unrefined as possible. Brown rice is excellent and so are the others, millet, kasha, etc.

Good air and sunbaths are important too.

Season your meals with aromatic plants.

ANEMIA

Under the term *anemia* are grouped all the defects which betray a poor quality of blood with diminution of one or several elements, or modifications in their inter-relations.

The diminution of red blood cells may very well be caused more by their abnormal destruction than by an insufficient formation in the bone marrow. Sometimes the red globules are stopped at a certain stage of their development.

In the case of chlorosis, there is at the same time a diminution of the number of red blood cells and a remarkable decrease of the hemoglobin rate. This would coincide with a lack of iron and may be caused by a liver deficiency.

Myeloid anemia (of the spinal chord) is caused by an injury in the marrow and in the spleen.

Leukemia is not grouped with anemias. The former is characterized by the increase of white blood cells with abnormal formations in the lymph and marrow and the latter is characterized by the decrease in red blood cells.

Before looking for what can contribute to the reconstitution of the red blood cells or hemoglobin, it would be proper to remedy the initial cause of the anemia.

Knowing that blood passes through the liver, where it is purified and 'completed', and where it receives most of the nutritive elements, and knowing that the liver produces a factor of maturation of the red blood cells and regularizes their iron content, it is easy to conceive how anemia takes place.

It is vain to fight anemia with calf-liver; this part of the animal introduces a large number of dangerous products which work against the process of assimilation. Do not count on blood transfusions either, as explained in the chapter on the liver.

Of all the errors made about anemia, the most common one is in looking for the strongest types of food containing the most reconstituents and trying to absorb as much of them as possible. Here is an error that no one should ever commit!

When blood is anemic, this means the whole organism is deficient. It is proper, then, to introduce change without shocks. In this case too strong a type of food can worsen the situation.

The Cure

Nature gives us remedies of all kinds, from soft to powerful ones. Nothing reconstitutes the hemoglobin better than carrot juice, and nothing is more favorable to the formation of red blood cells than spinach (raw) which is so rich in iron and chlorophyl. All green vegetables - and those having passed the stage of green at a certain point - are regenerators of blood, thanks to their chlorophyl, mineral salts and catalysts (vitamins, ferments). It is not enough to introduce nutritive elements in the organism, for there is no guarantee that the organism will be able to utilize them. This is when the catalysts must enter into play, transforming the nutritive elements, contributing to their assimilation, fixation and storage.

Many experiences have confirmed the useful role of clay in the reconstitution of the blood. Spectacular ameliorations in the composition of the blood occurred after a clay cure -- accompanied by a proper way of eating, of course.

To utilize meat requires a large effort, while to the contrary, the 'biotic' energy of the vegetable kingdom is activated at the very instant it enters the mouth. It is a direct source of energy.

The liver functions should be stimulated by clay applications (lukewarm) or raw cabbage leaves on the liver (3 layers). The decoctions for jaundice and cholemia (p.55) will act remarkably on the

THE PHENOMENON OF
BIOLOGICAL TRANSMUTATIONS

Many physicians and biologists are now discovering that living bodies at every level of life can perform operations of synthesis, that one element can give birth to another one. Eating only grass, herbivorous animals such as the cow can manufacture proteins and any other substances its organism needs. Every scientist knows that the animals which excrete the greatest amount of nitrogen are the herbivores, the very ones whose food intake contains the least of this element, for nitrogen is part of protein $(C_{720}H_{1134}N_{218}O_{248})$ but not of carbohydrates $(C_6H_{10}O_5)$. Another example is that after incubation, limestone increases inside the egg without anything brought from the outside. Also, after germination, seeds contain more sulphur and mineral salts than before. It is clear that elements in their natural state can change one into another in a normal biological (living) medium. Normal biological conditions are stressed, because bacterial flora or other living elements are usually needed as catalysts.

The French scientist and professor, Louis Kervran, in his book BIOLOGICAL TRANSMUTATIONS* discusses all these phenomena. He also shows that the human organism, when functioning properly, is capable of such transmutations; sodium can be changed into potassium in the body, and into calcium or magnesium as well; potassium can become calcium; sulphur can change into phosphorus and phosphorus into sulphur; silica can change into calcium, manganese become iron and many more.

Since the publication of this book - two years ago - now in its third printing, it has gone through a difficult period where it has been both ridiculed as being impossible and praised for being the best news for science since Lavoisier, the father of chemistry. How appropriate! Lavoisier proclaimed that elements remain unchanging in their structures until the end of days. Now Louis Kervran broke through to find out otherwise, for he proves that elements do change one to another. This is the phenomenon known as biological transmutations.

M.D.'s, nutritionalists and other scientists from all over the world are studying Louis Kervran's work and many of them have begun to practice his teachings, the most popular seeming to be that of silica changing into calcium in the body.

In his book, Professor Kervran also explains the fallacy of giving mineral calcium to correct a calcium deficiency, mineral iron for anemia, and other similar treatments, for it is very difficult for the body to retain and assimilate these elements in such a form; such work is alien to it. He warns doctors against prescribing medicine which may do more harm than good.

Instead, Professor Kervran strongly recommends that we take silica (an important element found in the outer layer of grains but usually extracted from the horsetail plant, which contains it in great quantities) to cure such ailments as rheumatism, arthritis, broken and weak bones, falling hair, nail breaking and numerous others. In fact, in Europe it has become a must for people over fifty to take silica in extract form since after that age the bones start becoming brittle.

According to scientific medical investigation, there are no harmful effects from the use of silica, or horsetail. It can be used in both plant and extract form. In the first case, one should be careful to harvest it in the spring and not in the summer, for at that time it turns into a mineral state; it absolutely must be picked as early as possible while it is still organic. Professor Kervran informed us that silica in its mineral form is not only worthless but dangerous for it produces the opposite effect: decalcification. It is in its extract form that silica does wonders, for it is in a concentrated state. Dr. Kervran also informs us that what a plant does in a year the extract does in a few months. There are some health food stores in the U.S. that now carry the kind specifically recommended by Kervran.

*published by Swan House, P.O. Box 170, Bklyn, N.Y. 11223
$5.75 cloth; $2.75 paper; 40¢ postage.

digestive and assimilating processes.

Take clay orally, 1 teaspoon in ½ a glass of water, in the morning on an empty stomach.

After a cure of three weeks of this decoction and clay, then a week of rest, start the clay cure again; however, this time take the decoction on p.108.

Massaging the spine with a mixture of 2 parts olive oil and 1 part grated garlic will activate the circulation and produce a salutary stimulation.

Have carrot juice twice a day. Raw spinach in salads (with grated carrots, for example), beets (raw, if possible), grapes (fresh and dried), apples, apricots, cabbage, (preferably raw), prunes, and plums.

It is evident that if any organs are deficient or injured (stomach ulcer, for example) poultices of clay should be applied on that area (for this will exercise an important action on the composition of the blood.

The reader should keep in mind that the opposite effect of elimination always precedes assimilation itself. A slight loss of weight in the beginning of the treatment should not be a cause of surprise or worry.

DEMINERALIZATION

Demineralization does not refer only to a deficiency of calcium. The skeleton may also lack phosphorus, the nervous cells may lack sulphur, the cardiac muscles potassium, the lungs magnesium and the blood cells, iron. And let us not forget silica, whose importance is not minimal; its deficiency is always found in lesioned tissues of the arteries, intestines, lungs and bones.

It is common to limit the phenomenon of demineralization to 'losses'. Some people, for example, complain of losing phosphates in their urine. It may be that these losses are the result of transformations or transmutations which are not taking place.

A major qualification must be made about these transformations, though, and that is, that they cannot take place without the presence of a catalyst or bacteria. How misleading and illusory are all the pills given for calcium, magnesium, and other deficiencies. Sometimes the organism eliminates more iron or calcium than it receives. Sometimes one element gives birth to another.

The ability of organisms to perform these transmutations is variable. Some might be able to do it immediately, some will only be able to after months or even a year or two of the right kind of eating restores the intestines with their bacterial flora to full-functioning. A catalyst will help accelerate and trigger these transmutations. The process is helped with aromatic plants.

Clay should be taken alternately with fenugreek every morning; one week clay, one week fenugreek (1 teaspoon of clay in ½ a glass of water; 1 tablespoon of fenugreek in 2 cups of water; bring to a boil, simmer until it is reduced to ½).

Stimulate the liver with a decoction prepared especially for this purpose

Avoid alcohol and any chemicals such as medications.

Take cold hip baths, when possible.

Knowing that sodium can change into calcium or magnesium, some might conclude that it would be good to eat a great deal of salt. Doing this would show a lack of knowledge about one of the qualities of salt: its ability to slow down the action of ferments which are present in food. The reason why some vegetables are preserved in brine is because the elements of fermentation are inhibited. Salt has the same action in the body. Therefore, if additional salt is desired, it should be acquired at times other than during meals.

Seaweed baths with salt are excellent for weakened organisms, especially for children temporarily deficient in some minerals. These baths help restore a good balance; they help eliminate and assimilate depending on the person. It suffices to put a few handfuls of seaweed in a ½-gallon or more of boiling water. Let macerate (soften) one day. Fill the bathtub with hot water and throw the seaweed and the water it was boiled in, into the tub. Put the seaweed in a bag so as not to clog the drain. Add 6-8 pounds of unrefined seasalt. Remain in this bath as long as the water is warm.

A cold hip bath should be taken every morning.

Put clay poultices on the liver every evening or on the areas particularly touched by the demineralization.

The sources of demineralization are often hereditary, that is why one can gain positive results only through perseverance.

No detail should be overlooked, whether it be nutritive or aesthetic. Food should look attractive and always be varied.

Good aromatics are parsley, chive, tarragon, basil, bay leaves, nutmeg, clove, and others.

Impotence

This may be of physical or psychological origin. In the former case, it is often related to problems of decalcification. In all cases it is necessary to treat the general condition to re-establish equilibrium and strength to all the functions. Take 1 teaspoon of clay in ½ a glass of water in the morning, alternating with a decoction of fenugreek seeds (1 tablespoon per cup of water).

Take the decoction for remineralization during meals.

Take a cold hip bath every morning. Apply clay poultices in the evening, one night on the lumbar region and the other on the neck.

Take sprouted wheat and have plenty of dried fruits such as dates, figs, etc.

In principle, follow the same treatment as indicated for decalcification.

For sterility, see 'women's ailments.'

TABLE OF DEFICIENCIES AND THEIR NATURAL REMEDIES

VITAMIN A

Its deficiency causes visual troubles which manifest themselves mostly at dusk; hardening of the cornea, hardening of the skin and of the mucous membrane, nails, brittle hair, nervous state, anxiety, insomnia, headaches, swelling of the abdomen, mammary pains a few days before menstruation, respiratory afflictions, paraplegic troubles, premature aging.

It is found in:
All green plants; fruits (mostly the yellow ones); yellow potatoes; oleaginous fruits; certain oils; garlic; onion; whole cereals; tomato; mushroom; lemon; orange; apricot; turnip; dried fruits; butter; egg yolk.

* *

VITAMIN B COMPLEX
(B_1, B_2, B_5, B_6, B_{12}, PP)

A deficiency may lead to troubles of the nervous system, or the digestive system, constipation, anemia, neuritis, muscular imbalance, ulcers, chapped skin, beri-beri, liver deficiency, intestinal insufficiency, defects in the oxidation of the carbohydrates.

It is found in:
Envelopes and germs of cereals; green parts of vegetables; most fresh fruits and vegetables; milk products; eggs; sage; honey.

* *

VITAMIN C

Its deficiency may lead to: scurvy, hemorrhage and swelling of the gums, loss of teeth, ruptured blood vessels various hemorrhages, especially in the joints, blood disease, improper growth in bones and teeth, affection of the digestive tube, tuberculosis, muscular weakness, cellulite by cellular asphyxiation. In the organic tissues an intercellular substance maintains the cohesion of the cells. When there is a lack of vitamin C this substance liquifies.

It is found in:
Lemon, orange, grapefruit; green and red pepper; cabbage; tomato; horseradish; watercress and green salads; onion; radish; aromatic plants and all fresh fruits and vegetables, especially in the peel. Whitened vegetables have lost vitamin C.

* *

VITAMIN D

A lack of sunbathing leads to a lack of vitamin D. Its deficiency may lead to rickets, perturbation in some of the operations of synthesis, a deficiency of the bones and abnormal development of the cartilaginous tissue; tooth decay, less muscular strength; incomplete growth, cutaneous tuberculosis, unjustified fatigue.

It is found in:
Olive oil, summer butter; fruits and vegetables - fresh picked; pollen; new honey.

* *

VITAMIN K

Its deficiency may cause hemophilia and a tendency to hemorrhage and anemia.

It is found in:
Tomato; orange; green vegetables such as cabbage and spinach; carrot; cereals.

This vitamin is mainly produced by a certain bacterial fermentation in the colon, but becomes active only in the presence of the bile in the digestive tube.

* *

VITAMIN E

Its deficiency may lead to a lowering of the neuro-muscular activity; sterility in both men and women, some eczema, and ulcers and sclerosis.

It is found in:
Sprouted wheat, whole wheat flour, some green vegetables such as lettuce and watercress, cold-pressed vegetable oils; butter.

* *

VITAMIN P

Its deficiency may lead to a weakening and hardening of the vessels, defects in the vascular permeability, hemorrhage in infants, tuberculous people, and people suffering from defective liver functions.

It is found in:
Buckwheat; green and red pepper; orange.

* *

CALCIUM

Its lack may lead to deficiencies of the bones, teeth, tendons; its lack may cause anemia, cerebral and nervous weakness; the organism is reduced to a state of low resistance, general deficiency, and a giving way of the defenses.

It is found in:
Turnips, cabbage; carrots; wheat and other cereals; spinach; walnuts; hazelnuts; almonds; grapes; onions; lentils; milk products.

Note: See silica for a more complete instruction in calcium deficiency.

* *

IRON

Its deficiency may cause anemia, growth trouble, weakening of the defenses, tuberculosis, constipation.

It is found in:
Wheat (mostly the germ); watercress; spinach; carrot; oats; hazelnuts; almonds; rye; date; rice; walnuts; lentils; lettuce; barley; onions; leeks; and other fresh vegetables; honey.

* *

MAGNESIUM

A lack of this element may cause: general deficiency, degenerative diseases (cancer, tuberculosis, diabetes), neuritis, all nerve diseases, weakness of the bones, anemia.

It is found in:
Dates; beets; spinach; oats; wheat; potatoes (grown without chemical fertilizer); carrots; almonds; walnuts; hazelnuts.

* *

PHOSPHORUS

A lack of it can cause bone deficiencies, nervous and humoral deficiencies, neurosis, tuberculosis, nervous disease, neuritis, neurasthenia, depression.

It is found in:
Almonds; wheat (mostly the germ); grapes (mostly in the seed); garlic; dates; oats; nasturtium flowers; barley; fresh green peas and beans; lentils; cabbage; spinach; onion; lettuce; carrots; apples; leeks; millet; egg yolk.

* *

SILICA

The deficiency of this precious element may lead to the deficiency of the bones, tendons and teeth, hardening of the vessels, arteriosclerosis, diabetes, rickets, weak kidneys and heart.

It is found in:
The peel of fruits and vegetables, but mostly in whole cereals; garlic; apples; fresh peas and beans; cabbage; chives; shallots; strawberries.*

* *

SULPHUR

Its deficiency can lead to infections, skin diseases, demineralization(defective assimilation of foods), weakness of the bronchia.

It is found in:
Garlic; onions; cabbage; leeks; watercress; radish; barley; peach; corn; rice; dates; almonds; string beans; apricots; strawberries; eggs; organically grown wheat contains some in its germ.

* *

IODINE

Its deficiency may lead to glandular deficiencies (mostly of the thyroid gland) weakness of the defenses, slowing down of the cellular exchanges, tendency to congestion.

It is found in:
Seaweed; garlic; watercress; string beans; onions; spinach; turnips; asparagus; cabbage; mushrooms; strawberries; rice; carrots; leeks; radish; cereals.

* *

FERMENTS

A deficiency in ferments may lead to a defective assimilation - the food cannot be completely transformed.

They are found in:
Raw food (fruits and vegetables); honey; cheese; eggs; At a temperature of 104°F. the ferments begin to be destroyed.

* *

CHLOROPHYL

Its lack may lead to anemia, weakness of the heart, muscles and nerves, deficiency of the smooth muscles of the intestines, risk of infection (chlorophyl is an antiseptic); fatigue.

It is found in:
Green vegetables and all fruits which have been through the green stage of development.

* *

AIR

Air is necessary to life, not only for its role in the purification of the blood, but also for the role that it plays in the process of nutrition: for example, air permits the process of oxidation and reduction and helps maintain a healthy bacterial flora. It also has a great influence on the pH of the blood.

The deficiency of air leads to a latent state of asphyxia, cardiac troubles (the symptoms of which are blue circles under the eyes, purple color of the face and nails), acidification of the humors.

* *

---

*See Buyer's Guide for organic silica tablets

VISUAL TROUBLES

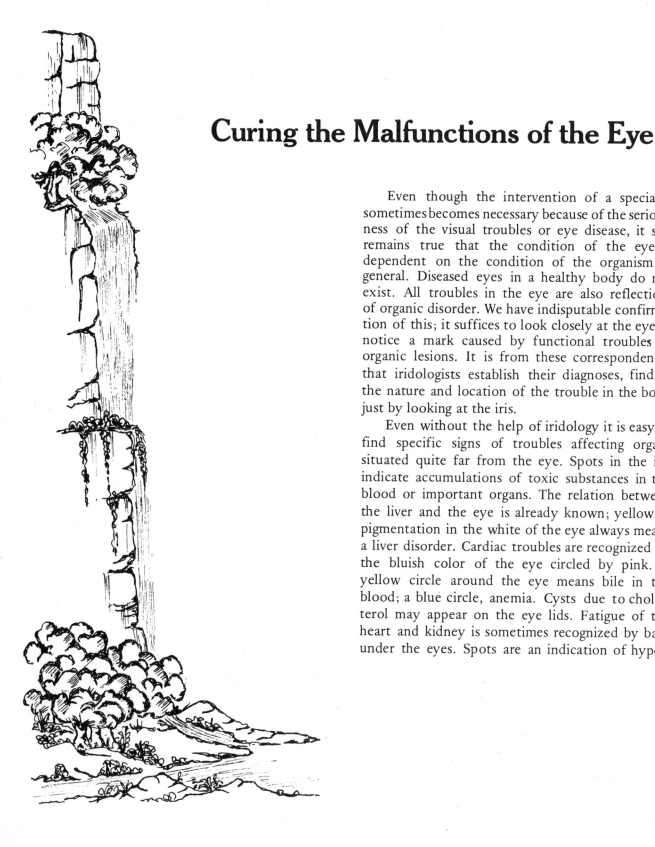

Curing the Malfunctions of the Eye

Even though the intervention of a specialist sometimes becomes necessary because of the seriousness of the visual troubles or eye disease, it still remains true that the condition of the eye is dependent on the condition of the organism in general. Diseased eyes in a healthy body do not exist. All troubles in the eye are also reflections of organic disorder. We have indisputable confirmation of this; it suffices to look closely at the eye to notice a mark caused by functional troubles or organic lesions. It is from these correspondences that iridologists establish their diagnoses, finding the nature and location of the trouble in the body just by looking at the iris.

Even without the help of iridology it is easy to find specific signs of troubles affecting organs situated quite far from the eye. Spots in the iris indicate accumulations of toxic substances in the blood or important organs. The relation between the liver and the eye is already known; yellowish pigmentation in the white of the eye always means a liver disorder. Cardiac troubles are recognized by the bluish color of the eye circled by pink. A yellow circle around the eye means bile in the blood; a blue circle, anemia. Cysts due to cholesterol may appear on the eye lids. Fatigue of the heart and kidney is sometimes recognized by bags under the eyes. Spots are an indication of hypertension or nephritis; sometimes they signal the rupture of small vessels. In any case they constitute the symptom preceding serious accidents of the arteries.

If the liver does not produce enough protective substances and does not neutralize toxic wastes, the latter circulate in the blood and prevent the good irrigation of the eyes by blocking certain vessels. The toxins obstruct first the small vessels - those of the eyes. The sclerosis of the vessels which follows reaches the choroid (a region particularly rich in vessels). At this time the eye cannot defend itself against the outside aggressions; infections or visual troubles may occur.

The liver participates in the production of vitamin A. A deficiency in vitamin A is disastrous for the eyes.

When one eye is slightly darker than the other, it means that the half of the body corresponding to the darker eye is more overloaded with toxins than the other half. Two very dark eyes generally indicate an obstruction of the gall bladder, sometimes accompanied by cardiac troubles of varying intensity.

Leon Vanier, M.G. Jausa, and other scientists have established the correspondence between the condition of the pupil and certain body injuries or psychological troubles. The contraction of the pupil is very significant, it may mean inflammation of the iris or foreign bodies in the cornea, uremia, meningitis, emaciation or intoxification from opium, chloroform, alcohol. The dilation of the pupil may be a sign of glaucoma, the effect of a trauma, a disorder in the sympathetic functions, syphilis, meningitis, or an abscess in the brain. If this dilation is permanent it indicates an intoxification from substances such as cocain, atropin, etc. When the pupil temporarily takes an irregular form, it may signify serious injuries of the nervous centers or of the bone marrow (paralysis and tabes). The vertical elongation of the pupils shows a tendency to cerebral congestion; the horizontal elongation mainly implies troubles in the nervous and glandular centers.

COMPLEMENTARY IDEAS

The great influence of a bad general condition on the vision has been demonstrated. It is sure that the iris will become clearer upon detoxification of the blood and organs. In families of vegetarians, those who are born and raised that way have clearer eyes than their parents who had been eating animal food.

The most amazing thing is that this can also be demonstrated in reverse. Professor Bonnier, quoting Dr. A. Leprince, explained this phenomenon: by compressing the eyeball there is a slowing down of the cardiac rhythm and a decrease in arterial tension. Even more compression can create feelings of warmth and cold, sweating, dizziness, headaches, colitis, nausea. This compression can stop a persisting hiccup, a sneezing fit, buzzing in the ears, contraction of the bladder (with a real need to urinate) or the large intestines.

It has been observed that the stimulation of the eye from a light source creates the stimulation of the pituitary and the genital glands. This action would explain the too rapid growth of near-sighted children. This will serve for the visual education of the children whose weak vision is hereditary.

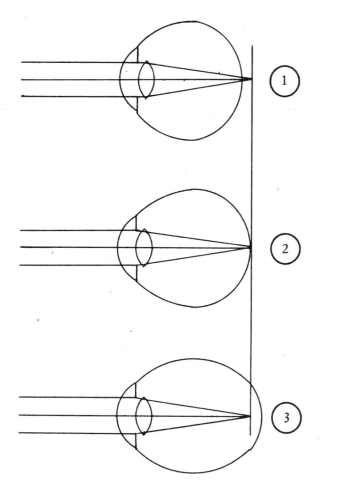

1   far-sighted eye: the image is formed behind the retina

2   normal eye: the image is produced exactly on the retina

3   near-sighted eye: the image is formed before the retina

Some causes of eye trouble

Bad working conditions may contribute to the degradation of vision, such as where there is pollution from alcohol vapors, perfumes or tobacco smoke, or eye strain resulting from the particular job demands, constant bad lighting, trepidations and excessive amounts of dust; all wear away good vision. Mental and physical strain leads to the production of muscular or nervous toxins. An increase of the rate of acidity and an overloading of all the humors, including the vitreous humor of the eye follow. Nervous intoxification is particularly deadly for the retina and its connections. Not sleeping enough, or sleeping too much are both bad for the vision.

Circulation troubles, especially hypertension, may have immediate effects on the vision. This may be corrected with a natural way of eating and with foot baths prepared with red-grape vine leaves.

Wearing sunglasses for a long time is bad for the eyes, for it leads to abnormal reactions when confronted with the modifications of the light rays. The recourse to eye glasses atrophies the mechanism of defense. This is also true for glass, which should be used only in case of absolute necessity.

EYE DISEASES

Cataract

Diabetes, syphilis, senility or other degenerative processes in the body may cause a white chalky, opaque spot to appear on the center of the pupil. This indicates that the accumulation of toxic substances, the sclerosis of vessels and necrosis of the eye tissues are being manifested by the opacification of the crystalline lens.

The vision troubles become so serious that the person may become blind if he does not remedy the general deficiency. Surgical extraction of the crystalline lens may bring an amelioration, however this solution is far from being ideal since the person then has to wear special glasses.

Any local cure is illusory if an efficient treatment for the general condition is not practiced at the same time. Toxins will continue to affluate and accumulate if not drained. Give special attention to the evacuations, using laxatives and diuretics in case of insufficiency. (Laxatives - buckthorn, cassia, senna, linseed; diuretics - corn, cherry stems, elder, ash, bearberry, etc.).

Since the cells of the eye suffer from malnutrition, especially in the case of diabetes, it would be proper to take the following:

Decoction for Aiding Assimilation

Blind nettle	35 gr.	Green hops	35 gr.
Black currants	35 gr.	Wild thyme	35 gr.
Wild geranium			
(alum root)	35 gr.		

Put 1 tablespoon of each plant (or 5 tablespoons of the mixture) in a quart of water. Bring to a boil and let simmer a few minutes. Drink when desired.

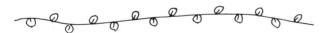

To contribute to the revitalization of the eye, apply clay poultices on the forehead (a little less than ½" thick) which should be kept in place approximately 1½ hours. Further poultices may be applied as desired. Complete the treatments with a poultice of elder-tree flowers (1 tablespoon of flowers and 2 of whole wheat flour). Soak in some water a few minutes, forming a heavy batter. Put in a cheese cloth and fold. It should be applied hot on the most injured eye just before going to bed and kept on overnight. "The most injured eye" is specified in order to be able to check more easily on the progress of the treatment.

Four times a day, proceed with eye cleansings with a lukewarm decoction of melissa, using 2 tablespoons of the plant per cup of water, boiling 10 minutes.

Conjunctivitis

This inflammation of the mucous membrane over the eyelids can be recognized by redness of the eyeball and excess tears due to the obstruction of the superior lachrymal channels. The eyes are often hard to open upon waking up, as if they were glued shut, and there is a sensation of sand under the lids.

This is a deep disorder and the draining of toxic substances is a necessity. Use clay-water, lemon, and diuretic and laxative plants. Take special care of the liver (see its chapter). Take cold hip baths.

Begin local treatments with eye lotions prepared with an infusion of elder-tree flowers. Use 20 gr. in a pint of boiling water; infuse 10 minutes. Apply several times a day.

Make clay applications on the back of the neck first to affect vital centers, then one on the eyes, and continue, alternating. The poultices on the neck should be 1" thick, and should be left in place for two or more hours; those on the eye should be a little bit less than ½" thick and should only be kept on 1½ hours. Use gauze between clay and the eye.

If the eyelids are sticky in the morning, every night put a drop of lemon in the inside corner of each eye. In case of persistency of the inflammation, apply humid compresses overnight, using an infusion of elder-tree flowers.

Detached Retina

It is a serious affliction which can lead to irremediable blindness; it should not be allowed to reach that stage.

People with a good nervous equilibrium do not run the risk of getting a detached retina. It is important to emphasize the fact that the taking of any kind of sedative only worsens the situation. The condition will worsen even more when any chemical salt is absorbed. The oculist Dr. Price pointed out the fact that "half an hour after the absorption of a chemical salt, traces of it can be found in the crystalline lens which takes 33 days to eliminate."

Any nervous person, especially if his eyes are clear, should watch out for the least visual trouble and act accordingly. This means a basic natural treatment supplemented by the following specific methods.

Apply clay poultices on the forehead and elder flowers in infusion, exactly as for cataract. Work as little as possible, even stay in bed if it might be a serious case. Using a light bandage, put an elder-tree poultice on the diseased eye, prepared as for cataract. It can be applied at the same time as the clay poultice is on the forehead.

An exercise (Bates method) is highly recommended: place an electric lamp (100 watts) 10"-12" from the face, while the eyes remain closed. It is important that the lamp have a shade in order to alternate a moment of light with one of darkness (which should last twice as long), for example, 2 seconds of light and 4 of darkness.

As soon as the troubles begin to go away, do the following exercise: open the eyes wide and look at the sky for a few seconds, then close the eyes for the same amount of time, and so on. This exercise prevents the detachment of the retina and will hasten the cure.

Glaucoma

This disease is revealed by an increase in size of the eyeball; there is increased tension and pain in the body of varying intensity. The eye becomes hard and painful. The dilated pupil takes on a grayish-green color. These symptoms are accompanied by headaches and sometimes vomiting.

A general treatment must obviously be started along with local measures which consist of hot foot baths, prepared with red-grape vine leaves (2 handfuls in a gallon of water, boil 15-20 minutes); take it daily. Apply clay poultices on the back of the neck and elder flowers on the diseased eye (see 'cataract' for preparation). The following decoction

particularly indicated for arteriosclerosis should be used:

Decoction for Arteriosclerosis

Bearberry leaves	2 oz.	Rest-harrow root	1 oz.
Couch-grass root	2 oz.	Hawthorn flowers	½ oz.
Meadowsweet		Heath	½ oz.
(flowered tops)	2 oz.	Shepherd's purse	½ oz.
Cherry stems	1 oz.		

Put 4-6 tablespoons of the mixture in a quart of water. Bring to a boil and simmer for 10 minutes. Drink during the day.

A few drops, two or three times a day, of a concentrated decoction of plantain leaves will contribute to the sedation of the pains.

Pay careful attention to urination. Do not hesitate to accelerate evacuation by applying a hot bran-cabbage-onion poultice on the kidneys. This poultice can be left in place overnight if applied before going to bed.

Inflammation of the Iris

This disease is a manifestation of the poor condition of the whole organism. The iris becomes dull and diminishes in diameter. The person cannot tolerate light.

A natural treatment which focuses on the general condition should be started; (see treatment for the liver) then local applications of clay on the forehead and eyes alternately; also a poultice of elder flowers (see 'cataract') on the diseased eye or eyes, one after the other.

****

CATARACT

An 82 year old lady was resignedly waiting for her cataract to 'ripen' before undergoing surgery. Then she agreed to try application of clay poultices. It has been a year since it last bothered her. The improvement has been witnessed by her oculist.

****

Cleanse the nose with clayish water (1 teaspoon in a cup of water). Sink the nose into the cup; close one nostril and breathe in slowly with the other. Let the liquid come out and do the same with the other nostril and so on, 5 or 6 times. These cleansings should be done morning and evening. Before going to bed it will be useful to put a few drops of lemon in each nostril and 1 drop in each eye.

Keratitis

This inflammation of the cornea on which may appear small blisters should be treated - in addition to the general treatment - with relatively thin clay poultices (3/8") on the forehead first and on the eyes afterwards. Begin with one poultice a day and increase to as many as possible depending on the seriousness of the case.

Follow procedure for the inflammation of the iris.

Keratitis indicates a degeneration of the organism. Children develop it at the same time as rickets. One should emphasize raw vegetables and various cereals such as brown rice, wheat, barley.

Blepharitis

This is the inflammation of the edge of the lid, which becomes red.

It means that the organism is suffering from a general deficiency. Fruits and vegetables (raw as often as possible) and cereal will be the main foods. These foods will be assimilated with the help of the following decoction:

Decoction for Remineralization

Blind nettle	25 gr.	Elecampane	20 gr.
Horsetail	25 gr.	Lavender	20 gr.
Rosemary (flowered tops)	25 gr.	Wild celery root	20 gr.
Small centaury (flowered tops)	25 gr.	Germander (flowered tops)	15 gr.
		Hop cones	15 gr.

A full tablespoon of the mixture per cup of boiling water. Let simmer gently 5 minutes. A cup at each meal or just before the meal.

Wash the eyes with an infusion of elder tree flowers (¾ oz. in a quart of boiling water, infuse 10 minutes). Do this several times a day.

At night apply a light clay poultice (3/8") on the eyes (with a cheesecloth intervening). Leave it in place 1-1½ hours. In case of persistency of the inflammation add the elder flower poultice (see 'cataract').

Inflammation of the retina

This disease can occur due to diabetes or syphilis, but mostly it results from nephritis caused by albuminuria. Concerning this it is necessary to point out the harmful action exercised on the kidneys by the anti-diphtheric vaccine; the vaccine, as other toxic substances, goes through the blood and injures the kidney, the troubles which follow may have an effect on the retina via the nervous relays.

It should be treated like the inflammation of the iris.

Sty

This little boil of a sebacious gland on the lid should be taken care of with elder-flower poultices (see 'cataract'). Keep these poultices on for approximately 1½ hours. Apply as many times as possible. The one applied at night should be thicker and can remain in place overnight.

When the sty has opened up, apply small clay poultices for a few more days, in order to prevent any scar or recurrence.

Certainly a natural way of eating would help prevent such occurrences.

****

EYE WOUND

In an accident, a patient's eye was struck by a well-handle thrown into the air. The cornea burst out, the iris was displaced and small crystal pieces from eye glasses aggravated the wound. Clay poultices were applied continually, renewed every hour. After the first day, the eye, which had appeared as a bloody paste, began to take on a better appearance. After three weeks, the cornea was rebuilt and the sight restored after three months. No surgical intervention was necessary.

****

WOMEN'S AILMENTS

It has become very rare to find a woman not suffering in some way from troubles in the genital organs. How rare is shown by the fact that the abnormal has come to be thought of as normal; the pains accompanying menstruation are considered unavoidable and profuse or insufficient menstruation is no longer a cause for concern. Menstrual pain is so common that most women, including teenagers, carry a sedative in their handbag.

The acceptance and generalization of all these inconveniences which women are subjected to now should under no circumstances cause them to lose determination or hope. All these abnormalities of the genital system are easily remedied with the natural harmonist method - excluding those few exceptional cases where a tumor has attained great proportions.

With the natural treatments, the immediate results can be somewhat deceptive for those who cannot expand their judgment beyond appearances. Not only may uterine discharges continue during the first few days of treatment, but they may even intensify! Soon afterwards, however, diminution begins.

Therefore, even though there exist specific remedies of proven effectiveness, emphasis goes to the basic treatment, which aims at re-establishing normality in all the functions. It is evident, seeing that the general treatment includes a change of food and stimulation of the liver, clay will play an important role in most cases. In truth, clay poultices applied on the lower abdomen are indispensable.

FIBROUS TUMORS AND CYSTS

Benign Tumors

Cysts are an abnormal formation of soft substances which develop to the detriment of the host organ, sometimes assuming great proportions.

Fibrous tumors are benign tumors formed by the exaggerated development of the fibrous tissue. The uterus is often the seat of such tumors, which are hard and protuberant.

Fibrous Tumors in the Uterus

There are fibrous tumors as small as the head of a pin and there are some which are so large that they may weigh up to 25 pounds and even more. The expansion of the fibrous tumor causes sterility. A woman may still become pregnant as long as it is not too large. In such a case the fibrous tumor diminishes in size after delivery, sometimes so much so that it disappears completely. Menopause often favors the disappearance of a uterine fibrous tumor.

The Symptoms

The presence of a fibrous tumor may be signaled by a more abundant flow of blood than usual during the menstrual period, by leucorrhea, or by slightly pink secretions between the menstrual periods. Sometimes great blood flows persist between the menstrual periods which themselves last more than the normal few days.

Some fibrous tumors are like sponges which hold a lot of blood and give it out rapidly. These are the least tenacious, and are eliminated more rapidly by natural medicine; there is another kind of fibrous tumor which is constituted of very resistant fibrous tissue. These fibrous tumors rarely cause blood to come out except at the normal time of menstruation.

Usually a fibrous tumor produces a sensation of heaviness in the lower abdomen; it often also gives pains in the same area, which radiate through the thighs. If it is too voluminous, the tumor may compress certain organs, vessels, nerves, etc. Many disorders can arise from these compressions: compression of the iliac veins manifests itself as edema of the legs; compression of the nervous ducts can produce a neuralgia of the sciatic nerve; compression of the rectum leads to constipation, while frequent urination is a result of the compression of the bladder and its opposite, uremia, may happen when the ureter is compressed and blocked.

The Causes

It is difficult to say with exact precision what causes the formation of these tumors, but it is probable that it comes from the accumulation of toxic bodies in a place already weak from birth. The localization of a disease is often the manifestation of a general disorder. The blood carries toxins brought by food, which thrive wherever the organism is weakened by fatigue and emotions. Therefore, these toxins are attracted to the organ whose defensive capability is lowest.

About Remedies

It is clear from the above that the basic remedy is to rid the organism of the toxins. This means no toxic foods of any sort. If it is true that deficiencies lead to biological imbalance it is equally true that the accumulation of non-used food is at the origin of these deficiencies. It does not always suffice to eat more in order to make up for the deficiencies. *What counts most is maximum utilization of nutritive elements, not the increase of their intake.*

The Cure

Lemon is good for accelerating the elimination of substances in excess and for contributing to the fixation of useful elements. Take 2-6 lemons a day, depending on tolerance.

Clay is an amazing remedy for fibrous tumors. It should be taken orally for the same reasons as the lemon. Take 1 teaspoon in ½ a glass of water, once a day on an empty stomach.

Used externally, clay accomplishes wonders when accompanied by natural medicine and food.

A woman with a fibrous tumor in her uterus which caused serious hemorrhages during menstruation was treated with clay. She drank it and applied poultices on her lower abdomen. After 3 months of treatment, an examination in a hospital produced this conclusion: "uterus is in the condition of a person of twenty." The patient was 50 years old.

In another case of a cyst on the ovary, even specialists feared the operation which seemed unavoidable. However, four months of clay applications resulted in a significant reduction of the cyst (at first to the size of an ostrich egg - it had been much larger), making it possible to avoid the operation. Applications of poultices continued until the total disappearance of the cyst.

Spectacular results are often registered after a few weeks of treatment; however, it should be made clear that usually it takes months (and sometimes years, in the case of fibrous tumors that do not bleed) to get rid of it completely.

Specific Treatment

For the first two months apply a poultice a day on the lower abdomen, interrupting it only at the period of menstruation (which is normally 4 days; resume the applications if the periods go beyond that time).

The poultice must remain in place at least 2 hours. It can remain overnight if applied just before going to bed, unless it is too bothersome. The poultice must be approximately 10"-12" large and 1" thick. The clay must be well against the skin (put a cheese cloth on hairy areas only). Begin first with cold clay; only if it is not tolerated should it be warmed up slightly.

It may happen that a bleeding tumor does not react quickly with clay. In this case, replace or alternate the clay poultice with the wheat bran-ivy poultice.

The Plants

If one has already used douches of a chemical nature, they can be replaced by clay, sea salt or walnut-tree leaf douches.

Put 4 tablespoons of clay or sea salt in 2 quarts of lukewarm water, or 2 tablespoons of each. For the walnut leaves put 2 full handfuls in 2 quarts of water. Boil 10-15 minutes. The temperature of the injections must be hardly lukewarm. The operation should be done rapidly.

In case of heavy losses of blood prepare a decoction of oak bark. Use 4 oz. per quart. Boil 10-15 minutes and use as a very slow douche.

Also take the following plants in decoction: wild geranium (alum root), bearberry, comfrey, persicaria, red-grape vine leaves, Shepherd's purse.

When there is no blood loss use the following depurative plants: bittersweet, borage, buckbean, hop, patience dock, sarsaparilla. These plants can be used individually or mixed.

DISEASES OF THE GENITAL ORGANS

Modern medicine gives different names to diseases of the female organs depending on where the troubles are located. For natural medicine this factor is of but secondary importance, for whereever the seat of the trouble, it is still the case that the abnormal phenomena come from the accumulation of toxins which slow down the circulation. A tumor or a cyst may develop if there is not immediate draining.

Most of the time the organism defends itself by secretions of mucous which envelop the toxins and secure their discharge. The injury of the mucous membrane manifests itself by an increase of those discharges which are first white, then yellow or green, or even bloody in some lesions. The mucosities may have pus in them (dead white cells and destroyed microbes). These mucosities often give an offensive odor.

The menstruation lasts too long, giving off too much blood, the person urinates too often. There are digestive troubles, nausea, nervous troubles (palpitations, irritability). The person loses weight, her complexion is dark and she has circles under the eyes. Sometimes the temperature is high and the pulse races. Two symptoms, constipation, and abundance of intestinal gases, demonstrate clearly an insufficiency in the evacuations of the neighboring colon. By osmosis, toxins pass through the intestinal walls and corrupt the genital organs.

The Cure

Begin by draining the accumulated wastes in the organism and then start the specific treatment which includes what follows:

Take a depurative laxative decoction before the main meals for 3-4 weeks. Then, in case of persistency of the constipation, continue to take that same decoction, but only before the evening meal or just before going to bed, and instead, take a decoction for the liver functions before the meal.

Depurative and Laxative Decoction

Buckthorn bark	30 gr.	Borage leaves	10 gr.
St. John's wort	20 gr.	Horsetail	10 gr.
Soapwort	20 gr.	Wild thyme	
Licorice root	15 gr.	(flowered tops)	10 gr.
Madder root	15 gr.	Senna follicles	10 gr.
Sarsparilla	10 gr.		

If the intestines are somewhat fragile, do not mix in the senna with the other plants; it should be added only after the pot has been removed from the fire. Use only 5-10 follicles. 1 or 2 tablespoons of the mixture per cup of water. Bring to a boil; simmer 5 minutes. Infuse 5 minutes.

Do not forget the clay-water every morning on an empty stomach (½ a glass of water to 1 teaspoon of clay). Take a cold hip bath every morning and apply clay poultices on the lower abdomen; every

2 or 3 hours in periods of attacks and once a day before going to bed at other times. Do this for a few months.

If the secretions are very abundant (or if one already had the habit of using douches) the best thing to do is to bathe with the following preparation:

4 tablespoons of clay diluted in 2 quarts of lukewarm water; or walnut-tree or box-tree leaves - a good handful in 2 quarts of water. Boil 10-15 minutes. The douche must be just barely lukewarm and be given once or twice a week.

In case of heavy losses of blood take oak bark baths (p.164).

Also take the following decoction:

Decoction against Heavy Blood Losses

Agrimony	20 gr.	Yarrow	20 gr.
Bearberry	20 gr.	Bistort	10 gr.
Cypress nut	20 gr.	Stinging nettle	10 gr.
Mistletoe	20 gr.	Wintergreen	10 gr.
Shepherd's purse	20 gr.		

2 tablespoons per cup of water. Bring to a boil and simmer for 2 minutes. Infuse 15 minutes. A cup every hour if necessary.

Do not be worried by the abundance of blood loss or the smell of the secretions at the beginning of the treatment. They are a most welcome phenomenon, and will soon cease with continuance of the natural treatment.

Painful Menstruation

Menstruation should not be the occasion for a liver attack, constipation, headache, dizziness, etc., it is a normal and natural phenomenon which should occur without any problem.

The period should last four days and the blood flow must never take on the appearance of hemorrhaging. Sometimes the flow is insufficient and the time of menstruation exceeds four days. It happens then that the blood comes out in the form of clots. All this is abnormal - this must be mentioned again and again since the knowledge of the *normal* has been lost to most people.

One of the functions of the liver is to stabilize the production of the estrogen hormones. The liver supplies the genital glands with most of the elements necessary for this and neutralizes all the excess.

Thus, it is illusory to pretend to have re-established the genital functions without having cured the liver. Use the following decoction for a congested liver from the beginning of the treatment:

Decoction for Congestion of the Liver

Licorice root	30 gr.	Horsetail	10 gr.
Woodruff	30 gr.	Marigold	10 gr.
Artichoke leaves	20 gr.	Rosemary (flowered	
Bearberry leaves	10 gr.	tops)	10 gr.
Black currant		Small centaury	10 gr.
(gooseberry leaves)10 gr.			

A full tablespoon for a cup of water. Boil gently for 2 minutes and infuse 10 minutes. 1 cup before each of the two main meals.

Diet must be improved, use raw vegetable dishes, including, in season, a few flowers of marigold, nasturtium and others which are rich in female hormones, especially when there is insufficient menstruation. Take sage infusions for the same purpose (1 handful per quart of boiling water).

Fruit cures can help very much. Eat only a single variety of fruit for 3 days, once a month (in season).

Stimulate the intestines with an appropriate laxative decoction.

A cold hip bath (60°-65°), lasting 3-5 minutes, every morning, will also help.

If major troubles occur - if the menstruation is very abundant, insufficient, too painful or accompanied by several clots, mucosities or skins, apply a clay poultice on the lower abdomen every night before going to bed. The poultice should be kept overnight, unless it causes discomfort. Otherwise, it is sometimes sufficient to apply these poultices only for 10 days preceding menstruation. Interrupt the application during the menstrual period, which is 4 or 5 days; after that, resume applying them, even if the reactions persist.

The applications can be continued even if the menstruation takes the form of a hemorrhage; be sure to slightly warm up the poultices in order not to create a congestive state. One of the best treatments for hemorrhage consists of applying fresh climbing ivy leaves on the top of the poultice, the stems against the clay. Renew the poultices every 2-3 hours during the day, and every time the clay becomes very warm during the night.

Menstrual pains generally yield to the application of the wheat bran-climbing ivy poultice (p.65). This poultice can be applied on the lower abdomen in case of pain, during menstruation.

When there is a liver attack at the time of menstruation this same poultice may be applied on the liver and stomach.

Lack of Menstruation

Called amenorrhea, it can be a trouble affecting young girls who never had menstruation, or else an abnormal suspension of the menstruations. These suspensions may be a consequence of an excess or a lack of folliculin - in other words, to an endocrinian imbalance. Sometimes they may be caused by a chemical treatment.

A lasting cure will be obtained only if the treatment is aimed at re-establishing the proper balance between the functions of the genital glands and the other organs. Knowing that the liver contributes to the regulation of the sexual hormones, it is easy to see how the imbalance of one of its functions can perturb the production of the precursors of hormones or the neutralization of the excess hormones.

Clay poultices must be applied on the liver and lower abdomen, alternating one with the other.

The general treatment, which includes a better way of eating, will be the one already used for the

****

FIBROUS TUMOR

A person of our acquaintance, after six months of repeated hemorrhages, was about to undergo surgery for the extraction of a fibrous tumor the size of an orange.

Approximately three weeks before the operation, she started application of clay on the lower abdomen. The operation was avoided; the tumor had gone down in the uterus and was evacuated through normal channels.

****

diseases of the genital organs (decoction for the liver functions or depurative-laxative, hip baths and clay-water).

Blood circulation should be stimulated with foot baths, prepared by boiling 2 handfuls of red-grape vine leaves in 2-3 quarts of water for 15 minutes. This bath should be taken every day; each one should last 20-30 minutes and can be used 2 or 3 times.

When the periods are momentarily suspended, the following decoction can contribute to their return:

Decoction for Glandular Troubles

Buckthorn	30 gr.	Absinth	10 gr.
Mugwort	30 gr.	Angelica	10 gr.
Yarrow	30 gr.	Marigold	10 gr.
Catnip	20 gr.	Sweet rush	10 gr.
Costmary	20 gr.	Wild celery	10 gr.

2 tablespoons of this mixture per cup of water. Bring to a boil and simmer for 2 minutes. Infuse 10. 2 cups a day, between meals.

If the lower abdomen seems congested, apply a hot poultice of wheat bran and climbing ivy, kept 1½ hours or overnight if applied before going to bed.

In the case of lack of menstruation on account of hormonal imbalance, stimulate the glands with female hormones. Raw vegetables and salads will include flowers such as marigold, nasturtium, dog rose. Drink infusions of sage as much as possible, which is richest in hormones. Put a handful in a quart of boiling water. Let infuse 10-15 minutes. Drink during meals and when desired.

Leucorrhea

Leucorrhea sometimes accompanies the beginning of the inflammation of the uterus and Fallopian tubes, however, it may have other origins, especially when it is the manifestation of some deficiency (calcium, for example). Many women and most young girls notice an increase of these phenomena at times of fatigue and depression. The white secretions may be simple mucous, or sometimes mixed with pus.

Sometimes a simple change of eating habits, such as the elimination of coffee and milk in combination, will see these secretions cease. Resting can sometimes be of great help.

Include cold hip baths in the morning, and clay poultices on the lower abdomen before going to bed as a part of the treatment.

Every day between meals, take 2 cups of the following infusion:

Infusion for Leucorrhea

Black currants	30 gr.	Birch bark	10 gr.
Blind nettle	30 gr.	Spotted thistle	10 gr.
Basil 10 gr.	10 gr.	Sweet rush	10 gr.
Bennet	10 gr.		

1 tablespoon per cup of boiling water. Infuse 10 minutes.

Vaginal Itching

This irritating manifestation may disappear after simply eliminating some bad eating habits and taking an herbal tea for the liver functions (p. 55).

Special treatments may also be necessary, if only to temper the unpleasant itching.

For this, take short lukewarm hip baths (aside from the cold hip bath used in the fundamental treatment) prepared with 4 handfuls of bran or 2 of walnut-tree leaves or 2 handfuls of both, or 1 handful of oak bark.

Apply a paste made of olive oil and clay powder or just clay powder alone locally.

Sometimes the edges of the vagina are the seat of small transparent blisters gathered on a reddish background. These inflammations (lesions, ulcerations) of the vagina are cured like all abnormal manifestations of the genital system - hip baths, clay poultices, etc.). In addition, a douche would be beneficial:

In 2 quarts of water put 4 oz. of garlic and 1 handful of thyme. Boil gently until it reduces to ½. The douche must be lukewarm and without pressure, the water must penetrate very slowly.

Whether the troubles are attributed to fungi or viruses, such as trichomonas, use a box-tree leaf decoction(1 handful per quart of water, boil 10 minutes), or externally in douches or compresses.

Collibacilli

When, due to an imbalance in the normal composition of the bacterial flora, one variety comes and proliferates, the germs who have become virulent can go through the intestinal walls and reach the bladder, kidneys and genital organs, sometimes affecting them very seriously.

The destruction of these collibacilli by artificial remedies does not solve the problem. New pathogenic germs will come and replace those which are destroyed by the chemicals. Often, these new varieties are even more virulent.

It may be that natural medicine does not give the immediate results that have come to be expected from modern medicine. Notwithstanding, it is the only way to a lasting cure.

It is possible that in periods of crisis, natural foods, which are normally good for health, may not be well-tolerated. Sometimes it is the lemon, the orange, the tomato; sometimes the pear or even the apple. In this case, interrupt having these fruits for awhile until the time when the organism can accept them.

Aside from these exceptional cases, follow the same rules as for the other diseases of the genital organs.

If lemon is well-tolerated, take its juice mixed in some hot water and sweetened with honey after the meal.

Sterility

More and more couples are sterile, and in two out of three cases it is the woman who is sterile. That is the reason why it is important to be watchful that young girls do not present any irregularity in the ovarian functions, that they have no secretions of any sort between the menstrual period. Young girls should be advised to stay away from taking hormonal treatments, for estrogens may block menstruation and favor the appearance of cysts in the ovaries.

Hereditary tendencies play a great role. Sometimes previous treatments, especially radiations, atrophy the genital organs. Or it can be a malformation in the anatomy or physiological make-up. Most of these causes can be remedied in the natural treatment. Even a malformed uterus can come back to a normal position under the influence of clay applications on the lower abdomen.

The treatment of sterility is hardly a matter of local treatment of genital organs, except when there is an affliction such as a fibrous tumor. Most of the time what is required is to improve the daily habits of life, starting with eating, to see a beginning of the return to health.

We have had several cases of women, who, with a natural treatment, succeeded in becoming pregnant after 10 years and even more of 'sterility.'

One excellent food for this treatment is *sprouted wheat,* especially abundant in vitamin E. Here is how to prepare it:

> Choose healthy wheat, unbroken; wash it and put in a bowl of lukewarm water. Let it soak for 24 hours, then rinse and place in a jar, which should be kept humid. Rinse every day; it should sprout in 3 or 4 days (2 in summer). It can be eaten at the appearance of the white spot. Add it to raw vegetable dishes, 1 or 2 tablespoons a day.

Frigidity

The remedy to this problem is not so simple; it requires first restoring most of the organic functions to normal. Only when the nervous relays are reestablished, can a psychological balance be reached. This may take time, but it is very rare that an amelioration is not finally brought about.

To the fundamental treatment, which should become a way of life, a few plants may be added which will help to wake up dull senses, especially by stimulating and tonifying the uterus. Saffron is good for that (used as a spice - with rice, for example); yellow rocket should be sprinkled on raw dishes; cow-parsnip in decoction; 1 tablespoon per cup of boiling water.

Menopause

The habit of accommodating oneself to this disease, giving it a character of fatality and finding it *where it is not* has perverted the mind enough to make of menopause a pathological state. Having passed the age of 40 a woman expects all the discomforts; she feels diminished by the suspension of ovulation. Menopause is becoming more and more a mental construction, linked to life conditions that are contrary to the order of nature.

168

In general, in a woman of good health, leading a life of normal activity, the end of ovulation does not occur before fifty - there are people living close to nature who pass even that limit.

This transition period does not have to force any modification in one's habitual way of living, if it is in concurrence with natural necessities. Unfortunately, years and sometimes generations of accumulated errors have indeed made of menopause a critical age. Troubles of diverse origin mark the four or five years of menopause; it first starts by irregularity in the frequency, the duration, and the amount of the menstruation.

These troubles are most of the time of a congestive order; sudden flushes, dizziness, congestion of the face, diffuse perspirations. They may come in different forms and manifest themselves by palpitations, hearing troubles, loss of figure, sensations of suffocation and even arterial hypertension.

Sometimes there is nausea or other manifestations of a liver disorder. These are most likely to occur if the menopause is artificial, caused by the removal of genital glands, or their atrophy by a treatment with radiation or any other dangerous method. As the liver exercises a regulating action on certain sexual secretions, it is easy to understand how this happens. Usually the more premature the occurrence of the menopause the more accentuated the troubles. After the age of fifty, things are generally better, with the exception for the case where the presence of a fibrous tumor in the uterus is postponing the time of menopause. The occurrence of menopause, when not in the proper time, frequently creates psychological troubles such as anguish, irritability, asthenia, obesity, change of character, but when menopause happens in its proper time, the whole organism is gradually brought to this new rhythm; there is *no broken line or anachronism.*

The Cure

It is preferable not to wait for the 'critical' age to adopt a way of life which will be a precursor to calm and equilibrium.

Foods of the vegetable kingdom 'alleviate' the humors, relieve congestion, favor the glandular action and strengthen the nervous system. Some buttermilk (if possible without its acid liquid), a moderate quantity of eggs, are the only animal products that should be eaten. Natural honeys are excellent. Completely eliminate meat, sugar, alcohol, coffee, tea, or any chemical type of food as soon as possible. (read the chapters on 'circulation' and 'liver' for more details).

Lemon should be given an important place, for it acts favorably on the circulation. *Garlic* and *parsley* are also valuable. Also use chervil, tarragon, shallot, sorrel, chive, horse radish, nutmeg, etc.

Among herbal plants, the *sage* stands out above the others because of its richness in female hormones. It should be used as an aromatic herb in cooking and infusions.

Other good plants are red-grape vine leaves which accelerate the blood circulation in foot baths; hawthorn and passion flower, which temper the disruptions of the heart; mistletoe, which moderates nervous digressions; and persicaria, which diminishes the intensity of the blood flow, if the latter is too intense. These plants may be used individually or in combination, in infusions. Take 2 or 3 infusions a day.

Sudden flushes can be taken care of with red-grape vine leaves in foot or hand baths. The same goes for congestion of the face, hypertension, etc. The bath is prepared with 2 or 3 handfuls of leaves in a gallon of water, boiled 10-15 minutes.

Take cold hip baths (60°-65°), sun baths, and clay poultices on the lower abdomen (in case of prolonged or painful menstruation), and breathing exercises to help bring calm and equilibrium.

For sudden flushes use the following decoction:

Decoction for High Blood Pressure

Rosemary	50 gr.	St. John's wort	25 gr.
Mint	30 gr.	Shepherd's purse	25 gr.
Elecampane	25 gr.	Vervain	25 gr.
Mugwort	25 gr.	Oak apples	25 gr.

A handful of the mixture in a quart of boiling water - let stand overnight. Strain in the morning and take for 10 consecutive days. Rest 2 days and renew the treatment.

SKIN CARE

Getting Rid of Acne, Eczema, Sporiasis

ECZEMA

In modern medicine, skin diseases are the object of a meticulous classification. The medical treatments are so specific that this classification becomes indispensable. To those that are familiar with natural medicine it is known that these subtleties are of only secondary importance. It is more important to find out what the causes are than to classify the effect; it is within everyone's ability to start the natural treatments by himself, as there is not a risk of a slight inaccuracy being dangerous, which is one of the inconveniences of chemical medicine.

Whatever the various aspects of eczema are, one thing is certain, that the source of them all is an arthritic condition. Asthma itself is a manifestation of an arthritic condition. There are many occurrences of eczema which had been treated in 'isolation' transformed into asthma, and there are many whose asthma regresses at the time of an eczema attack.

An acute crisis is often welcome, for then the seriousness of the condition is realized and a big effort to get rid of it will be mobilized.

Treating eczema exclusively with skin medication leads to a worsening of the internal condition with all its consequences: blood poisoning, asthma, nervous imbalance, etc.

Eczema is tenacious and difficult to cure since the nervous system has suffered from it or has accomodated itself to it. Sometimes it is after a psychological crisis that eczema manifests itself. If the organism accomodates itself to this condition, a new equilibrium - an unstable one - is created, and that has to be broken before the return to a normal condition will be possible.

The appearance of eczema is known. It can sometimes be mistaken with other skin problems. such as eruptions, shingles, hives, impetigo or even psoriasis.

With the oozing eczema the surface of the skin is red and humid; it dries up, forming small crusts which flake off when others are formed.

The dry eczema is red, shiny, even 'varnished.' Skin may be chapped. The skin is constantly renewed through peeling.

Itching, pruritis and a feeling of heat accompany the various manifestations of eczema. These often occur in the head, hands, rectum and genital area. That is where eczema persists, even after treatment.

Troubles such as lymphangitis, adenitis, abscess, chills, fever, etc. might occur. There is often nausea, which shows an imbalance of the liver functions.

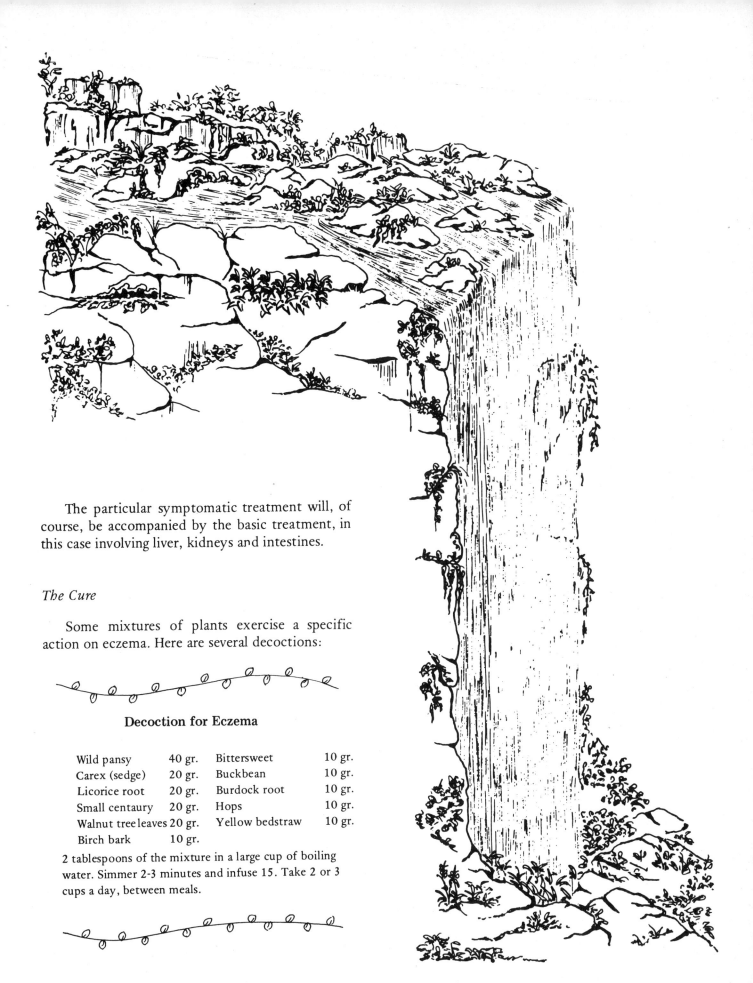

The particular symptomatic treatment will, of course, be accompanied by the basic treatment, in this case involving liver, kidneys and intestines.

The Cure

Some mixtures of plants exercise a specific action on eczema. Here are several decoctions:

Decoction for Eczema

Wild pansy	40 gr.	Bittersweet	10 gr.
Carex (sedge)	20 gr.	Buckbean	10 gr.
Licorice root	20 gr.	Burdock root	10 gr.
Small centaury	20 gr.	Hops	10 gr.
Walnut tree leaves	20 gr.	Yellow bedstraw	10 gr.
Birch bark	10 gr.		

2 tablespoons of the mixture in a large cup of boiling water. Simmer 2-3 minutes and infuse 15. Take 2 or 3 cups a day, between meals.

Infusion for Liver and Gall Bladder

Horsetail	30 gr.	Yellow bedstraw	30 gr.
Licorice root	30 gr.	Marigold	20 gr.
Rosemary	30 gr.	Mint	20 gr.
Woodruff	30 gr.		

2 tablespoons in a cup of boiling water. Infuse 15 minutes. 1 cup after the two main meals.

Children may take the above infusion. However, there is one that is especially indicated for children:

Infusion for Children's Eczema

Anise	15 gr.	Cherry stems	10 gr.
Black currants	15 gr.	Olive tree leaves	10 gr.
Boldo	15 gr.	Sarsaparilla	10 gr.

1 tablespoon in a cup of boiling water. Let infuse for 10 minutes. You may give 2 or 3 teaspoons of this infusion to an infant before breastfeeding; if he is older, give a ½ cup before the meal.

Take clay-water in the morning (1 teaspoon in ½ a glass of water) for a week and olive oil-lemon, (1 teaspoon - ½ a lemon) the following week.

Every morning a short cold hip bath (3 minutes) should be taken. If the parts to be immersed are affected by the eczema, coat them before the bath with a mixture of clay powder and olive oil. Put thick clay poultices on the liver and lower abdomen in the evening, one day on one organ, the next on the other, and so on. Bandage and leave overnight.

Local Treatment

One should experiment with different systems. In general, the dry eczema is treated with a mixture of olive oil and clay (2 tablespoons of oil, 1 of water, mix thoroughly and add 1 tablespoon of clay powder. Mix well). Coat the affected part and bandage.

The oozing eczema is treated by simply powdering it with dry clay. However, in case of inflammation, use a poultice of clay which will be kept on approximately two hours. The poultice must be broad and thick.

Chapped eczema should be given special lotions and local baths in an infusion of wild geranium (wild alum root) and absinth: a heaping tablespoon of each in a quart of boiling water. This preparation cleans the skin and activates peeling. In certain cases, both the baths and the mixture of clay-oil may be used.

If the eczema is infected, put a handful of box-tree leaves in a quart of water; bring to a boil and simmer 10-15 minutes. Alternate it with the clay poultice.

When the eruptions are accompanied by burning sensations, swelling and other discomforts, apply hot poultices of a mixture of elder-tree flowers (4, 6, or 8 tablespoons, and enough whole wheat flour to make a paste when the water is added). Cook the mixture in a small amount of water for a few minutes. Put in a cheese cloth and apply hot.

The following preparation is excellent for rebellious eczemas. Use walnuts that are still in their green envelope. Crush or press them, trying to retain as much liquid as possible. Rub the juice on the eczema.

These local treatments will help a lot. However, a true and complete cure can be obtained only in combination with treatment of the fundamental problem (see 'liver').

ACNE

The causes and treatments of any eruption resembling acne do not diverge. Two hypotheses are acceptable; either it is a discharge that remained in an incomplete stage, or the phenomenon resembles what sometimes happens with diabetes when the troubles of nutrition lead up to a toxic condition.

It is certain that malnutrition and devitalization are the causes of acne; that is why it would be vain to treat the eruption with local treatments. These come only after starting the basic treatment.

One of the most currently common forms of acne is the one that is characterized by the appearance of nodes localized on the face and on the upper part of the chest and back.

People like to believe that acne is a juvenile problem, and yet people of all ages seem to suffer from it. Among older people acne comes in different forms; a variety of crusty seborrhoea is manifested by the appearance on the nose and cheeks of yellow or gray crusts.

In all cases of acne, the primary step is to bring the intestinal functions to normal. Either the evacuations are insufficient or the feces lack consistency or color or else they are too colored.

The Cure

As the intestines are dependent on the liver, the treatment will have to act jointly on both organs. The person suffering from acne has brought himself to such a toxic and devitalized condition that he must categorically eliminate all harmful products, and take only such food as fruits and vegetables (often raw), cereals, dried fruits, honey, yoghurt, buttermilk, and fresh eggs.

Clay (1 teaspoon in ½ a glass of water) every morning on an empty stomach will get rid of a great part of the toxic products. The liver should be stimulated with the olive-oil lemon juice mixture (1 teaspoon of each, mixed) in the morning. Alternate this with clay-water weekly.

Before the meals take the following decoction:

Decoction for Congestion of the Liver

Licorice root	30 gr.	Horsetail	10 gr.
Woodruff	30 gr.	Marigold	10 gr.
Artichoke leaves	20 gr.	Rosemary	
Bearberry leaves	20 gr.	(flowered tops)	10 gr.
Black currant		Small centaury	10 gr.
(gooseberry leaves)	10 gr.	Yellow bedstraw	10 gr.

1 tablespoonful for a cup of water. Bring to a boil. Simmer for 2 minutes. Remove from fire and let infuse 10 minutes.

After meals, drink a cup of hot water mixed with the juice of ½ a lemon.

Before going to bed take the following decoction which is good for the bowel movements:

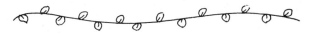

Decoction for Constipation

Althea	20 gr.	Linden flowers	20 gr.
Bittersweet stem	20 gr.	Nettle root	20 gr.
Buckthorn	20 gr.	Wild chicory	
Black currant		leaves	20 gr.
leaves	20 gr.	Rhubarb	
		(rhizome)	20 gr.

1 tablespoon of the mixture in a cup of water. Bring to a boil; remove from fire, add 1 teaspoon of senna and let infuse 10 minutes.

Before going to bed, apply a clay poultice on the liver or the intestines, alternating each night.

A cold hip bath every morning (4-5 minutes) up to the groin will revitalize the person.

Treat locally as needed. Sometimes two or more preparations should be used. Don't be afraid to experiment.

Begin the clay treatment by making a paste either with water or with olive oil and water (mix 1 tablespoon of oil and 1 of water with 1 of clay powder). This paste may be put in place either with the hand, or with a soft brush (soak the hairs first). Afterwards, rinse and wipe with a little lemon juice. The paste prepared with water only should be removed and renewed rapidly, whereas the one prepared with oil can remain in place for hours, even overnight. In the morning, aid the cleansing of the organs by drinking lemon juice or a mixture of olive oil and lemon juice, or an infusion (10 minutes) of equal parts of absinth and wild geranium (wild alum root).

Sometimes the deficiency is so bad that it takes a few months to completely get rid of acne.

ABSCESSES, BOILS, ETC.

Whatever the cause of these troubles, whether internal or external, the treatment has to start with a good draining of the liver, intestines, kidneys and bladder. It is only after this has been started that one can proceed to complementary local measures. Proceed in the following manner:

In the morning on an empty stomach take 1 teaspoon of clay in ½ a glass of water.

Before lunch have the decoction for the liver described in the section on acne.

Before dinner take the following decoction to depurate the blood and activate the evacuations:

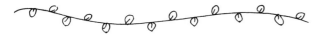

Decoction for Blood Purification

Buckthorn bark	30 gr.	Wild thyme	
St. John's wort	20 gr.	(flowered tops)	10 gr.
Soapwort	20 gr.	Sarsaparilla	10 gr.
Licorice root	15 gr.	Senna follicles	10 gr.
Madder root	15 gr.	Horsetail	10 gr.
Borage leaves	10 gr.		

1 or 2 tablespoons in 1 cup of water; bring to a boil and let infuse 15 minutes.

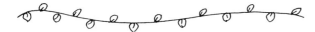

After the evening meal, drink a cup of water with ½ a lemon and 1 teaspoon of honey.

Put a clay poultice on the liver before going to bed. In the morning take a short cold hip bath.

Never touch the afflicted area. This would retard the healing processes which depend so much on cleansing and purifying.

Apply clay poultices locally, renewing them every 1½ hours, sometimes even every hour or ½-hour. The clay should be prepared soft, for it dries very quickly. Clay poultices are the most active of all auxiliaries; they are best in helping pus eliminate through the outlet of the infection (the boil or abscess). Apply the clay until there are shooting pains. Then temporarily interrupt the clay treatment and use one of the following: a poultice of cooked onion, or a plaster prepared by diluting 1 or 2 teaspoons of sea salt in some water and placing it on a flame, stirring constantly. Add clay powder until it becomes a heavy batter. Continue to stir for awhile and remove from fire. Place in a thin cloth and apply this very hot against the skin. Put 1 plaster on at night and 1 in the morning. Keep in place permanently. Raw cabbage leaves may also be alternated with the clay poultices; apply them as they are after soaking for several hours in a mixture of equal parts of lemon juice and water.

Once the abscess has 'ripened,' resume the regular clay poultices for the daytime. For night, use a large wet compress (cheese cloth plunged in clayish water). Do not cover with anything that does not let it breathe; rather, cover with a cabbage leaf which will maintain the humidity and let air enter. A cheese cloth will be placed on top of the cabbage.

Keep the area humid, so that the cavity does not close, keeping non-evacuated matters inside.

By prolonging the clay applications, even when the abscess or boil is well-emptied, the chances of a scar remaining are reduced considerably. Space the poultices further apart and leave them on for 2-4 hours. Between poultices wash the area with unboiled salt-water (1 handful salt in 1 quart of water).

People often believe that if the pus reaches the bone it will be necessary to cut very deep and scrape off the pus. It has been observed several times that where the bone has been touched, the cure was made complete without cutting.

Without the treatment of ulcers and tumors as also with all suppurating sores or those capable of suppuration, the first effect of clay is a drastic cleansing of the ulcer and a closing of the surrounding area. This is followed by an apparent aggravation and extension of the ulcer, both in size and depth. It will take on a disagreeable aspect; pus lodged in the surroundings gives a violent aspect to the dead skin, which will flake off before the replacement with new and healthy cells. Do not be affected, but continue the treatment with confidence; new flesh will not delay in appearing.

RELATED AFFLICTIONS

Many people suffer from these in the cold season. They erupt because of diverse causes; sometimes from excesses, sometimes deficiencies.

The thickening and overloading of the blood, whose circulation becomes difficult, are the main causes of chilblains. Young girls and women who experience painful menstruation know this problem too well. The blood does not circulate well, substances are stuck, obstructing the capillaries. The non-irrigated skin, which is badly nourished, dries up and develops cracks. The skin expects these excesses which are blocking its nourishments to be discharged through normal eliminatory channels. When this is not accomplished, it responds to the urgency itself by opening up channels of evacuation towards the outside. This does not help the situation, for while the skin is trying to reject the poisons it is opened up to all outside elements including many harmful ones.

The Cure

The first measure is to stop eating foods which create a toxic condition; no meat, white bread, white sugar, alcohol, etc. Then take care of the intestines with a laxative decoction and purify the blood by taking the clay-water (1 teaspoon in ½ a glass of water, once or twice a day on an empty stomach).

Do not think this is a substitute for lemon juice, whose action is irreplaceable. Begin with 2 lemons a day, the juice in some water, without sugar, for one week. The second week, take 4 lemons a day, the third week even 6, coming back to 2 lemons afterwards.

Eat fruits exclusively for a few days. Then fruits and raw vegetables (carrots, beets, turnips, grated; raw cabbage and lettuce in salads). Some dried fruits.

Use wheat in all its forms (raw, cooked, ground, in grain forms, sprouted).

Take a hip bath every day. It should last 3-5 minutes in 60°-65° water.

Local hot baths prepared with red-grape vine leaves (2 handfuls) for feet and hands activates the circulation. To soften the skin, take a bath prepared with 2 handfuls of wheat bran and 1 of walnut tree leaves; boil 15 minutes. After the bath, massage the hands with the white part of a lemon peel.

PSORIASIS

This is cured by most people to a certain extent by exposure to the sun. However, some people experience a recrudescence by doing so. Those who could never tolerate sunbathing and ocean swimming will probably not find relief in this practice.

Those for whom being near the ocean is favorable should know that only by coming back to it for 2 or 3 consecutive years can they hope for a lasting cure. In the meantime, they should pay close attention to their way of eating.

See the section on eczema for specific treatments.

SEBORRHOEA

This exaggerated secretion of the sebaceous glands may be dry or oily. It is often a corollary of diverse skin diseases such as eczema or psoriasis.

This affliction, although superficial in appearance, is a deep one, for it betrays an advanced case of an arthritic condition.

The way of eating must be changed. Fruits and vegetables should be given primary importance.

Follow the same basic treatment as for eczema. It would be advisable to read the chapter on the liver.

PERSPIRATION OF THE HANDS AND FEET

After having switched to a vegetarian way of eating and beginning to drain and stimulate the liver, kidneys and intestines with the appropriate decoctions (see 'acne'); after having started drinking clay, take the following baths for hands and feet:

1) Wheat bran-walnut tree leaf baths to tonify the tissues.
2) Red-grape vine leaf baths to stimulate the circulation. Prepare the same way as the preceding bath.
3) Oak bark baths to tighten up the skin. Put 4 oz. in a quart of water and boil 15 minutes.

If the perspiration persists after 2 months of this treatment, take thick clay 'mud baths'. Afterwards, massage lightly with lemon juice.

HIVES (Urticaria)

Sometimes urticaria is accompanied by hay fever, asthma or eczema. They all have the same origin: failure of the liver, which does not neutralize certain toxins or which cannot secrete all the substances that are necessary to the integral transformation of foods.

See the eczema section for treatment.

CORNS, CALLOUSES, AND WARTS

To the regular skin treatments already mentioned, add foot or hand baths in a solution of red-grape vine leaves and water (boil 2 handfuls of leaves in a gallon of water for 15 minutes).

A Special treatment for Warts

Scoop out the inside of an onion; put sea salt inside. Daub a small piece of cotton with the juice that comes out of the salted onion and apply it on the warts very often.

A Special treatment for Corns

Cut a round slice of garlic exactly to size. Attach it to the corn with a sticky dressing. Renew it morning and evening.

Corns and callouses that are massaged every night with lemon juice can be reabsorbed if there is enough perseverance. The massage of the whole foot makes the sensitive skin firm. It also is a preventive against chilblains.

SHINGLES

Use clay poultices immediately after the appearance of the blisters and feelings of pain. There is no reason to hesitate; even if it is the wrong diagnosis,

there is no risk with clay; it only helps.

At the beginning of the treatment, renew the poultices every 2 or 3 hours. Later on, when the eruptions and the pain lessens, reduce the number until they are being applied only once or twice in a 24 hour period. Do not stop the poultices abruptly, continue for a few weeks to make sure that everything has been eliminated.

Follow the general treatment recommended for eczema.

Important note: The reader should refer to p. 51 to find out what the daily meal should consist of, and to p. 47 to become acquainted with the type of food to use. P. 29 provides information on measurement and preparation of herbs.

USING CLAY FOR COSMETICS

Clay's invaluable properties make it an ideal base for skin care products. Although most active in its virgin state, clay may be blended with other natural ingredients to become highly effective deep cleansing masks, toothpaste, shampoo, and even soap. You may mix your own cosmetics or buy them ready-blended. A reputable beauty and hygiene company in France, appreciating the value of clay in skin care, has formulated an excellent group of products using green clay -- considered to be one of the most active of all. These clay-based toiletries have been widely used in Europe for over 10 years and are now available in the U.S.*

Deep cleansing masks

Perhaps the easiest way to use clay is as a skin beautifier. When applied to the skin as a mask, oxidation and circulation are accelerated, defensive functions stimulated and body temperatures lightly raised. Thus clay acts rather like a light massage. In addition, clay, as with every natural product, is

a balancer and revitalizer.

To mix your own masks, make a paste by adding ½ a glass of water, ½ a cucumber, tomatoes, or grape juice to clay powder. Apply thinly and uniformly all over face, back, or wherever you have over-oily or troubled skin. Leave the pack moist as long as possible to give skin flexibility with no sensation of tightness. Then allow to dry and rinse off.

Clay, being very absorbent, thoroughly, but very gently, cleanses the tissues. Because it is so kind, it may even be applied to dry and delicate skin, without drying at all.

A more soothing cosmetic cream can be made by mixing clay powder with olive oil, or you can use the French masks, ready-blended with pure olive oil and sweet almond oil.

Treat any unwanted growths or blemishes with clay. Apply very thickly on a pimple or wrinkle at night and leave until morning.

Wash irritated, pimply, grainy, or very delicate skin with clayish water, without soap, then rub it with the inside of a lemon peel.

Under-eye sacs are very much relieved or even

---

*See Buyer's Guide

disappear with clay applications and complementary treatment of heart or kidneys, whichever is responsible.

Shampoos

Clay is excellent for regular hair washing as it has a natural acid pH that is similar to the skin. It is particularly recommended for a greasy scalp. To combat this, make a clear paste with water and apply as a shampoo. Leave on for at least ½ an hour and rinse off. The European shampoos contain olive oil and plant-based foaming agents to bring hair back to its natural lustre.

Toothpaste

One of the best natural toothpastes is clay, or a mix of clay and seasalt. Being so absorbent, clay is completely non-abrasive. It lifts off dulling film, removes mouth odors naturally, and acts as a gum stimulant.

Soaps

Blended with honey and olive oil, clay makes a very effective soap. It removes deep-seated grime, acts as a natural deodorant, and balances the skin. The added ingredients bring their own softening and soothing qualities for first class skin care.

NATURAL RECIPES FOR THE SKIN

How to make an ointment

Prepare the appropriate decoction among those indicated below. For conversion tables and complete directions on preparation, see p.29.

To the chosen decoction add 3 oz. of olive oil and ½ oz. of virgin wax (heaping tablespoon).

Place over fire: simmer until the liquid has completely evaporated, which may take a ½ hour. Let it cool off. It should be an unctuous paste. Place again over fire if there is any water left. If the paste is too firm, heat it in a double boiler and add some oil. If, on the contrary, the dough is of a soft consistency, put it in the double boiler and add a little bit more wax. Keep stirring while it is cooling off in order to keep it homogenous.

The Different Decoctions

Put the chosen plant in 1 cup of water. Bring to a boil and let simmer gently. How much of the plant should be used and for how long the decoction should simmer is given next to the plant. Prepare, if possible, in the evening and let macerate overnight.

For a softening and decongesting ointment - for eczema, inflammation, pruritis, painful ulcers, etc.

Mullein: 1 oz.; simmer 10 minutes
Althea: 1 tablespoon of the root or 2 of the leaves; boil 10 minutes.
Birch-tree leaves: 1 oz; simmer 10 minutes
Wild geranium(wild alum root) and absinth(wormwood): ½ oz. of the mixture; boil 2-3 minutes
Walnut-tree leaves: 2 tablespoons; boil 15 minutes
Bittersweet berries: ½ oz.; boil 10 minutes
Elder tree flowers: 2 tablespoons; boil 2-3 minutes

For an astringent action - for varicose veins, hemorrhoids, chapped skin, dilated skin, etc.

Oak bark: 1 oz.; boil 15 minutes
Quince: ½ oz. of the dried fruit; boil 10 minutes.
Silverweed: ½ oz.; boil 2-3 minutes
Birthwort: ½ oz.; boil 2-3 minutes
Comfrey: 1 oz. of the root; boil 15 minutes
Mistletoe: 1 tablespoon of the leaves; boil 15 minutes
Plantain: ½ oz. of the leaves; boil 15 minutes

For the massage of painful areas - in case of rheumatism, arthritis, sciatica, etc.

Climbing ivy: ½ oz. of the leaves; boil 15 minutes
Seaweed: ½ oz. or mixed in equal parts with climbing ivy leaves; boil 15 minutes

For the reconstitution of tissues and the healing of sores - in cases such as ulcer, scab, ulcered chilblains, etc.

Box-tree leaves: 1 oz.; boil 15 minutes
Sage (leaves and flowers): ½ oz.; boil 10 minutes
Milfoil (yarrow): 2 tablespoons of the chopped plant; boil 10 minutes
Marigold: 2 tablespoons of the flowers; boil 10 minutes
St. John's wort: 2 tablespoons of the chopped plant, boil 10 minutes
Veronica: ¼ oz.; boil 10 minutes

DAILY SKIN CARE

To tonify, revitalize and make the skin firm, get rid of wrinkles and blackheads.

Lotions: with the juice of a carrot, tomato, quince, or cucumber

Mask: Mix 1 teaspoon of honey, 1 teaspoon rye flour, 1 egg yolk. Keep on for 20-30 minutes.
For dry skin: add 1 teaspoon of olive oil.
For oily skin: replace the egg yolk with the juice of ½ a lemon.

Ointment: prepared with 1 oz. of each: honey, onion juice, virgin wax, bulb of lily. Boil gently the lily bulb in 1 cup of water until it reduces to half. Strain and add the honey, wax, and onion juice. Cook in a double boiler until the wax melts. Keep stirring while it is cooling off to keep the mixture homogenous.

Pollen Mask: Grind 1 teaspoon of pollen in a coffee grinder until very fine. Mix with a fresh egg yolk. Use this pomade as soon as it is made on the face, neck, massaging gently. Keep on for a ½ hour.

Lotion with a decoction of quince: Use 3 quinces, fresh or dried; cut them into small pieces, put in a quart of water and boil 20-30 minutes.

FOR IRRITATED AND INFLAMED AREAS, FOR ULCERS, CHILBLAINS, ECZEMA

Poultice: prepared with the pulp of a carrot
Mixture: made of equal parts of lemon juice and honey
Mixture: prepared as above, but adding an infusion of rose petals
Maceration: a handful of quince seeds in a cup of hot water (for chilblains, certain hemorrhoids, breast chaps, scurvy, etc.)
Agar-agar decoction: Cook 2 teaspoons in 1 cup of water for 15 minutes
Pomade: prepared with 2 oz. grape juice, 4 oz. almond oil and 2 oz. of virgin wax. Cook everything in a double boiler until the wax is completely melted. Mix well during cooking.
Mixture: prepared with equal parts of sweet almond oil and cocoa butter. Melt in double boiler. Mix well (excellent for cracked hands).
Mixture: prepared with an egg and 2 tablespoons of sweet almond oil. Mix thoroughly (good for inflamed areas, hemorrhoids, for example).
Poultice: prepared with rice or barley flour.

HAIR CARE

Hair washing

Dilute a few tablespoons of rye flour in cold water (find out the ideal quantity). Bring to a boil, stirring constantly. Let it cool off a bit. Use as a shampoo. Rinse with lukewarm water.

Treatment for oily hair

Mix 3 oz. of clay powder and ¾ oz. of sulphur (4:1). Apply this on the scalp. Leave on overnight. Rinse with lukewarm water in the morning. Repeat as often as necessary.

Rinse for blond hair

Put 2 handfuls of chamomile in a quart of water. Boil for 15-20 minutes.

To fortify the hair

– 1 handful of nasturtium leaves, 1 handful of its flowers, and 1 of its seeds in a quart of water. Bring to a boil

and simmer 10-15 minutes. Use as a lotion for the scalp,
— 2 handfuls of flowered tops of small centaury in a
   quart of water. Bring to a boil and simmer 10 minutes.
— massage the scalp with raw watercress juice
— rinse with lemon juice

Hair coloring

Prepare a dough with Henna powder.* Apply hot. Keep on for 2 hours. Aside from that put 1 pound of walnut-tree leaves in 2 quarts of water; bring to a boil; leave over fire until it reduces to half. This preparation will be used as the last rinsing water. This gives a fawn-colored tint to gray or white hair.

Capillary lotion
To prevent loss of hair and activate its growth

Mix 4 oz. of each: nasturtium seeds, box-tree leaves, stinging nettle leaves and burdock root. Put 2 oz. of the mixture in a quart of water. Bring to a boil and let simmer gently without a lid until it reduces to half.

To give hair its natural color

—a concentrated decoction of thyme (also effective as capillary lotion)
—rinsing with a decoction of thyme and bay leaves, to which the juice of a whole lemon has been added.

To make white hair slightly blond

Put 1½ tablespoons of henna powder in a bowl; add some water to make a smooth dough. Bring to a boil and remove from the fire. Use a soft brush to apply to the hair. Keep on for 20 minutes, and then rinse.

—————————————————————————————————

*Henna is a brownish (green when fresh) powder sold in most artist supply stores.

* *

ACNE

A man had suffered a bad case of acne for ten years. Doctors' and dermatologists' prescriptions were without effect. He turned to natural remedies; for two months he took clay orally and applied it in the form of poultices. A great amount of pus and blood was discharged through the skin, after which the acne cleared up completely, leaving no trace whatsoever.

* *

CHILDREN'S DISEASES

A healthy child may still have some toxins to eliminate, either of hereditary origin, or from pollution of the air or even from certain foods, chemically treated, as there was no supervision of their source. A healthy child will undergo such eruptive diseases as measles, chicken pox, and perhaps mumps, but this should never take a serious turn.

MEASLES

All traces of this disease must be erased by the tenth day.

Continue the nose and throat cleansings (see p.109) that will have been started at the appearance of the head cold.

During the period of fever, darken the room and maintain a 72° temperature. The child should not lie completely flat on the bed; raise him up with pillows to prevent congestion of the lungs.

Give lemon-water and thyme tea.

Give 2 hip baths a day. Apply 3 clay poultices for 2 hours each on the abdomen every day of the fever.

When the first difficulty of breathing is noticed, make a mustard plaster and apply it twice a day until the end of the fever. Read the section on fever.

Introduce food gradually.

MUMPS

This inflammation of the salivary and parotid glands may affect the testicles, ovaries, mammary glands, pancreas and thyroid.

Follow the general treatment: vegetarian food (in small amounts), hip baths, clay-water and herbal teas according to need.

The child must remain in bed only if there is fever. In such a case, he should get up only to take the hip baths 2-4 times a day, depending on the temperature. If there is temperature, do not give food.

Apply clay poultices ½'' thick, 3-4 times a day. Keep each one on for 2 hours. Also apply poultices on the genital organs, salivary and parotid glands, alternately.

To prevent possible meningitis, apply a helmet of cabbage leaves (3-4 layers) on the head, maintaining it in place with a bandage. It should be replaced after 8 hours.

WHOOPING COUGH

Even though it is characterized by its cough, whooping cough is most of all the manifestation of damage in certain nervous centers.

Take care of it with cold hip baths (2-3 minutes long), clay poultices on the back of the neck, wheat bran-climbing ivy poultices on the solar plexus and one of the following preparations:

Decoction of Garlic and Thyme

1½ oz. garlic   ½ oz. thyme

Put them in a quart of water; bring to a boil and simmer gently until the liquid is reduced to ½. Take every 3 hours, 1 teaspoon up to 1 year old, 1 tablespoon above that age.

Garlic Syrup

Place a thin layer of crushed or grated garlic on the bottom of a dish. Sprinkle on the garlic an equal and uniform layer of cane sugar (brown). Leave it aside a few hours and then collect the juice that is produced. Give it in doses of a teaspoon or mix it with some water or thyme infusion.

In case of a persistent cough, use the following:

Infusion for Cough

Bittersweet	15 gr.	Peach-tree	15 gr.
Corn-poppy	15 gr.	Valerian	15 gr.
Golden rod	15 gr.	Peony	15 gr.
Mistletoe	15 gr.	Arnica	5 gr.
Narcissus	15 gr.	Wormwood	5 gr.

For 2-5 years old, 1 teaspoon; age 5-10, 1½ teaspoons. Above that age 1 tablespoon. Put the mixture in a cup of boiling water. Let infuse a few minutes. Take 1-4 cups a day.

TONSILLITIS AND ADENOIDS

As they shelter multiple lymphatic masses that are destined to produce white blood cells and other protective substances, tonsils constitute organs of defense of the respiratory channels, and to surgically remove them is a mutilation. With adenoids, it is quite different; they appear to be a formation of parasites resulting from hypertrophy of the adenoid tissues in the pharynx. Even with natural treatments it is not always possible to remedy this situation, and surgery may prove indispensable. In such cases, be careful to ensure that the adenoids alone are removed, nothing being done to the tonsils.

In general, hypertrophy of the tonsils ends when the child reaches the age of 10. Make an effort to let him reach that age with his organs intact.

The Cure

For tonsillitis either water-sea salt mixture or lemon juice can be used, or both alternately. For example, salted water in the morning and lemon drops in the evening.

A mixture of honey and lemon attenuates the inflammation of the tonsils; place a piece of cotton in a special stick made for this purpose, then imbibe it, with the mixture of honey and lemon juice (equal parts) making gentle contacts with the tonsils.

Every day, give a cup of the following decoction before going to bed:

Decoction for Inflamed Glands

Buckthorn	60 gr.	Couch-grass root	30 gr.
Ash-tree leaves	30 gr.	Hyssop	30 gr.
Hulled barley	30 gr.	Licorice root	30 gr.

Use 1 or 2 tablespoons of this mixture per cup of water; bring to a boil and remove from fire. Use the buckthorn only if a laxative effect is also necessary.

****

TONSILLITIS

One patient developed tonsillitis with high fever. The doctor that was called feared a serious inflammation and prescribed antibiotics. But instead of using them this boy continued the clay poultices which he had already started. The third day the fever began to go down, the fifth day it was normal.

For precaution's sake, and to ensure the cure he continued taking clay-water and applying poultices on the liver for awhile.

****

Do not neglect attending to the liver functions, together with the function of elimination, for, depending on hereditary predisposition, the toxins which are insufficiently neutralized by the liver, or not well-eliminated by the intestines, kidneys, or bladder, inevitably aggravate the inflammation of the tonsils.

IMPETIGO

It is an alarm signal. It shows that the child is not eliminating the toxins through natural channels.

Local treatment

Coat with a mixture of clay and water that resembles mud, 3 times a day after a cleansing with a box-tree decoction.

Have the child clean his nasal ducts with a solution of sea salt and water or with equal parts of olive oil and lemon juice.

Put 3 layers of cabbage leaves on the liver overnight.

The child must have regular bowel movements. If not, give him the following preparation:

In the evening put senna follicles (one follicle for each year of age) in a cup of cold water. Let macerate overnight and give in the morning on an empty stomach.

Every day, if possible, give a little of the following:

Infusion for Tonsillitis

Birch-tree buds	1 oz.	Wild pansy	2 oz.
Borage	1 oz.		

1 teaspoon of the mixture per cup of boiling water. Infuse 5 minutes.

Of course, take the natural harmonist approach to eating to ensure a good general condition. If the child is more than 1 year old, give fruits for 3 weeks, 1 teaspoon of sprouted wheat and plenty of carrot juice.

POLIO

As a general rule, polio occurs to those who have undergone long periods of medical prescriptions. Polio can come only to the child who has lost his natural immunity. There is no example of a harmonist child who has been victim to a clear and distinctive case of polio.

Polio may be curable with natural methods, but we do not have the confirmation which allows us to present an efficient remedy.

Knowing that polio injures only deficient children, act accordingly by nourishing them with the right foods. The deficient state cannot be treated 'specifically', the attenuation of the symptoms has nothing to do with the cure. What is primarily recommended is to treat the liver. Clay poultices on the back of the neck will be of great help after the liver treatment is well under way.

If there is an acid blood condition, adequate protection of the organism is not guaranteed. The harmonist child has a slightly alkaline pH level in the blood due to the richness of its basic elements and his vegetarian foods. All fruits and vegetables (except walnuts and legumes) are alkalizing. Bread is also, but only when made of whole wheat flour and natural leavening and not baked in gas ovens.

The best and surest 'vaccination' is a cold hip bath each morning, for this accelerates the vital exchanges, and helps build up defenses.

Clay taken orally fortifies the organism and maintains a balanced intestinal flora, thus enabling good utilization of food. Lemon-water will serve as a purification. In case of an epidemic, insist on the use of clay, lemon, and garlic, which contain many protective elements.

Parents who live according to harmonist principles do not ignore the above measures. Many write and share their joy of their children's health and freedom from serious diseases.

THE EAR

The cause of the infection of the ear is like that of sinus infection - the liver is suffering an obstruction and the humors are polluted because of it.

Ear infection signals itself by sharp pains which increase in intensity at night. Deafness occurs at the same time with a buzzing feeling and pulsating of the vessels. The fever generally attains 100°-101° but may go even higher. Even if the fever is not too high, it is preferable not to eat.

General rule: Drink a lot to clean the blood and the viscera. Favor the evacuation with laxative and diuretic decoctions. Take clay-water, lemon-water (with a large amount of lemon juice), infusions of thyme, linden flowers, eucalyptus, etc.

Apply clay on the back of the neck. The poultices should follow one another, each one lasting 2-3 hours. They should be 1" thick, covering an area that reaches both ears. It is even recommended to cover the ears themselves, first putting a small piece of cotton inside the ear, bandage it to the forehead and not to the neck.

If there should arise a feeling of hotness in the head, then apply the poultices cold and thick. Protect the hair with gauze. In serious cases, cold poultices must be renewed every 1½ hours and even more frequently if clay becomes heated. If this heating is not too quick or if the patient feels a sensation of internal cold, stop the cold applications and continue with clay heated in a double boiler.

It is advisable to precede these clay poultices behind the neck with compresses of hot water for dilating the pores, aiding the elimination of toxins and soothing the pain.

During the period following an acute crisis and also in the case of chronic or slight affections, 2 poultices a day should be sufficient. Sustain them for about 2 hours.

Clay poultices should also be applied on the lower abdomen (3-4 a day) and kept on 2-3 hours. Give cold hip baths if they are well-tolerated. They should last 3-10 minutes. Do this 4-6 times a day.

Wash the ear with lukewarm salted water and, once a week, put about ½-1 teaspoon of lemon juice in each ear (except if the tympanum is perforated); leave for ½ an hour. Do this with one ear first, and then after 3 or 4 days, with the other. If lemon produces violent pains, put a teaspoon of hot oil in the ear at night and lemon the following morning.

For cases of 'hard wax' in the ears, it can be softened by mixing the lemon juice with the juice squeezed from raw cabbage.

It will also be necessary to cleanse the nose several times a day either with clayish water, saltwater, or a decoction of thyme. It suffices to put the nose in the liquid and breathe in with each nostril alternately.

****

EAR CANCER

There was a case of ear cancer in a patient 78 years old who had already been operated upon. The consultant specialists considered this relapse a forerunner to the unavoidable end; all medical or surgical treatment was considered a failure. The patient turned to clay.

Repeated applications of clay on the actual tumor produced the elimination of pus and black blood. Tissues began to be rebuilt after 8 months of treatment and the tumor closed almost entirely. Two years after his fatal condemnation (at the time of this report) the patient is still living, the trouble rapidly diminishing.

****

LOSING WEIGHT IN GOOD HEALTH

Problems of obesity can start from various causes - grief or a psychological shock of some sort can be the original source. Lesions of the central nervous system may lead to exogenous obesity by an increased food consumption. Endogenous obesity is probably caused by metabolism troubles because of a defect in the regulating nervous center.

Obesity which comes after menopause would more likely be the consequence of a perturbation of the hypothalamus. Not only do treatments which involve ovarian hormones not help one to lose weight, they sometimes even cause the contrary.

Some tuberculous people gain weight after an antibiotic 'cure'. Some mothers gain after giving birth.

There are people who suffer from an obesity caused both by the accumulation of fat in the fatty tissues and retention of water in the tissues and muscles. This form of obesity happens most often to women, and not always heavy eaters. This is why we find people gaining weight by eating large amounts of fruits - because of circulation trouble.

Bad arterial circulation impedes the normal nutrition of the cell. Defective circulation in the veins prevents the channeling of the wastes towards the organs of neutralization and elimination. Organs that are improperly irrigated or insufficiently drained will imperfectly produce the elements that are the precursors of hormones; thus the good function of the endocrine glands is impaired. Improperly irrigated, the nervous centers will transmit disordered commands; the whole organism will suffer.

The deep fatty tissue contributes to maintaining the organs in place; it is richer in water and less in fat and, as a whole, constitutes important energetic reserves. The fats must pass through it before being utilized when necessary.

It would seem that the obese - having more fats and reserves - possess more resources than other people, but this is not so; on the contrary, the problem is that he cannot utilize all the reserve fats which have accumulated. *The fats are immobilized.* His case can be likened to a full bowl which loses only the water that is added to it from the top.

In order to be utilized, the reserve fats must be

broken down first. It is the liver which does most of this operation, with the kidneys and the lungs supplying secondary participation. A deficiency of the liver functions does not allow this rational utilization of the reserve of fats. These obstruct the fatty tissue, overcharging its cells and causing expansion of the body.

It is essential to understand that obesity may be caused by both deficiency and overcharge together. Some organisms subjected to the repeated effects of overeating cannot get basic nutritive elements from the excessive amount of food. Thus overeating has repercussions affecting all the organs of digestion and assimilation and precedes troubles in these functions. It leads directly to deficiencies.

The Cure

Nothing is better for these deficiencies than natural elements, not only for their vitamins and amino acids, mineral salts, but also other important substances such as ferments, enzymes, and other elements which are necessary for the proper utilization of food elements.

Look not only for the 'rich' elements which the body needs, but also for those which will favor assimilation.

Losing weight very fast is not significant. It rarely lasts. It is better to strive for a reconstitution of the failing functions, which will secure a good equilibrium.

A basic treatment on the liver (see 'the liver') helps assimilation, neutralization and evacuation. Stay away from toxic foods such as meat products, fish, animal fats, alcohol, and alkaloids.

The liver and fatty tissue itself can utilize the products resulting from the breakdown of natural sugars and proteins to make fats. Thus the organism can produce a fat reserve even if the food brings little of it; it suffices that the food be rich in starches, natural sugars, etc.

It is important to make a distinction between natural and industrial sugars, olive oil and other fats, whole cereal and bleached flours.

The re-establishment of the organic equilibrium is not exclusively dependent on food restriction. On the contrary, eating too little sometimes may intensify the psychological troubles, the role of which is certainly important here. Of course, this does not sanction not trying to eat progressively less and less instead of continuing to eat large quantities.

One way to reconcile these two needs - not to suffer from hunger and not to eat too much - is to select food rich in cellulose. These types of foods help secure an efficient draining of food wastes, residues of metabolism and dead cells.

The natural sugars of fruits and honey constitute an important source of energy. With such sugars, all the different functions of the body will have enough time to allow a reducing cure, which excludes food that is too rich in starch, protein, and lipids.

This elimination of toxic and excess food should be practiced before or during a natural way of eating.

Note: No single method is likely to give the best results for everyone. The system we discuss here, although it has demonstrated its efficiency, may not fit everyone's specific needs.

During the reducing period exclude, for 1-3 months, starches (bread, rice, noodles, etc.), fats, (except for some olive oil for seasoning), legumes, oleaginous fruits (except for some olives).

Have only fresh fruits and vegetables (raw or cooked), dried, sweet fruits (figs, dates, raisins, prunes, etc.) honey, cheese at one meal, yoghurt at another, 2 or 3 eggs a week, seaweeds. Season the vegetable dishes with lemon, garlic, and other aromatic plants, olive oil and sea salt.

THE NATURAL TREATMENT

Since the common factor in the diverse forms of obesity is the disorder of the metabolism which leads to the accumulation of wastes, act accordingly by using clay, which eliminates the impurities. Take it every morning, 1 teaspoon in ½ a glass of water.

Drain the liver, intestines and kidneys with two herb teas. The first one will act mainly on the liver and kidneys (p.55). The other decoction has a depurative and laxative effect (p.91).

Take lemon-water after the meals (½ a lemon in a glass of hot water, sweetened with some honey). As a matter of fact, this drink can be taken as often as possible over a long period of time - 2-6 months, or even for years. It is particularly recommended for losing weight without incurring deficiency. It also favors the fixation of calcium due to its potassic salts and its glucose, which exercises a tonic action on the heart. It is a good depurative and diuretic and it fluidifies the blood without preventing coagulation.

If the eliminations by the kidneys and bladder are insufficient, accelerate them with the following decoction:

Decoction for Kidneys and Bladder

Bearberry leaves	40 gr.	Licorice root	20 gr.
Ashtree leaves	20 gr.	Mint leaves	20 gr.
Horsetail	20 gr.	Blackcurrant leaves	20 gr.
Buckthorn bark	10 gr.	Wall pellitory	20 gr.

3 tablespoons of the mixture in a pint of water. Bring to a boil, simmer a few minutes and let infuse 10 minutes. Drink during meals or when desired.

Increase the volume of urine to drain excess water by applying a hot wheat bran-ivy leaf poultice (p.143) on the kidneys.

Eat plenty of food rich in cellulose; this helps get rid of waste and gives consistency to the stools.

A cold hip bath every morning (3-4 minutes) accelerates the exchanges.

Apply a poultice on the liver before going to bed, either lukewarm clay or wheat bran-ivy leaves.

If the heart is strong enough, take hot baths twice or four times a month. Put 1 pound of seaweed which has been soaked overnight in the tub. Add 2 pounds of sea salt before taking the bath. These baths tonify the organism and, when taken very hot, help the organism build defenses and accelerate elimination.

Here is an efficient method that will take care of deficiencies, eliminate excesses and bring the organism into order: *undertake 3-day periods of fruit eating in season.* Every time a fruit comes into season, eat it exclusively for a three-day period. This should be done at least once monthly, with cherries, strawberries, plums, apricots, peaches, raisins, figs, etc. Apples and pears which appear in winter will then follow in the treatment and then oranges, tangerine, grapefruit. From time to time lengthen the cure to 2 or 3 week periods. However, vary the fruits to avoid saturation and monotony.

Hunger should be satisfied during these periods, even if it is still artificial; it will gradually change to normal hunger. For some people eating fruits exclusively takes care of all the functions; others would have to find out what is best for them.

The harmonist method concentrates on reestablishing the functions as a whole. Specifically directed actions are usually avoided, since the correct one would be practically impossible to determine. All the interactions and reactions of the different organs and glands are yet unknown. That is why we focus more on a treatment that aims at reconstituting a normal medium in the equilibrium of the internal and external forces.

Losing weight should never entail an extreme campaign to get rid of excess volume quickly - this attitude can lead to ill consequences: the person will have a fast loss and then an equally fast regaining of weight all as a result of attacking the symptom and not the cause.

CANCER

It would be hopeless and even dangerous to pretend to solve the problems of tumors in a few lines.

It is true that facts have shown no other treatment to be as effective for these troubles as clay, but we must not forget that it is a very complex problem and we can only localize its manifestations.

The cellular imbalance, characteristic of these troubles (see section on cancer in 'the liver') all begin to be corrected only with a truly physiological feeding diet.

Laboratory research has brought scientific confirmation that the terminal phase of cancer, which is generally accompanied by significant loss of weight does not have its remedy in eating a lot to make up for that loss. Not only does overeating not bring an amelioration, but on the contrary, it favors the expansion of the tumor. It is only through caloric restriction that it is possible to stop its evolution.

The harmonist position goes even further than that. It is not enough to adopt a diet that will succeed in slowing down the development of the tumor, it must accomplish a gradual regression of the cancerous condition.

The patient must be given to eat only as much as he needs. Do not starve or overfeed; these methods can be very dangerous.

There must first be 15-20 days of general preparation, including a cleansing diet of mostly fresh fruits and raw vegetables and absolutely no meat, sugar or chemicals, clay taken orally, and clay applications on the lower abdomen; only then is it possible to begin with local applications of clay on the cancer itself.

If the tumor is external, apply very thick (1") poultices on it the size of a small saucer; place the clay on the wound and leave for 1 hour (1½ hours maximum) unless the sensation of local warmth becomes intensive, in which case the poultice should immediately be replaced with a fresh one.

Poultices should continue day and night. However, it is possible to place poultices only during the day and, in the evening, apply a pack of salt and clay, prepared by putting 2 spoonfuls of unrefined sea salt in a non-aluminum pan, with sufficient water for its solution. Place it on the fire, stirring with a wooden spoon. Add clay powder as necessary to give the consistency of an ointment. Spread it on a clean cloth and apply it well heated to the affected part. Put one pack on in the morning and leave for the whole day and another at night, to be left on all night. When pus appears, apply only cold poultices during the day, while continuing to use the salt-clay pack at night for a few more nights.

Alternately, at night, apply a large moist dressing soaked in a decoction of box-tree leaves (1 handful of dried leaves per quart of water; boil until reduced to ½ the liquid; cool and filter it). It is sometimes necessary to change those dressings which have been applied cold or tepid.

If the affected area is able to bear it, take baths with this same decoction during the day, lasting for a ½ hour. Throw it out after use. These tepid baths can be taken once or twice a day.

During the day, the 'ripening' of the abscess may be hastened by alternating clay poultices with those of onions, roasted in the oven, than applied hot and left on for 1 hour. When suppuration is completed, it is necessary to apply fresh clay poultices to be left for a longer period (1½-2 hours). Between poultices, wash the area with unboiled salt water. For 1 quart of water add a handful of sea salt.

****

BREAST CANCER

A patient with cancer of the nipple had the nipple removed by surgery. After this, followed by radiation and radium applications, nodules appeared on the other nipple (a common occurrence -- removing a cancerous growth is not at all curing cancer). An operation was foreseen with prospects of a limited life.

The patient changed to natural medicine, she modified her diet, took teas for the liver, and applied clay on the nodules and ganglions. Her state improved progressively. Unfortunately she then became the victim of an auto accident and had to be fitted with a plaster cast for a vertebral fracture. The surgeon agreed to open a window on the plaster to allow clay applications on the fractured area.

It is now more than ten years since this patient followed clay treatment and her present condition would appear enviable to many others.

****

The treatment of internal tumors requires extra precaution, as a vital organ may be very near. It is necessary to watch that the tumor does not extend itself, as sometimes happens at the beginning of many clay treatments. *The poultices must be very thin(¼")*, which will still be very active, but will not provoke any strong reactions. At first, one every day will be sufficient; after a week, increase the frequency gradually, and also the thickness of the poultices, until arriving at 2 or 3 poultices a day nearly 1" thick.

If the tumor is affecting a deep organ, the clay should not be kept in place for more than 3 hours because its radiations become negative on contact with the ailing organ.

Use cold clay in most cases, but not for tumors in the spinal column or neighboring regions; for these, clay should be heated in advance. In other places, it can also be applied heated but it is better to apply it cold whenever possible.

In brief, the definite treatment implies 2 or 3 poultices, nearly 1" thick, applied daily directly onto the skin, and leaving on for 2 hours minimum, 3 hours maximum.

If it is certain that surgery radiations can aggravate the situation, they often succeed nonetheless by according a forced rest, which allows the patient to radically abandon his old bad eating habits and orientate himself towards harmonism. We have many amazing examples of such types who outlived their predicted time.

Those who expect miracles from the harmonist method will perhaps be disappointed, it must be understood that the appearance of a tumor, the identification of a cancerous state, indicate such a profound and old trouble that nature seems to lose her right.

One should not wait to have a cancer before changing one's way of life. After more than twenty years of practice, we have never observed a cancerous growth among people who follow this method.

TIPS ON FIRST AID

BURNS

Burns treated with clay heal better and more rapidly and leave less traces than with other methods, especially if the clay is applied immediately.

Apply cold clay, in thick poultices, with gauze between the clay and the sore. After 1 hour, remove the poultice, leaving the gauze if it has adhered. Equally, in cases of deep and extended burns where rags or cloths have adhered to the wound, leave them and apply the clay as above. The clay should have several points of contact with the burn, though.

Clay eliminates all risks of infection and absorbs all the impurities and foreign bodies apt to be found in the burn. It also eliminates the destroyed cells, enabling cellular rebuilding.

Renew the applications each day and night, changing them every hour, until the appearance of new tissues. Then reduce the frequency of application, but not to less than 3 or 4 poultices a day, and leave the poultices in place for 2 hours each, until the tissues are virtually rebuilt.

If the burns are on the feet or hands, dip them directly into a container of clay paste. It is necessary to remain immersed for 1 hour so that no trace of the burn will remain on completion of this mud bath. For extended burns, it is advisable to dip the whole body into a large container of clay. Do not forget all other measures for maintaining a general healthy state.

Acid-burns can also be treated with clay; alkaline ones should be treated with lemon-water.

WOUNDS, CUTS

If it is recent, put clay powder directly onto the wound, then cover it with a large cold poultice. Bandage firmly.

After this poultice, which should be kept in place for a maximum of 2 hours, wash the wound with salted or lemon-water; after that, use a compress of clayish water.

If the existence of foreign bodies in the wound is feared, continue the clay poultices until there is no more doubt. *All the foreign substances will be absorbed by the clay, and later found there.* There have been many cases where foreign bodies that were impossible to extract surgically have been drawn out with clay.

When the state of the wound allows it, *expose it to the open air in order to hasten its healing.* Sometimes it is necessary to apply a dry dressing in order to avoid friction or any other contact. This dry dressing may stick to the skin and present difficulties in removing it, so to avoid this, use the following antiseptic pack: peel an onion; take out a layer carefully and extract the very thin membrane that is between two layers of onion. This pellicle is applied directly onto the wound which it protects and disinfects. Add the dressing and bandage. This precaution is also very useful for any kind of dry dressing in general, such as on ulcers and sores.

SPRAINS

The most simple and efficient way to treat a sprain is to first place the injured part under a thin stream of cold water for 20-30 minutes.

Then apply thick poultices of clay that should be left in place for 3-4 hours. The one applied before going to bed can remain in place overnight.

Hot baths with salted water contribute to the sedation of pain. After the first day, take one

every day for 15-20 minutes. After 2 or 3 days of clay applications, it may be lightly massaged with a mixture of olive oil and grated garlic (2:1).

It is important to leave the injured part under cold water as often as possible.

BONE FRACTURES

The use of clay, rather than plaster, is recommended. It allows for faster results and eliminates the complications which might result from the use of plaster.

Plaster has only a passive action - that of immobilizing the parts to be rejoined. Clay is an active agent; with its vitalizing radiations and absorbent power, it participates effectively in the repair of the fracture.

First fix the bone in place with splints, although if the parts are displaced, as in a compound fracture, a specialist should be called. If plaster is unavoidable, ask the specialist if it is possible to leave some 'windows' through which clay may be appplied.

Apply a uniform layer 1" thick, cold or slightly lukewarm. If there is a sore, change the clay every 2 hours. Otherwise, twice a week will suffice. Shave the hair or put a cheesecloth between the clay and the skin (but direct contact is always preferable). Wash the skin with plain water, no soap or alcohol, between the poultices.

BRUISES, BUMPS, ETC.

We cannot neglect any discolorations or swellings, as some ligaments or vessels may be broken, or some nerves injured.

For healing the congestive state, it is necessary to apply cold clay poultices from ½"-1" thick.

Leave on for 2 hours, or less if the clay heats or dries rapidly.

There is no danger in continuing to apply poultices. The more are applied, the faster will be the healing. It is necessary to continue the applications until total disappearance of pain.

Every night, use a compress of clayish water and leave overnight.

MALFORMATIONS AND WEAKENINGS

Affections or malformations should be treated either with dense baths of mud or with hot or cold clay poultices, it all depends on the tolerance of the individual.

In cases of loosening of the foot arches, bunions, and other malformations or osseous or muscular weakenings, cover the whole foot with a thick cloak of clay. In cases of comparable afflictions of the hand, treat similarly.

These mud baths should last about 30 minutes, while poultices should be left on for 2 hours or more. Complete the treatment with a massage using a mixture of equal parts of oil and garlic.

HERNIA

Possibilities of healing depend on the age of the hernia. A total healing of a hernia one or two years old is almost certain, but for one older than that, we can only hope for a complete cure.

The first element of treatment is the bandage for supporting clay poultices; it is necessary to make it solid in order to maintain support for some months of use.

The affected part is generally inflamed, so cold clay will be well tolerated. Apply poultices which

191

are more than ½" thick, and somewhat longer than the affected part. Keep in place with a bandage for 2-4 hours. If it is not possible to change poultices every four hours, at least remove it and replace it with a cotton pad (prepared in advance) the same volume as the poultice. *Do not leave the hernia without support until it is completely reabsorbed.*

Morning and evening, lightly massage the treated part with a mixture of olive oil and chopped garlic. This massage must be carried out by another person, because the patient must be lying down.

Do not make any effort or movement when the bandage is not in place. This is the secret of the treatment's success. As the hernia is being absorbed, the use of poultices and pad should be gradually diminished until the final disappearance of the hernia.

Clay treatment can be complemented with compresses of evergreen oak bark (4 oz. per quart of water, boiled for ½ hour) kept on overnight with a bandage.

IN CASE OF FEVER

Whenever there is a fever, four main steps must be taken immediately:

1 - cease taking any solid food
2 - drink liquids. However, the liquids should be such as lemon-water, clay water, infusions. No vegetable broth or fruit juices, which are too nutritive, unless they are mixed with a large amount of water.
3 - insure regular evacuations. Give a decoction of buckthorn - 1 teaspoon or 1 tablespoon, depending on age and case in a cup of water; bring to a boil and let simmer 2 minutes.
4 - apply clay poultices on the lower abdomen: 2-4 a day, depending on the temperature. Leave in place for 2 hours, even less if the clay gets warm quickly.

To these four main measures, add hot foot baths with red-grape vine leaves, depending on the case. These baths will relax the head, heart and respiratory channels. If they are well-tolerated, without chills or cold sensations inside the body, administer 4 or 5 of them a day, every 2 hours, each bath lasting for 10 minutes. Apply clay poultices on the back of the neck or forehead in case of bad headaches (a little bit less than 1" thick for the neck) and a ½" on the forehead. The poultice on the neck should last for 2 hours and the one on the forehead for 1 hour.

Apply mustard plasters on the calf of the leg if congestion seems to localize in the upper part of the body, most particularly the head. An enema will also help.

Perspiration will help, give the patient a decoction of box-tree leaves.

Put 1½ oz. of dry leaves in a quart of water; boil and reduce fo 3/4 of its volume. Drink in one morning in 3 doses, waiting 15-20 minutes between each drink.

Cover the patient well, and if need be, put either a hot bottle in his bed, or cover him with an electric blanket.

Perspiration may also be created with the *wet towel:*

Lay a thick material across the bed, wider and larger than the following compress: soak a towel in cold water (or lukewarm, if one lacks confidence); squeeze it and place it on the top of the thick material. Attach with pins and put a hot bottle (or any object that retains heat) on each side of the body. Cover well with warm blankets.

After perspiration, if it be spontaneous or provoked, quickly uncover the patient, take off his bedclothes, massage him gently with a sponge soaked with cold water. *All this should be done as quickly as possible;* change his clothes and cover him with warm blankets.

In order to conduct all the indicated treatments well, eliminate any kind of fear which may upset the results. As this system has already been widely used, there is no need to fear any harm whatsoever; all it takes is to behave calmly and with confidence when confronted with any reaction, whatsoever its apparent violence. Do not forget that a feverish body is an organism which is defending itself. The most serious type of disease is the one where no fever is able to be produced.

Fever, eruptions, expectorations, mucous secretions, all of these indicate an intense and salutary battle. It would be a crime to thwart the elevation of temperature with unnatural means.

****

HERNIA

A mother tells how she cured her ten year old son who had had a hernia since he was one. She succeeded in making it disappear in two months with clay poultices, applied locally every evening.

****

****

CRUSHED FINGER

A friend had her finger crushed by a door, but unfortunately did not think of clay until the next morning, after a bad night. After 48 hours of application of clay, the pain finally calmed down. Whenever the pain manifested itself, clay would soothe it.

After a few days, seeing her finger black and swollen, her daughter, who is a nurse, advised her to have it opened in a clinic, telling her that she would be given antibiotics. This woman preferred to continue with clay. Her nail fell off, but in a very short time her finger regained a normal appearance and the nail grew back.

****

****

LEG INJURY

One correspondent relates, "six months ago, a friend fell from his bicycle, wounding the front of his leg seriously. I immediately proposed clay poultices. The only answer he gave was a disbelieving stare.

Five months later he visited me again and his leg was in a very bad state. He had followed the standard treatment as was prescribed to him: pomades, cleansings, Seeing that finally he was really worried, I repeated my advice. He agreed, and I gave him clay on the spot (I always have some prepared). The best that could have happened, did. One and a half months later, everything was cured. There is only a bluish trace left, but no more pain."

****

****

SEVERE CUT

A woman we know had a deep cut in the right thumb caused by a kitchen appliance. Clay poultices were applied immediately. The extensive bleeding of the wound stopped with the first applications. In the beginning the poultices were renewed as soon as the clay dried.

After eight days the flesh was reconstituted and her finger was returned to normal.

****

****

BURNS

A woman burned herself quite badly. It was taken care of in eight days by clay applications. Three poultices a day were applied - two during the day and one at night. There is now only a slight mark, even though the individual appearance of the burn was quite bad.

****

****

SEVERED FINGER

A 17 year old boy sliced his left index finger with a sickle. It was so deep that the finger was attached only by some flesh around the joint.

Twenty minutes later, without using a disinfectant, a clay poultice was applied and renewed frequently, day and night, for two days. Between the poultices a pellicle of onion (which is found between the layers), a natural antiseptic, allowed a dry bandage. From time to time the finger was exposed to air.

All the flesh then formed a crust of protection. In less than two weeks, everything was healed and even the traces disappeared.

****

****

BIRTHMARK

A birthmark on a patient's face was getting bigger. After putting clay on it for months, although quite irregularly, it almost disappeared, leaving only a light brown spot, like a beauty mark.

****

****

DISLOCATED COLLARBONE

One woman writes that her son had his collar bone dislocated when he fell from his bicycle. Overnight clay poultices were applied every night for three months. The collarbone gradually came back to its normal place. She said afterwards, "I must confess that I was skeptical about getting the dislocated bones in place!"

****

ADDITIONAL USES OF CLAY

There are other forms of living earth for healing purposes, and they may be put to work for other purposes as well.

CLAY POWDERING

Finely ground clay is advisable for powdering babies, instead of talcum, which generally has medicinal substances but not clay activity. Don't hesitate to use clay powder on childish pimples or have them drink it, if necessary.

On ulcers, powdered clay performs an antiseptic action, favoring the rebuilding of harmed tissues. Powder sores, scars, inflammations, eczema, etc.

The use of very fine clay powder for a massage increases its efficiency.

SLIME MUD

This is the sandy clay deposits left by water on their withdrawal. Its properties are variable but definite.

Ancient deposits of slime mud constitute the 'loess', of which successive layers present different aspects. The inferior (lower) loess (yellow earth) is virtually arable and predominantly chalky. It is the "argilette" of Normandy and the "terre douce" (sweet ground) of Picardy.

The upper level, reddish and rather sandy, is very rich in arable clay. It is the "terre a brique" (brick ground) of the districts of Paris.

All these grounds may be used when true clay is unavailable, but only for external use.

CLAY BATHS

The use of mud with high mineral content is very common at present in health resorts and clinics. This is a good idea, because its actions are powerful and helpful, although for maximum benefit it is necessary to complement them with a natural way of eating.

If it is not possible to go to these spas due to

the inconvenience or expense, you can take advantage of the benefits of mud baths with a mixture of clay and water.

If you have a garden, dig a hole sufficiently long and deep enough in which to dip your whole body, once the hole has been filled with mud. To protect against cold, do this in the open air only during warm periods when the clay can be exposed to sunlight.

These baths can be taken inside in a trough, cask, etc. but never in a bath-tub as the clay would obstruct the drain-pipes. Mix the clay and water so as to obtain a clear paste. This bath can be used several times; each time add a little water, cold or hot, according to need.

Begin with daily baths of 5-10 minutes duration, then increase to 15-20 minutes. If they tire, take them every second day or twice a week. After a month of treatment, rest for one month before resuming.

These baths are recommended for treatment of rheumatism and arthritis, or osseous afflictions, for certain skin and blood illnesses and for certain kinds of paralysis.

Bathing specific parts of the body is equally possible, and is very effective; especially foot and hand baths in cases of rheumatism.

SAND BATHS

Of everyone who has lain on sandy beaches, exposed to the sun's rays, how many know that the sand on which they were resting is as beneficial as the sun or sea? We could profit more from its beneficial influence by covering ourselves with it -- that is to say, by taking a true sand bath.

It is known that sand, especially marine sand, can contain certain radioactive substances, particularly Uranium. This explains, though only partially, its wonderful action on osseous afflictions. Rickets, weakness, decalcification, all troubles of the osseous system such as arthritis, rheumatism, lumbago, nephritis, sciatica and many other illnesses are helped with sand treatment.

These baths are taken in the sunshine with dry sand; dig a little so that the body is well-buried, and then cover with a thick cover of sand, leaving out only the head, which will be under the shade of foliage or an umbrella or cloth, placed at least a yard away from the head, so as to permit air circulation and avoid a concentration of heat.

The sandbath sometimes produces an active perspiration. If this happens, interrupt the bath immediately and cover yourself again with dry sand, repeating this procedure 2 or 3 times, if necessary, to end perspiration.

Always finish the bath before arriving at a feeling of fatigue or cooling, which would be fatal. Keep in mind the length of this tolerance, and in subsequent baths increase only gradually. Begin with sessions from 10-15 minutes and increase them gradually to 1 or 2 hours, 2 or 3 times a day. Do not take them during digestive periods because they produce energy reactions.

Once out of the sand, dip completely in water; then cover yourself and rest before taking sun or renewing the bath.

Apart from sand baths, which can be local (and in this case rather longer), sand can be used in poultices - either for increasing the results of sand baths, or as a separate treatment for the same troubles and afflictions treated with sand baths.

Heat the river or sea sand in an oven or frying pan. Put it into a bag, prepared beforehand, and sufficiently large enough to cover the part to be treated - about 1" thick. Apply it well-heated and leave for 2-3 hours. Repeat it as many times as necessary.

Techniques of sand baths have hardly changed over the centuries; the following text from the Greek, Herodotus, reported by Dr. Hector Grasset, is more than two thousand years old:

"Sand treatment benefits those people suffering from asthma, pneumonia, gout, progressive paralysis, dropsy, and everyone who has chronic pain, because every ailing person, with the exception of small children, adapts himself to this treatment. Summer is the best season, choosing the most sunny days. In the morning, we prepare two or three graves of the same size as the patient for his use, leaving them to be dried by sun heat. At home, the patient's food has to be well-distributed and he must previously have had good walks or other passive movements. When air heat is strong and sand sufficiently heated, the patient lays in the grave and is covered with as much sand as he can support. He must cover his head in order to avoid sunrays, placing over his eyes some protective object. Choose the best position for him; towards South at midday and during the first half of the day; towards North in the second half. Dry his face with a sponge soaked in cold water, and, if he suffers very much, also soak his mouth. If the patient feels that he does not heat himself or is cold due to sweat, he must say so; then, the assistants can remove the sand which covers him, take him out of that grave, and place him again in a new one. If necessary, the change can be carried out once more in accordance with the illness and strength of the patient . . .

"We must bury in an inclined position those patients with asthma, pneumonia, stomach troubles, those who have a bad appearance of anasarca hydropsy and, in a sitting position, the hydropsical with ascites and, if necessary, those who suffer from colon, liver, spleen, hip, gout or paralysis of feet or legs. At the end, we completely bury the patient because it is good that relaxation spreads throughout the whole body, and the useful effects of this treatment encompass the healthy parts also, especially with those who intend to take a cold bath immediately afterwards. Near the graves, it is necessary to have cabins of transparent material, pails of natural water, and also bathing-suits, which are used by patients when they finish perspiring; after the bath, give them showers or massages with oil . . .

"with intermittent illnesses, the number of days of treatment are not less than 14 nor more than 21; but with hydropsicals, the number of days is in accordance with the remissions of the body's volume. If, after the 21st day of treatment, on arriving at a 'dead point' in its efficiency, it is advisable to take 2 or 3 days of rest and then renew the treatment again."

ANIMALS AND CLAY

A person who observes nature can witness the fact that animals instinctively use earth to cure themselves. Indeed, we owe much of our discovery in this field to animals. There is a sea resort in the Siberian forests of the Oussouri where the discovery of the curative properties of the earth was the result of observations of wounded animals, wild pigs, roe-deer, red deer and other animals who came to wallow in the benefactory mud. Dr. Em. Grommier has told the story of the elephant "Fil," who, with his kindred, purged himself with silicic-magnesic clay-marls and daubed himself with mud.

The French Army used it recently for veterinary purposes - when horses were afflicted with hoof gangrene, they were put in a stable, the floor of which had been dug up and kept wet so that the horses could kick in the mud. The animals went instinctively to the clay-mud where they found a remedy for their disease.

Animals seem to know instinctively the usefulness of contact with clay when they are ill or wounded. Those living wild do not hesitate to dip the affected area in mud. Domestic animals, too, turn to clay. A cat that is abscessed or wounded or ill will lie on a clay case (a large bin of clay covered with a cloth). Even when not ill, she will prefer this bed to one more comfortable.

Domestic and farm animals can be treated with clay. The method of treatment is the same as for human patients, the only difficulty being in the docility of the animal in accepting the treatment. Farm animals can be persuaded to dip themselves into a mud bath prepared by digging a large enough hole filled with clay and water. Cows have been cured of foot-and-mouth diseases (apthous fever) with applications on the feet and daubs in the mouth. In certain countries, seriously ill animals are saved by daubing them completely with a mixture of clay and vinegar. Good results are also obtained by replacing vinegar with very salted water (sea salt).

For internal use, clay is also effective. It can be added to the drinking water (4 soupspoons per quart of unboiled water) and even mixed with food. It can be used in the fur - particularly for cats, who constantly lick their fur, thus absorbing it easily.

****

ECZEMA IN A CAT

Mrs. B. relates, "Our little cat was struck with eczema. I lotioned her sores with a decoction of Box-tree leaves and applied clay. I also put clay and olive oil in her food.

All trace of eczema disappeared and a new, healthy skin was formed."

****

AGRICULTURAL USES

Clay is able to replace all chemical fertilizers and can be used in the form of packs, daubings, cements, powders, etc.

Clay is the best pack for tree wounds. Make thick applications which will only stay on if the clay is solid enough. Once the clay has been put in place, it cannot be re-applied.

When transplanting or replanting, soak the roots of small plants in a clay bath and daub the roots of trees, bushes and big plants. For 5 quarts of mud add a coffee-cup full of a decoction of chamomile (1 oz. of flowers to 1 quart of water) - this is the maximum dose.

In acidic ground, recognized by the presence of daisies, moss or buttercups, clay can be added to improve the balance of the soil. When the soil is rather light (too sandy), prepare clay as if for a poultice, grind, let it dry, and spread it over the soil.

Added to organic debris, clay increases the

production of humus and also the amount of carbon fixation in the soil.

CLAY IN INDUSTRY

Clay has many industrial uses. Many centuries before our era, the Chinese people used a certain kind of clay for decoloring greasy oils, according to M.C. Alexanian, Doctor of Physics. He adds that the Egyptians, Greeks and Romans clearly knew of this scouring and decoloring property. The frescoes of the 'fullonica' of Pompeii show the Roman bleachers trampling the cloths in clay-water - clay derives one of its names from this: "Fuller's earth."

Clay is still used today for decoloring oils, both mineral and vegetal - attapulgite, sepiolite, illite, etc. (5 grams of good clay being sufficient for decoloring 10^3 cm of a water solution to 0.1 of Methylene blue. It is also used for treating margarine, giving it the taste of butter). In the U.S. alone, 300,000 tons of "Fuller's earth" are used every year, of which 180,000 tons are used for treatment of oil-bearing products.

In North Africa, more than 100,000 tons of Bentonite are mined. Most of this is used in the petroleum industry. Here, clay, a natural silicate, is used as a catalyzer (it has remarkable resistance to being affected by chemicals) in the genesis of petroleum, determining a series of transformations of several organic materials. The essences of cracking are purified, passing under pressure over an absorbent clay. Thanks to clay, the 'catalytic cracking' allows the transformation of the gas-oil into a liquid burning essence, then into polymerizable gas, used in the manufacturing of synthetic rubber and other products. A white clay is used as a strengthening charge in the manufacture of natural rubber, for certain synthetic rubbers, thermoplastic material (such as vynilic resins), anti-acid paints, hydro-carbonated soaps.

Certainly, as time goes on, more experimenting and more research will be done with clay, and many additional uses are sure to be found for it, healing and otherwise. It is sincerely hoped that these uses will be in accord with nature and not against it.

BUYER'S GUIDE

Buying the needed kind of food and herbs should not be difficult now. Years ago it was so, when health food stores were a rare thing and only carried a few items.

Organically grown vegetables were always available, but always expensive. When you think about it, though, it is not really much more expensive than the ones sold on the regular market, since a small amount of the organically grown is far more satisfying in taste and in nutrition. People tend to eat a lot more vegetables when the taste is not there, they are trying to "catch" the true flavor of the carrot or cabbage.

If you find that vegetables, fruits, and grains are too expensive in a health food store, you might try to form a co-op (just a few families) and make a big order to the wholesaler; this can give you savings of up to 40% off the retail price - and that is a lot if your main food is vegetables, fruits, and grains. If you should buy grains in bulk, make sure to put them in a cold place, otherwise they get wormy after two or three months, more or less, depending on the temperature. Always keep them tightly covered in glass or earthenware jars.

Powdered clay can be purchased in bulk at all wholesale clay potter supply houses. Ask first for Jordan or Gorden clay, which we know works efficiently for external treatments. **Do not use it for internal purposes,** it is too rough. If Jordan clay is not available, try other kinds but make sure they are pure.

Stewart Clay Company and *Newton Potters Supply* both carry Jordan Clay. They will ship it anywhere. It might take time to get it, but it is well worth it. Write to:

Stewart Clay Company
400 Jersey Avenue
New Brunswick, New Jersey 08902

Newton Potters Supply
96 Rumford Ave. Box 96
Newton, Mass. 02165

The following company in California carries a clay that might prove itself good. It should be given a try. It is always good to use locally-mined clay. Write to them for full price information:

Cal-Min Company
P.O. Box 500
Brawley, Ca. 92227

The following companies supply clay which is excellent for oral purposes, as well as for poultices. They have all been tested, and found to be beneficial. Write to each for more information:

French green clay -
Pierre Cattier   The Three Sheaves Company
100 Varick Street
New York, N.Y. 10013

Volcanic Ash -
The Herbalist
934 N. Western Ave.
L.A., Ca. 90029

West German clay -
George Comfort Products
P.O. Box 742
Soquel, Ca. 95073

Desert Mineral clay -
H. R. Enterprises, Inc.
P.O. Box 4321
Fullerton, Ca. 92634

Big Horn Mountain clay (pascalite) -
P. & S. Mining Co.
P.O. Box 104
Worland, Wyoming 82401

Nevalite Products
Box 628
Verdi, Nevada 89439

Be careful about trying untested clays, for we have evidence that the surface lead content in many of our soils is very high, and can cause serious problems.

All clay products may be purchased from health food distributors and health food stores across the country. Cattier has come up with some fine products from toothpaste and soaps to skin care. The Cattier toothpaste, by the way, can be used for oral treatments. Use the natural one, of course, not the flavored one. Cattier is now manufacturing large tubes which will be available soon.

IMPORTANT NOTE:

If you are confused or unfamiliar with clay products or if you wish to know anything about buying clay we suggest that you write or call the following company; which carries all the Cattier and other products:

Pierre Cattier
The Three Sheaves Company
100 Varick Street
New York, N.Y. 10013

Organic silica can be purchased directly from the following distributors. The cost is $6.25 for a bottle of 100 tablets.

If you live west of the Mississippi, write to:

Alta Dena Health Foods
1860 North Allen Ave.
Pasadena, Ca. 91104

East of the Mississippi:

Pierre Cattier
The Three Sheaves Company
100 Varick Street
New York, N.Y. 10013

A word about the dosage - Research by doctors has found that 250 Gr. of organic silica taken in one month should be effective for calcium deficiency. M.D.'s advise to begin with less and observe the progress of the treatment before increasing.

Do not become too dependent on supplements. It is always better to eat the right type of food. Supplements are good in certain cases, such as a severe deficiency in an element. Of course, it must be from an organic source, for in its mineral form, an element has an opposite effect. It might temporarily supply help for certain body organs so that one feels good that day;however, it can not satisfy the organism as a whole.

Shop and eat in good health!

INDEX

D

HERBAL INDEX